sportsproview

www.sportsproview.com

Praise for *Second City*

"The most entertaining and insightful account of the life of a League of Ireland footballer that you will ever read"

Daniel McDonnell, *The Irish Independent*

"An essential antidote to the caricature of the pampered professional footballer, this remarkably candid player's account of a season in hell for Cork City also succeeds as a love letter to the enduring power of dressing room solidarity – not to mention the benefits of gallows humour – in the face of almost daily adversity"

Liam Mackey, *The Irish Examiner*

"Horgan captures one of the most turbulent seasons endured by an Irish football club with an account that will have you bubbling with anger and laughing on the same page. Some of the off-the-field tricks pulled on the players – from a lack of payment to the infamous story of the bus driver that refused to travel to an away game – will leave you startled, but the obvious camaraderie within the team during such difficult times is vividly brought to life. This book is not just a must-read for League of Ireland supporters but an account that any football fan should read"

Alan Smith, *The Guardian*

"Once again Horgan succeeds in bringing us inside the dressing room, the team bus and the mind of a League of Ireland player in a way I don't think anybody else has. Second City is a thoughtful, astute and brutally honest account of life at one the country's biggest and best football clubs during what were particularly challenging times for it and an already troubled league. It is a wonderful account of the often bizarre world Horgan and his team mates inhabited, one told with affection and, sometimes, justifiable anger. I laughed a lot only for it dawn on me more than once that I should have been crying, but I have a better understanding now of the league I've been covering for 25 years and the people who play in it than I had before picking this up. Anyone, regardless of their club loyalties, who wants to know what is really going on in the game they love should read it too. That they'll enjoy the read immensely might be considered a bonus"

Emmet Malone, *The Irish Times*

From 'The Fall, Death and Rise of Cork City FC'

An autobiography of an Irish footballer

Part Two:

SECOND CITY

Season 2009

by Neal Horgan

Published by Sportsproview

ISBN 978 0 9930622 5 4

To Kate & Hannah, Conn & Muirne, Ella & John, and Jo & Lola.

Neal Horgan is a practising solicitor and a frequent contributor to *The Irish Examiner*'s sports pages. Neal spent 15 seasons playing as a conservative full-back for Cork City FC in the League of Ireland and loved (almost!) every minute of it. His debut book, *Death of a Football Club?* was published in 2014. This is his second book.

Also by Neal Horgan
Death of a Football Club? The Story of Cork City FC, Season 2008 – published by Sportsproview

Contents

Preface

Did you ever wonder why there is no fully professional football club on the island of Ireland? Or why the Republic of Ireland is an outlier amongst our European neighbours as a country with a population of more than 4 million that has no professional football league? Does the existence of the GAA in Ireland explain this anomaly, or is that just a convenient answer to a more complex issue? Could we, in the near future, have a professional soccer league in Ireland?

While the questions are clear, the answers are not. But before we come to any conclusions we should at the very least examine the evidence. The experiences of players should not be ignored. This book, along with its predecessor, *Death of a Football Club?* (which chronicled the 2008 season), offers my first-hand experiences as evidence in respect of Irish football's recent relationship with the professional game.

Second City examines Cork City FC's controversial 2009 season, which brought my club to a new low.

Introduction

The League of Ireland's constant 'state of chassis'

"The whole worl's in a state of chassis"
'Fluther Good' in *The Plough and the Stars* by Sean O'Casey

Following publication of my book about Cork City's 2008 season, I was tempted to leave it at that. While I had also kept a diary of the 2009 season, I was not as enthusiastic, initially, about publishing that. In fact I was worried that it might do some harm. On the other hand, the 2008 season, after the looming spectre of financial and sporting disaster at the club, had ended on a high, which gave a positive slant to the whole book. There was a new owner at the club, and the Setanta Cup victory had brought a sense of security for players and fans alike. And while on the last day of the season there was still some uncertainty in terms of tying up players' contracts, this was a feel-good ending – which was important.

Having enjoyed playing in the league for about 15 seasons, I was conscious, when writing about the 2008 season, that the book should not turn out to be overly negative. The league takes enough hits from people who know nothing about it. I was, and remain, most interested – like many others out there – in seeing the league progress onto more stable and fruitful grounds.

So in the context of the long-term view of the League of Ireland, the 2008 season documented something more important than that oft-told tale of victory after a crisis. It's a season that, despite the particularities of full-time football, the withdrawal of Arkaga and the entry of the club into examinership, is symbolic of the continuing condition of the League of Ireland that has prevailed over the last 60 years or so. As such it was a season that, despite the positive ending, represented the 'status quo,' whereby the struggle for survival has taken priority over any efforts towards real progress.

In this regard any League of Ireland club's five- to ten-year period over the last 60 years might run something like this:

- The club performs to their best within the (deficient) structures of Irish football. It focuses on doing well in the league or in the FAI Cup in order to bring in bigger crowds. Every now and then it might sell a promising player to an overseas club, and this money helps with payment of wages. When things are going well the club manages to keep its head above water.

- Then the club has a bad year and, fairly quickly, finds itself in financial trouble. This can be brought about by any number of factors – a director might've pulled away funds, a debt might've surfaced from somewhere, there may have been a downturn of results on the pitch leading to lower attendances… Any of the above will do, and they cause the same result: money running low. (The bad year may have been preceded by a few successful years or a few barren years in terms of winning silverware – it doesn't seem to matter either way in the League of Ireland.)

- Attendances fall (or continue to fall) and cash runs dry. The owner or directors suddenly find themselves on their knees, gasping for air, praying for time in order keep the creditor sharks at bay.

- For the main part the end game – the death of a football club – comes threateningly close, perhaps two or three weeks away. But somehow the club is saved. Maybe – as in our case in 2008 – the court protection offered by the examinership process is a lifeline. An unexpected cup win could bring relief. A new owner might bring in fresh funds; or, if the club's lucky, the FAI will lend a financial hand to allow them the breathing space they need to survive.

- Once back on its feet the club returns to the first stage of this process, but the next stage is never too far away, and any effort at real progress is undermined by what Fluther Good would describe as a constant 'state of chassis' (chaos).

This depressing state of affairs was acknowledged in 2005 by a report entitled 'White Paper on the Strategic Development of the Eircom League,' commissioned by the FAI and carried out by Scottish consultant firm Genesis – which had produced an earlier report focussed on the Irish national team in the aftermath of the troubles involving Mick McCarthy and Roy Keane at Saipan in the build-up to the 2002 World Cup.

Genesis' second report focussed on the League of Ireland (then called the 'Eircom League') and is commonly known as 'Genesis II'. It makes for interesting reading:

"Over the last 20 years the eircom League and its member clubs have struggled to survive. By any rational analysis of financial performance, attendances and sponsorship it is clear the eircom League is near to being economically bankrupt and is unsustainable in its current format and incapable of sustaining itself into the future.

[...]

"The eircom League is currently trapped in a downward spiral. A poor product with unattractive facilities leads to a lack of support, minimal sponsorship and low levels of income. The challenge for the league is to shift from that downward spiral to a virtuous, growing spiral where a strong, superior product with attractive facilities leads to increased support, higher levels of sponsorship and an improvement in performance and income for the league and its clubs.

[...]

"Making small, incremental changes to the League will not have the desired effect. Transformation is required to change

structure, management, performance and behaviour - all four vital ingredients of any process of change. What is needed is a 'whole new ball game'".

('White Paper on the Strategic Direction of the eircom League', by Genesis, 2005)

As such, my reluctance to write about the 2009 season was not just based on the fact that it was, overall, a negative experience; it was also based on the fact that 2009 was a less accurate reflection of the league than 2008 had been. 2008 was a clear example of the survival game that has come to dominate League of Ireland life, involving a status quo whereby clubs just about get by, from week to week, season to season. This is the life that, for the most part over the last 15 years at least, has been eked out by even some of the most successful Premier Division clubs. The top Dublin sides such as Shamrock Rovers, Shelbourne, Bohemians and St. Patrick's Athletic have all experienced hardship and threats to their existence over the last decade or so. Drogheda United, a top club in the mid-2000s, were another that barely managed to survive into the current decade. Many observers have blamed the rise of full-time football for the financial problems faced by these clubs after the financial crash hit our shores at the end of 2007. And there may be some merit to that argument.

However, part-time clubs, most of which resided in the less glamorous First Division, were not immune either. During this period Cobh Ramblers left the league before returning; Limerick 37 were rebranded as 'Limerick FC'; and two Galway clubs (Salthill Devon and Mervue United) were merged into Galway FC. And unfortunately the survival game continues to dominate, as this current year (2016) financial problems have been documented at Athlone Town and Waterford United. All of these clubs would have experience something similar to our season at Cork City in 2008 whereby efforts at progress inevitably gave way to the needs of survival.

Disappointingly, since the publication of *Death of a Football Club?* in 2014, the League of Ireland has not improved. The standard of football (besides that of one or two teams at the top of the league) has deteriorated. Attendances around the country (again, excepting one or two clubs) remain at a dismal level and, as mentioned, a few more clubs have recently skirted dangerously around the brink of extinction. Even worse, a much-vaunted report by the FAI into the League of Ireland (the Conroy Report, 2015) failed to even mention – never mind plan out – a route towards sustainable fully professional football in Ireland.

And so my reluctance to write about the less representative 2009 season gradually gave way to a stronger feeling that I needed to show just how bad things had actually become, so that this dark year might serve as proof of the urgent need for transformative changes in our league – especially in light of the view, in my opinion, that the Conroy Report represents: that incremental changes will suffice.

At this point it should be noted that the death of a League of Ireland club, whilst uncommon, is not exactly unheard of either. In fact over the past 10 years (2006–2016) we've witnessed the demise of Dublin City (2006), Kilkenny City (2007), Kildare County (2009) and Sporting Fingal (2010), while Monaghan United left the league in 2012 in order to focus on their underage and amateur players. The bigger clubs haven't been immune either. Derry City and, as we will see, Cork City, died before returning as ghosts (or zombies) in the clothes of their former clubs in 2010. Clubs have died, and have continued to die even after the FAI took over the running of the league in 2007. '*Which club will be the next to go under?*' This remains a hushed talking point among insiders at League of Ireland grounds around the country.

So who cares? What exactly is the reaction when a club is on the way out? Well, as this book will show, when it becomes clear that a League of Ireland club is in serious financial difficulty, some of our national media get more interested in the league than usual. And when a club's woes become a public interest story, the press tend to highlight unsustainable player wages and financial mismanagement by the club's officers, together with a lack of support for the league by the FAI. The relative disinterest of the general public is also often mentioned as a factor.

This disinterest doesn't stop the general public from espousing a range of views as to why we can't or shouldn't have professional football in Ireland. '*The GAA is too strong*' is a reason favoured by many. '*We're foolish to attempt it – especially with England at our doorstep*' is another. '*Sure haven't we seen how [full-time football] is unsustainable, when all those clubs went belly-up back in the 2000s?*' would represent another commonly held view.

Even among footballing people there is a degree of acceptance that the survival game is the way it always has been and always will be here in Ireland. '*We're just not up to it – we're too small.*' However, very few of these reactions are informed by an experience of professional football. Fewer still are informed by a proper analysis of the viability of professional football in this country, or by a comparison with soccer in another similar-sized country. *But who cares?* Perhaps there seems a certain inevitability or predictability that, in our impoverished state, we will stay tied to the survival game and 'off the radar' in terms of European club professional football.

Following the death of a League of Ireland football club the response from the club owners and the FAI tends also to be predictable. The club owners, finally freed from any constraints that the FAI may have held over them, often cast blame and disappointment upon the FAI for not supporting them or the league sufficiently.

For their part, the FAI hates the bad press that a club in trouble, or a club on the way out, brings on 'the Association' – especially when they want the world to think all is rosy in the garden. So the individual club owners are often blamed. It's a convenient enough but somewhat fickle position for our sport's governing association to take, and it was demonstrated by the FAI's chief executive John Delaney when he described the SSE Airtricity League as a 'difficult child' during an interview on RTÉ's 2fm on 30th September 2014, whilst at the same time dismissing the suggestion that the domestic game was in trouble.

As previously mentioned, the FAI commissioned the SSE Airtricity League Consultation Process Report by Conroy Consulting (known as the 'Conroy Report') (2015) – a report that, in my opinion, painted a picture of the League of Ireland in need of only small, incremental change rather than anything more transformative. Whilst it contained some good initiatives, its main strategic recommendation seemed to be limited to changing the number of clubs in the top league from 12 to 10; a very conservative suggestion – and something that had already been implemented between the 2008 and 2009 seasons in the League of Ireland. Hardly the 'whole new ball game' that Genesis II envisioned. In fact some commentators have even stated that the Conroy Report is merely a survival guide for clubs in the league. But it's time for us to leave the survival game behind, to get out of the downward spiral.

At some point while keeping my diary during 2009, and as things were getting progressively worse around me, I became aware that the club would probably not survive the next few months. And while the eventual death of Cork City (before its subsequent rebirth) is an event that does not make for light reading, I now feel that the experiences of the players during that dark period need to be published – not just for our club but for the entire league and the greater game in Ireland. And so I am glad that I took the time, back in 2009, to note down the goings-on, unknown to my fellow players, day after day, as we moved ever closer to the abyss.

There remains a real danger, in the absence of an overarching plan for professional football in Ireland, that these events will re-occur. *But who cares?*

Before you read on, please heed the warning: 'Abandon all hope, ye who enter here.'

Chapter 1

December 2008; pre-season and early-season form 2009

The players at Cork City FC had journeyed through a storm during the 2008 season. It had begun with a new manager, Alan Mathews, representing just one of the many signs of the increasing input from our mysterious and somewhat elusive new owners, Arkaga. Whoever they were, Arkaga, through their various representatives, soon made it clear that they were promising to take football at Cork City FC to new heights, both domestically and on the European stage. As if to back up this claim, among other things, a new 'state of the art' multi-purpose stadium was promised for the city and for the club. Soon, more lucrative and longer contracts were agreed with many of our more important players; this was accompanied by the addition of some key playing and administrative staff. Here was a club 'on the up', and we were, they kept telling us 'very lucky to be part of it.'

However, on the 14th of August 2008, just four months into the season, it was announced, without any prior notice to the players, that Arkaga were leaving and withdrawing their support from the club. And so it was that we, the players, fell sharply from the promise of decorated full-time football and off-field progress into all-out chaos. Faced with this sudden shock, and with increasing uncertainties all around us, we did what all players should do in any such times of such crisis: we got our heads down, trained and played hard. We battled to stay afloat, winning most of our matches and, effectively, winning a new chairman – and all while the club was embroiled in the examinership process. Our success in the much maligned (but well-funded) All-Ireland competition, the Setanta Cup, may have played some part in the decision of new club chairman, Tom Coughlan, to take over the reins, as the club emerged from examinership and into his hands in October 2008.

Unfortunately, Coughlan was an unknown quantity amongst the players and so there was some uncertainty as we closed the season and took a much-needed break in November 2008. Over Christmas we were probably all thinking the same thing: 'What lies ahead in 2009?' Like all players, while dreaming of medals and glory we mostly desired progress. But following the turbulence of 2008, some of us suspected that for 2009, stability would be a finer thing.

Mathews leaves Cork (*Irish Times*, 9th December 2008)

Cork City will begin the search for a new manager in the coming days after announcing the departure of Alan Mathews today. The former Longford Town boss only joined the club in January and led the Leesiders to the Setanta Cup title last month.

But after a turbulent year off the field – the club were docked 10 points after financial problems led to them entering examinership during the summer – the Cork City board today withdrew their offer of a revised contract to the Dubliner.

"Alan has been a tremendous leader throughout the examinership process and is a very talented football manager," Cork chairman Tom Coughlan said in a prepared statement.

"I would like to thank him for efforts in this difficult time for the club. I have no doubt he will have a great future in football."

~~~~

Most of us felt that Alan Mathews deserved better and were sorry to see him leave. After all, he'd just guided us to an unlikely Setanta Cup victory (with a resultant financial windfall). He'd also managed to keep our league form very respectable – this despite the forced departures of many of our key players. And had we not been deducted those 10 points by the League for our financial irregularities, we would've qualified for Europe. These must be considered significant achievements in themselves, let alone in the context of a season torn asunder by the shock exit of club owners Arkaga.

But as the club emerged from examinership, and into the hands of new chairman Tom Coughlan, it became only too clear to us that Mathews' days were numbered.

We first witnessed the negative body language between the two at a meeting on 23rd October 2008 in Kenmare, at which Coughlan seemed to prefer to address the players rather than Mathews. Coughlan's mentioning of new players that the club were hoping to sign – without ever looking over to Mathews for his confirmation – did not, we all knew, augur well for our manager. We witnessed a deterioration in their relationship as we approached the end of 2008, and so on learning of Mathews' departure we weren't really surprised.

However, as sorry as we might have felt for the departing Mathews, our minds – by necessity – moved to the question of his replacement.

There was much talk around the city about whether Coughlan could pick the right man to lead the club into the next season and beyond. Some of the people I spoke to harboured serious doubts. There were alarming rumours of Gaelic Athletic Association (GAA) managers being approached, but nothing was clear.

As far as the players were concerned, those of us that had met with Coughlan, and were made to feel part of his plans, felt contented for a period. For my part, it seemed as though he considered me one of our more important players, which is quite often enough for a footballer. And for a time it was enough for me.

I'd met with Coughlan at the Clarion Hotel in Cork before Christmas, following the departure of Mathews, to discuss my position. I was out of contract and had been somewhat unemployed since the end of the season. On entering the lobby of the hotel, Coughlan warmly invited me to sit with him and it was clear that he was very excited about the year ahead. He seemed genuinely happy that I was interested in signing back for the club. We got down to business and I told him it had previously been agreed with Mathews that I could start my professional training course to become a solicitor at Blackhall Place (the course had recently become available in Cork as well as Dublin) in the coming September.

'Not a problem,' he said, which was a big relief.

On this basis I agreed to take a 33% cut in my gross wage and to sign for one more season.

The previous year's problems at the club had influenced my decision to move on with my life outside of football in the League of Ireland, and this deal would allow me to do that. All things considered, I was happy enough to sign up, and Coughlan seemed happy too.

When we shook hands in agreement he said something like, 'Here's to agreeing to make Cork City FC the best club in Ireland,' and I felt he really meant it. To this day I still feel that this was his genuine, if somewhat misguided, intention – although he may have hoped to get some positive PR in the process.

Unfortunately, as things would turn out, there were problems before pre-season even began. My first wages under my new contract didn't come through as promised, and so just before Christmas, with my wages a few weeks overdue and without an incumbent manager to turn to, I approached the club shop (which had now moved to Sullivan's Quay) looking for answers.

Eventually Tom turned up and wrote me a cheque for the money I was owed. I can't remember whether he apologised or offered an explanation; I was just happy to see the money and lodged it straight into my bank account. Checking online later, I saw that the money had cleared into my account. Great stuff – full steam ahead.

However, a few days later, on Christmas Eve, I received a letter from my bank: 'Cheque bounced – refer to drawer'. Unfortunately this was to prove a portent for the season to come. When the players later met up I found out that most of us had been in the same boat over the off-season, experiencing problems with delays, partial or non-payment of our wages.

Then, before we met back for pre-season, the new manager was announced. It was a big surprise when we learned that Paul Doolin – the tough, shaven-headed manager of Drogheda United, our main rivals over the previous few years – was to take over the reigns. Doolin had been one of the most successful players in the league over the last 20 years or so, and had recently experienced a golden period as manager of Drogheda, winning the league and FAI Cup before financial difficulties had engulfed them. During this period, the strength and depth of their squad was of particular note: Doolin had amassed 20 to 25 full-time players of the highest quality in the League of Ireland – something not even Shelbourne in their prime had managed to do.

Doolin's Drogheda side had beaten us in two cup finals: the 2005 FAI Cup and the 2006 Setanta Cup. The guy had hardly enamoured himself to us. We were a strong group, loyal to Cork City FC, while Doolin was a hard Dubliner and the type of person, we felt, that might view the rest of the country – including those living in our city – as soft 'culchies'. As such, there was some apprehension amongst the players as to how we'd get along with him.

Also over this period, by the usual highways and byways, I'd learned with much regret of the departures of players Darragh Ryan, Liam Kearney, 'Crazy Daz' Murphy and 'Superkeeper' Mick Devine to pastures new. Darragh was moving to St Pats and would go on to play his part in their successful European odyssey during the 2009 season. He would subsequently move to the Victorian League in Melbourne, Australia, to finally enjoy the footballing lifestyle he had so long desired.

Liam, unimpressed with the scale of the reductions on offer from Coughlan, was snapped up by Derry City manager Stephen Kenny. Crazy Daz was off to try his hand in England: he soon joined Stevenage Borough in the Conference, who he went on to assist in winning back-to-back promotions over the next few seasons, bringing them up to England's League One. 'Superkeeper' Mick had been seeking a route back to part-time football for some time; he was probably relieved to join part-time Waterford United – the club from whom Cork City had bought him in 2001.

These were big losses, but in football, as with everything else, you move on.

Those of us that remained hadn't expected many new signings, given the pay cuts and problems with wages, so it was to our huge surprise that we signed not just five players to replace those that had left, but nine full-time professionals, ready for battle at the top end of the league. These included central midfielder Stephen O'Donnell from Bohemians; left-winger Billy Dennehy from Derry; and goalkeeper Dan Connor and striker/midfielder Faz Kuduzović from Drogheda. Such players wouldn't have been signed on the cheap; every club in the league would have wanted them.

On top of these, two Latvians – a striker named Guntars Silagailis and a centre-back named Robert Mežeckis (a senior Latvian international) – signed up. They were joined by a young midfielder from Limerick named Shane Duggan, who signed with us from UCD on returning to Ireland from Plymouth. We also signed talented and tricky Cobh Ramblers winger Davin O'Neill.

I was also particularly happy to see the return of Greg O'Halloran to the club. Greg had played with Cork City as a 17-year-old back in 1998, and was part of the team that won the league with us in 2005 before being signed by Shelbourne for the 2006 season. Since then he'd travelled Ireland, playing with Derry, Galway and more recently Cobh Ramblers. He could play in most positions, was two-footed, talented and strong.

Greg was very talented off the pitch too. His ability to accurately imitate every player, from past to present, often made the long bus journeys to Dublin more palatable for the rest of the lads. He once pulled off a 10-minute impression of Pat Dolan onstage in a bar in Malmö, which ended with rapturous applause from our travelling supporters just as Dolan, having tracked us down, entered the room. Dolan was duly informed of the nature of Greg's performance but, perhaps high on our win just a few hours earlier against the former European Cup finalists, let the matter go.

Inevitably, Greg saved his best performances for impressions of Denis Behan, and Denis couldn't help but provide an ongoing supply of his usual indecipherable material. As Denis and Greg were best friends, it worked a charm. No serious casualties – just good laughs, with Denis often throwing his head back in hysterics at Greg's interpretations of his own self.

In any event, there seemed quite a lot of signings for a club that had been through examinership the previous year and had recently asked players to renegotiate their contracts due to lack of funds during the off-season.

It seemed, with these new signings, that Doolin was setting out to build a squad of a similar size to that which he'd gathered around him at Drogheda. Whether this would be achieved under Tom Coughlan's stewardship, and whether the two of them would get on, would remain to be seen. In retrospect there's a degree of inevitability; they were a volatile combination. But things had started on a high note.

~~~~

Doolin: Future's bright for Cork – New boss insists long-term success possible at City (Aidan Fitzmaurice in *The*

Herald, 16th January 2009)

Success at Cork City FC seems to be the kiss of death for a manager as former coaches Damien Richardson and Alan Mathews left the Turner's Cross post just weeks after winning a major trophy for the club.

But new City boss Paul Doolin, a league-winning manager with Drogheda United in 2007, believes he can achieve long-term success with the club despite the turmoil that has surrounded Cork in the last six months.

City's five-week search for a manager, which at times had elements of farce such as the bizarre approach to former Cork GAA boss Billy Morgan, was formally ended yesterday when Doolin was unveiled to the media in Cork's city centre.

Doolin, who has watched his league-winning Drogheda side broken up in recent weeks, knows there are no guarantees of trophies on Leeside, especially as doubts remain over City's ability to meet their financial liabilities to players and former manager Alan Mathews, but he feels the club has a future – and a successful one.

"No-one knows what is going to happen with the clubs. The only thing I did say, and I said it to them in Drogheda, there is no point getting involved if in six months you're not going to be here," said Doolin.

"If you want to start something, you start it. He [club owner Tom Coughlan] seems really enthusiastic about what he wants to do with the club."

[...]

"Bohs will still probably have the strongest squad because they haven't lost too many at the moment and they may have signed one or two, Brian Shelley I think signed for them. They will be strong.

"Derry will probably be the same – decent. St Pat's I think will still stay full-time despite what they have said."

[...]

"In the league, Setanta Cup and FAI Cup, we would like to do well in them all," added Doolin.

Cork's hunt for a replacement for Mathews was a long and painful one, with City fans frustrated by the lack of real progress and the unsettling attempt to hire GAA boss Morgan, but owner Coughlan insists that Doolin was his first choice all along, though Doolin himself doesn't care how the hiring came about.

"I'm not bothered who was or wasn't asked. That's none of my business. I'm sure there were others. I'm probably 25th on the line. I'm waiting for someone to say that," he said.

"In fairness to Tom, so far he has been very, very good. He seems like a very genuine fellah. I wouldn't dare judge anybody. He doesn't know me at the moment and I don't know him and we have to build up a relationship.

"However, he seems like he wants to take the club forward. He has started work on the training ground in Bishopstown which is important."

~~~~~

Money was indeed spent at Bishopstown. The inside walls were repainted and, on the instructions of Doolin, our lunches were now presented to us in the old meeting room, which was set up as a players' food mess. Big hot bins of soup would be delivered in, along with the contents for sandwiches which we would make up after training or between double sessions.

On anticipation of a new manager, because so much depends on his opinion of them, players will often piece together whatever knowledge they have of him and construct it into a positive vision of falling under his favour. For example, when Pat Dolan was announced as the new boss in 2003 I took encouragement from the fact that he'd attempted to sign me for his club St Pats in 2002. At the time I'd moved to Dublin to do a law course at DIT, and before I did so, whilst out of contract, I'd met with Dolan along with my Dad to discuss my footballing plans. While Dolan was impressive and charismatic from the get-go, in the end we didn't agree terms.

And so I felt two years later, when he became our manager at Cork, that this might help my cause somewhat, because at least he knew who I was. And for a while it did help. Similarly, I drew comfort when Dolan was sacked and replaced by Damien Richardson (Rico): some years before, a moustached Rico had spoken in glowing terms on national TV of a last-minute goal that I scored against Derry City.

Along with most of my teammates, I'd been involved in a few previous interactions with Doolin. He hadn't spoken very well of us, or of Rico, during a fairly heated recent rivalry while he was manager of Drogheda; I'd also been part of a team that denied his Shelbourne side a league title on the last day of the league back in 2001, at a time when he was coming to the end of his playing career, although I doubt he'd remember my role in that game. But after I'd broken my leg in a league game against Waterford in early 2003, he later approached me while I was on crutches at a game in Cork, while he was manager of a visiting team, and had a few words of encouragement for me. That was somewhat promising. Overall, though, we all felt a little uncertain about how he would take to us, and to Cork in general.

In his first meeting with us it was clear he hadn't forgotten the rivalry. After the usual introductions he let us know where his office was located in Bishopstown, and in his strong Dublin accent left us in no doubt as to who was in charge: 'I'm telling youse, if any of youse want to have it out with me, youse know where to find me. Just knock on my door, and we'll have it out, one on one.'

He was also quick to criticise our defensive record over the previous few years; he said we'd gotten into bad habits and it would have to change under his watch. He was convinced that the team with the best defensive record had won the league every year for the last 10 years. While he was wrong on that score, overall there was some merit to what he was saying. I, like most defenders, was very aware of our goals against column. I knew we'd slipped from being the team with the best defensive record in 2005 and 2006, to the sixth best in 2007 and the joint fourth best in 2008.

'Work hard', he said, 'and things will be fine. It'll be a blank page between youse and me and that's all I can ask.'

Doolin initially tended to mix my name up with that of a guy he used to play with, and so I was called Neilly Ogden for the first few months, which kept the rest of the lads amused but which, I admit, was slightly insulting. His assistant manager was Tommy Dunne – a left-back from Rovers whom I'd played against at some stage also. Tommy was genuinely funny and would remain very loyal to Doolin. They also brought a goalkeeping coach, and on the recommendation of Joe Gamble, a new fitness coach named Mark McManus.

Doolin's training sessions were top class. All ball-work and football-related fitness work. There was a lot of focus on flexibility and a never-ending series of passing drills. Everything was prepared well in advance and planned out to the last second. It was all very demanding.

Due to a particularly cold period of weather during pre-season, our training pitch at Bishopstown was often frozen and dangerous, in which case we would get changed at Bishopstown and then travel 10km to Blarney United FC's AstroTurf pitch for training. On top of the eight new signings, there were (as always) a few trialists hanging about. The local papers got very excited when they learned that three Brazilians were training with us. One morning during the car journey to Blarney with Lordy and myself, the only one of them who could speak English asked us, 'When you play Glasgow Celtic?' He and his compatriots were very aggrieved when they found out, on their second week of training in the freezing cold, that they'd been duped. By whom? By their agent, perhaps? Nobody knew.

From that point onwards it was as if the wind had been taken from the Brazilians' sails. They'd mope about

Bishopstown, shivering and sniffling and whispering between themselves in Portuguese. We all felt quite sorry for them. During training, Doolo would shout at them, in the depths of winter, 'You, get over there!' or 'You [pointing to the one who had the best English], tell him to go over there!' They weren't bad players, but it became clear that they weren't suitable for our league, and when one of the poor guys actually developed frostbite on his leg, that put an end to it. They were gone. Nobody knew where.

However, some of the lads had enough on their minds without worrying about the trialists. A few of the players, such as Joe Gamble, Danny Murphy and Lordy (Cillian Lordan), who were on contracts that hadn't expired at the end of 2008, had been having problems getting paid in full. Unlike the others (including me), Coughlan didn't have an opportunity to offer those lads new contracts on less money. So the club had only paid some of their wages.

Due to this, and the various difficulties we'd all encountered with payment over the off-season (some of our back payments from the previous year were also overdue), we asked that we all be paid directly into our bank accounts on the same day from February onwards. The club agreed, but when the date for our February payment arrived there was no sign of the money in our accounts. Because it was a monthly payment, there was an increased anxiety about receiving it. One of the lads, Alan O'Connor, having had enough of the delays and problems, decided not to train until he was fully paid.

True to character, Doolin summoned Coughlan to attend the following Monday's training. While the payments arrived into our accounts that Monday morning, Doolin insisted that Coughlan should still come into a meeting and give the players an explanation.

We all gathered in the meeting room with Doolin and Coughlan at the top, in the same place that the examiner had met us the year before. Doolin spoke first, outlining the problems we'd all encountered and insisting that for the sake of the season ahead – which was due to start in a few weeks' time – we needed to iron out these problems now. Coughlan listened, staring down at us, waiting for his chance to reply. When it came, it was clear he wasn't happy. He reacted defensively, reminding us that he was a Cork man and that he'd put thousands of euros into the club to keep it alive. In the end, though, he calmed down and told us that our wages would never be late again.

'Alright,' said Doolin.

As Coughlan walked out of the room we basked in the comfort of having Doolin to fight our battles. We hoped that would be the end of it.

Chapter 2

Start of season to May 2009

After a few months of intense training we were very fit and counting the days to the start of the season. At some stage it became clear that Doolin was going to employ a 4-3-3 formation for the year ahead, and we were all interested to see how we might fit into his system in what had become a fairly large squad.

Perhaps partly due to the extensive personnel changes, together with the new formation – or maybe just for the sake of tradition – we were inconsistent in our pre-season and early season matches. In our opening league match, away to Sligo, we conceded a last-minute goal to draw 1–1. But with six players making their league debuts for the club that night, the feeling was that we'd get stronger.

Saturday 7th March 2009
League of Ireland Premier Division
The Showgrounds, Sligo
Sligo Rovers 1–1 Cork City

CCFC team sheet: Dan Connor; Neal Horgan, Robert Mežeckis, Dan Murray, Danny Murphy; Pat Sullivan, Colin Healy, Joe Gamble, Billy Dennehy; Fahrudin Kuduzović (Stephen O'Donnell 66, Greg O'Halloran 89), Denis Behan (Guntars Silagailis 79). Subs not used: Mark McNulty, Davin O'Neill

On our return from Sligo, instead of getting our heads down to focus on the next few games, we were brought on a trip to Reading FC near London. It was undoubtedly a good experience staying at the hotel situated within the Madejski Stadium, training at Reading's training ground and playing against their reserves in a friendly. However, given the financial situation that we'd just come out of, it also felt slightly bizarre. Had we come so far from last year's troubles to be able to afford this? Were Reading paying for it? We didn't know, but we certainly weren't looking like a club with financial problems.

Our poor form continued on our return to Ireland, and we lost to St Pats (Daz Ryan getting the winner against us) and Derry (with Liam Kearney playing) in succession. However, the real bad news came from Dublin, where it was emerging that Bohemians FC were in trouble. There were rumours of a big property deal – negotiated during the Celtic Tiger – involving the sale of their pitch at Dalymount Park to a company owned by property developer Liam Carroll, which had gone sour. Loans had apparently been taken out by the club on the strength of the proposed deal – loans that had helped pay for their league-winning team over the past few years. Now it seemed the deal was dead, and Bohs were reportedly in debt to the tune of a few million euro.

Back in Cork, it emerged that Danny Murphy's wages had been left short in the March payment. Murph thought this was due to the club continuing to renegotiate his wages without his consent; he brought the shortage to the club's attention but was only told that 'things are tight at the moment.'

'We can afford to fly the entire squad to London for a few days, though,' Murph pointed out in disgust. Tom Coughlan was out of the country on holiday, apparently.

Jerry Harris and his grandson Caen Harris (who had taken over the kit washing and handling duties) also don't receive their wages for March. Caen said, somewhat despairingly, 'I wouldn't have minded so much if they'd told me about it first, but when you're expecting the money to come and it doesn't… then the situation is far worse.'

All other staff and players seemed to have been paid, so most of us at least felt that maybe we were getting there.

Friday 27ᵗʰ March

Given Murph's problems getting paid, I couldn't help feeling alarmed when I read this in the *Irish Times* this morning: 'The key early indication that a business may be in trouble is where it becomes slower at paying its bills or is looking to renegotiate credit lines.'

League of Ireland Premier Division
Turner's Cross, Cork
Cork City 2–1 Bray Wanderers

We were all very relieved to have won at last. But the relief didn't last long, as we heard alarming rumours emerging from around the city that the club's in financial trouble again.

Friday 3ʳᵈ April

For the most part, since his arrival, I've gotten along fairly well with Doolin. That said, during recent one-to-one meetings in his office he's said he finds it unusual that I'm starting a college course a few months from the end of the season, and he's not delighted either about the blog I've started posting on the club's website. He's suggested that I might be distracted a little, and he's probably right. However, after last year's problems I know it's time for me to move on and I'm not about to change any of my plans. It's probably partly due to this – and mostly due to Pat Sullivan's good form – that I was dropped for the match away against leaders Bohemians in Dublin tonight. I haven't been setting the world alight, to be fair. Anyway, I came on for the last 20 minutes when we were 1–0 up and we held on.

League of Ireland Premier Division
Dalymount Park, Dublin

Cramped together in the small cabin-like dressing room in Dalymount, Doolo was overjoyed with all of us and about as emotional as he's ever likely to be. He shouted, 'Yez c*nts!' before embracing us and telling us we were fantastic – even me.

'You done well, Neilly fella, when you came on. Fair play to ya.'

Despite the rumours about their financial problems, Bohs are still the team to beat in the league, so this is a great result.

However, on the bus home we discovered that some of the lads had heard a rumour that Tom has come up with a scheme to let everyone in for free for Tuesday's game against Drogheda.

'There are posters up advertising it,' said Murph. 'It's because there's a Champions League match scheduled for the same night, so he's trying to boost our crowd, but I don't think it's allowed by the FAI. You have to charge a fee, I think.'

Whether it's allowed or not, it's been making the news and social media.

It's a strange strategy, it must be said.

Tuesday 7th April

Last year's gaffer Alan Mathews is now manager of Drogheda, who we played tonight at home. He made some comments about the state of our club in the media, essentially saying he's worried for the players and fans here. Just 2,100 people turned up to watch (for free), which is disappointing considering we beat the league leaders last Friday. It seems fans are staying away. Anyway, we won one-nil and I remained on the bench as Sully's playing very well at right-back.

League of Ireland Premier Division

Friday 10ᵗʰ April

We played Shamrock Rovers tonight at their new ground, the Tallaght Stadium. While South Dublin County Council owns the ground, it's definitely a move in the right direction for the league in terms of facilities, with a car park, a nice modern stand and club shop.

Tallaght has a big population and is nicely linked to Dublin city centre by the LUAS, so Rovers moving there makes sense. We've actually been driving past the foundations of the stand in the bus for the past five years or so, waiting for the chance to play there while a dispute with a local GAA club delayed the completion of the stadium.

It's great news for the league that Rovers finally have a solid base. They were renting Tolka Park the last few years, and before that they were playing at the Morton Stadium athletics ground, which was far from ideal and hardly appropriate for a club with the most prestigious history in Irish football.

The pitch in Tallaght has good potential as it's long and flat, but the surface was in bad condition tonight. Still, that's no excuse for the poor fare offered up by both sides. Long balls were battered from one end to the other; there was little or no emphasis on build-up play. It was entirely about not getting caught out – a kick and rush, territorial affair. Progressive footballing traits – passing ability, good ball control, clever movement and one-twos – were not present tonight. Somehow the league has to move on from this in order to grow.

I started on the bench again but came on after 25 minutes for Davin O'Neill, who hurt his ankle, with Sully moving to right wing. We scored from a free-kick, Colin Healy getting his first league goal for the club with a lovely shot up and over the wall. But they equalised in the last 10 minutes. Just a long ball, we didn't deal with it, and Gary Twigg scrambled a goal for Rovers.

League of Ireland Premier Division
Tallaght Stadium, Dublin
Shamrock Rovers 1–1 Cork City

We weren't happy coming off. Nobody was. A horrific game.

On the bus home Muzza told me he'd heard a rumour that Tom Coughlan is to walk away from the club over the weekend. I'd heard the same from a supporter who told me that the club is in debt with the taxman. Muzza also said there's supposedly money still owed to the Deanrock Bar for a remaining debt relating to the provision of players' lunches during the Arkaga period. We don't know if any of these rumours are true.

Nonetheless these are not good signs and the boys are worried.

Davin O'Neill, even though he's a part-timer, is quickly becoming an important player for us on the right wing, and Doolo has been asking him recently to go full time.

'I'm not gonna pack in my job [as a fitter in the Irish navy] – no f**king chance. You'd have to be crazy!'

Denis also voiced his concerns to the lads on the bus, saying he's spent his life savings on his wedding (which is at the end of the year) and the Little Kickers soccer franchise he's bought into. He said he'd be screwed if the club goes under.

At the back of the bus, I chatted to Guntars and Robert – both of whom have experienced similar payment problems in Latvia. Guntars said he wasn't paid for a whole three months during a time when his club were travelling around Europe beating teams such as Bohemians, amongst others. So maybe the problem is wider than our own league. Maybe it's about smaller leagues attempting to pay full-time players.

Saturday 11th April
A few of the lads got together to have lunch and Liam Kearney showed up. The boys wasted no time in mocking his new foxy haircut, and Liam replied with typical speed, mocking Danny Murphy's 'slippers' and my 'un-ironed' shirt. Kearney explained that the Derry lads know he'd prefer to still be in Cork, but given the rumours we're hearing around Cork we tell him he's probably be better off staying where he is. They seem a more secure club.

Easter Sunday 12th April
I received a missed call and voicemail this morning from an *Evening Echo* reporter. I replied by text, telling him I don't feel like doing a piece at the moment. He texted back saying he doesn't want to do a piece, he was just wondering whether I'd heard anything more regarding the rumoured Tom Coughlan situation.

I replied, 'No, just heard rumour and hopefully untrue.'

He texted back saying he'd called Coughlan, who didn't deny it but just gave out to him for ringing him on Easter Sunday.

Monday 13th April
At the end of training, Doolin brought us together to ask why the training had been so poor. We said nothing, so he went through possibilities: 'Are fellas tired?' The boys said no. 'Is it due to the rumours youse heard the other night?'

Nults was the first to reply: 'Well it's definitely the first thing we were all speaking about this morning.'

Doolin said, 'Well, I don't know if anything's going on or not, but I do know that youse can't let it affect youse boys. I know it's hard, and to be honest with yees it's been a pain in my balls since I got here. Every time a payment's due there's something wrong, someone hasn't been paid or somtin. It's not the bleedin' right way of doing things, but we gotta get on with it. To be honest with yis, I don't think it's any bleedin' different from before I heard the rumour, as I'm thinking it's dodgy whether or not we get the payment every bleedin' month. So I'll ask youse now: do yis want me to bring him in?'

Again nobody answered, so Doolo continued… ''cause the only thing I'd say is it would probably not make any bleedin' difference if we brought him in anyways.'

Tommy chipped in, 'Ya Paul, and it would only be confrontational and that isn't a help at the moment.'

'Look, we're all in it the same,' Doolo went on, 'I have a wife and kids in Dublin; I'm down here to win things. I'm no different from yees. The only thing I'd say is yees'll probably get clubs anyways if it goes under, but yis can't be thinking that way – just gotta get on with it, 'cause it could make yis unfocused and that might cost a match.'

Muzza agreed this was the best approach but pointed out that the fact it keeps happening every month is obviously not helpful.

Doolo wrapped up by telling us we need to focus on tomorrow's match against Kerry in the League Cup at Tralee. 'Bus is leaving from here at 1.30. Alright boys, that's it.'

We piled back into the dressing room.

Stevie O'Donnell, who was limping around with an injury, was first to offer his thoughts: 'Well boys, ye'll see me passing yee on the bin truck if the club goes under.'

We all laughed, but Stevie said he wasn't kidding.

Denis told us he still hasn't received all of his back-money from last year, and somebody else said former player Gareth Farrelly is taking the club to the High Court next week for the money he's owed. Murph said he'd heard that the FAI are coming down next week to ask why Coughlan broke the regulations in admitting spectators for free. (There's supposed to be a charge of at least €10, apparently.)

Later, my old friend and ex-City player Mark Herrick called me from Galway, where he'd heard a rumour that Coughlan's going to pull away from the club tomorrow. We talked about how terrible it would be for the league and for Cork football if it's true.

Things are definitely starting to look grim again.

Tuesday 14ᵗʰ April

League Cup
Mounthawk Park, Tralee, Kerry
Kerry District League 1–3 Cork City (AET)

At the start of the second half I jumped up to head the ball away, climbing above a Kerry player, but then I landed the other side of him on my elbow, dislocating it. The pain was worse than anything I've felt before. The game was halted while I was brought to the sideline. A doctor and ambulance crew were at the game, but they advised against re-setting the elbow at the ground. A plan was formulated to bring me back to CUH in Cork, two-and-a-half hours away.

Tom Coughlan's parents, who'd been watching the game up to this point, were brought over to assist. I'd met his father before and he'd seemed like a nice man. Together with his wife he helped me out of the ground and into their car and dropped me all the way back to Cork with my elbow out of place. I've never felt so sick with pain in all my life as I did on that journey. I couldn't thank his parents enough for what they did; if it weren't for them I would've had to wait for the lads, and with the match going to extra time that would've been a nightmare.

In Cork University Hospital the doctors knocked me out and put the elbow back into place.

Wednesday 15th April

Doolo and Coughlan were already at Bishopstown when I arrived this morning with my x-rays to show the lads. Within a few minutes we were brought into the meeting room and Doolo said, 'Well lads, Tom's here to explain what's going on at the moment, aren't you Tom?'

'Thanks Paul,' Coughlan began. 'Well, I wanted to come in and tell you lads that there's no truth to the rumours you've been hearing. I'm not a quitter. As you know, there's an unprecedented economic situation and the state have just announced a special budget. But we'll get through it. I also wanted to say well done with the results lately. You and Paul and Tommy have been great. You just need keep on going.'

He continued for a few more minutes before leaving, but probably due to the effect of the painkillers I was on, I didn't take much of it in.

'Well, that's it lads,' said Doolo afterwards. 'You've heard him: he says there's no truth to the rumours, so yees have to get on with it now. We've a big game tomorrow.'

Friday 17th April

League of Ireland Premier Division
Oriel Park, Dundalk
Dundalk 1–2 Cork City

I remained home tonight while the lads travelled to Dundalk. I can't say I was disappointed to miss that bus journey. Later I picked up the result on the radio: George O'Callaghan, playing in midfield for Dundalk, set up Dundalk's opener before Billy Dennehy got an equaliser, and a then last-minute winner came in from 'Ding Dong' Denis Behan.

Wednesday 22nd April

Lordy texted to say he reckons we're not getting paid for another week – even though our monthly payment is due tomorrow. Apparently we're getting paid in the last few days of the month from now on instead. The lads are somewhat suspicious of the reasons for this change. At home, nursing my injury, I feel removed from what's happening at the club.

Friday 24th April

League of Ireland Premier Division
Turner's Cross, Cork
Cork City FC 1–0 Galway United

Another good win tonight for the lads. Billy Dennehy scored his second goal in two games, set up nicely by Faz. The team seems to be finding form.

Wednesday 29th April

I went in this morning to speak to our physio, Alex, and to get a recovery programme from fitness coach Mark McManus. We were due our wages today but only about half of the players received a payment. Danny Murphy and others (including me) who haven't been paid are seriously depressed about it. Murph tried to ring Coughlan but couldn't get an answer.

'Seems like there's a problem every f**king month now,' said Muz.

The wage problems are starting to affect the lads away from the training ground. Young Timmy Kiely, who rents an apartment in town with his girlfriend, has been told by his landlord that he has to leave because of his irregular rent payments – which are a direct result of the delays with players' wages. He's been given a month to get out.

Timmy said, 'He [the landlord] is a nice fella and all, and I can understand it, but it's a disaster.'

Friday 1st May

League of Ireland
Turner's Cross, Cork
Cork City 1–0 Sligo Rovers

The lads continued their winning streak, with Faz scoring a nice header from a Colin Healy cross. Meanwhile I'm spending my time on a stationary bike and cross-trainer, and doing every damned PR event possible for the club (as injured players often do).

The remaining lads to receive payment, including me, finally got paid today; and perhaps because of this we were in generous form. We collected some cash for the girl (Laura) in the office who we found out has resigned, and gave it to her with a card wishing her the best.

Monday 4th May

League Cup
Turner's Cross, Cork
Cork City 1–1 Wexford Youths (Wexford win 5–4 on
penalties)

Lightning strikes again. Just like last year, we've suffered another embarrassing defeat to Wexford Youths in the League Cup. This time we lost on penalties, with Gamble missing the decisive penalty, driving the ball incredibly high over the Shed End and out into the street.

Saturday 9th May

I'm back running, but I'm still not allowed into contact training yet. Meanwhile the team bounced back from Wexford Youths to defeat St Pats away in Dublin and go joint top of the table with Bohemians.

League of Ireland Premier Division
Richmond Park, Dublin
St Pats 0–3 Cork City

The game was live on national TV and the lads looked very impressive. Ding Dong Denis got the opener, with his buddy Greg getting the second before Faz curled a lovely shot around the keeper and inside the far post. After the game it was announced that Doolin's been awarded 'Manager of the Month'.

Wednesday 13th May

Revenue seeks to wind up Cork City *(www.rte.ie)*

The Revenue Commissioners have reportedly applied for a petition to wind up Cork City Investment FC, the holding company of Cork City. The petition is due to be heard on Monday, 25 May.

In a statement released tonight, Cork say they wish to confirm that the club is currently in negotiation with the Revenue regarding the club's tax liabilities.

They say that when the club emerged from examinership in October last year, a settlement was reached with Revenue.

However, the statement adds that additional tax liabilities have subsequently emerged which resulted from the club's previous ownership, and the club is currently addressing this matter with Revenue in a bid to bring the issue to a swift and successful conclusion.

The fact that the liabilities have arisen subsequent to the examinership is an issue which the club intends to pursue with the examiners.

The club's legal and financial advisers intend to meet with the Revenue as a matter of urgency in order to come to an agreement.

Cork City are currently joint top of the Premier Division and face Derry City at Turner's Cross on Friday night.

Thursday 14th May

While the lads arrived in dribs and drabs this morning, Muzza was busy reading an article about us in the paper.

Stephen O'Donnell walked in and said, 'How about the club, lads? Sounds like we're f**ked, aren't we?

Muzza stopped reading and added, 'Again.'

That's how it feels: just like when examinership broke last year.

While most of the players had heard the news, it was easy to spot the ones that hadn't. Billy Dennehy came in whistling and smiling. Muzza asked him, 'Surely you f**king heard, mate? No? Look at this!' He showed Billy the paper.

We all talked about the news and wondered whether we're done for. Most players are optimistic, though. Greg O'Halloran thinks it's debt from before examinership, and 'it'll all be cleared up – don't worry.'

But Denis knows exactly what the winding-up petition means. 'We either have the money by the 25th of May or the club is gone.'

'What do you think, Hog?' the young players Timmy and Shane asked me. I feared the worst, but didn't want to affect the boys for tomorrow.

'I don't know, wait and see,' I said.

I was halfway down the corridor towards the physio's room to get my elbow strapped when Doolo called me and said to tell the lads down there to come for a meeting. Shortly afterwards we all headed back to the meeting room, where Coughlan and Doolin were ready to begin.

Coughlan started this time.

'Lads, I wish I was coming in here to talk about the great run yee are on and the fantastic performances yee've been putting in. On the football side of things, yourselves, Paul, Tommy and the playing staff have been outstanding. However, in regard to what we're seeing in the papers this morning, all I can say is I'm as surprised as you.'

There were a few sideways glances amongst the audience.

'I was in getting a haircut when I received a phone call with the news. I can tell yee that this Revenue bill is something that was left over from the previous owners. We came to an agreement at the time of examinership, but now there's a problem. We'll get it sorted but you'll have to be patient as there are some changes in backroom staff at the moment too, which makes it difficult. We'll get it sorted though, and I'm not walking away from it. I've never walked away from anything in my life. I'm here to build the club over the next four or five years and that hasn't changed.'

Nobody seemed to know what to say.

'Alright lads,' he continued. 'All the best for tomorrow night. Focus on that, and thanks for the good work yee are all doing. OK? Thanks, I'll let you at it Paul.'

As Coughlan left the room, Doolo remained in the same position he'd adopted throughout the speech: standing with one foot on a chair in front of him, facing down at the lads. After a pause to check that the door was closed and the coast was clear, he began to talk.

'Alright lads, look at it this way: we have been getting paid, and whether Tom's paying the tax or not, and whether youse believe him or not, we've got to do our jobs and forget about all of this. I know it's not easy, but youse need to try and keep focussed on tomorrow. OK?'

After the meeting I travelled to training to use Blarney's AstroTurf with Faz, Guntars and Timmy. Timmy reckons that so long as Coughlan pays *some* money back, we'll get another date from the court and then he'll have to pay back more on that date, and that it might continue like this for some time until the debt's been paid.

Faz asked me, 'Do you think he was surprised?'

'No, Faz,' I replied. 'Maybe he didn't know that the Revenue were going to petition the club, but I think every dog on the street knew of the tax issue.'

'Well, I'd prefer if he wasn't surprised by it,' said Faz. 'At least then I'd know we're not dealing with a complete idiot.'

At training the players were in good form, messing and joking before settling down to business. I got involved in a game for the first time since the dislocation, but I'm still not allowed to do any contact work.

We drove back to Bishopstown for lunch and Coughlan was there again.

'Christ, a double show from the big man – something must be up,' whispered Stevie.

~~~~~

Cork City play down Revenue wind-up fears (*Irish Examiner*, 14th May 2009)

CORK CITY have sought to play down fears about the club's future following the announcement that the Revenue Commissioners are petitioning to have the company which owns the club wound up.

A hearing is set for May 25 but the club has expressed confidence that it will overcome what it called "short-term problems" relating to outstanding tax liabilities which, according to unofficial sources, could be in the region of €300,000.

[...]

Not for the first time, it seems that City are doing a fair impression of a swan – serene on the surface but apparently paddling like mad just to stay afloat.

The timing of the revelation that the Collector General has petitioned to have the company wound-up could hardly be worse ... tomorrow night, Cork have the opportunity to go clear at the top, at least for 24 hours, when they host third-placed Derry City at Turner's Cross.

[...]

The FAI will also be nervous onlookers. A third of the way into the 2009 campaign, they will have been relieved that, thus far, the season has not been disfigured by the kind of seismic financial problems which rocked the likes of Cork, Drogheda and Shels.

For a number of years, Irish club football has stood accused of living beyond its means, but as the domestic game belatedly cuts its cloth to cope with the harsh realities of the recession, the revelation that one of the best and best-supported clubs in the country is once more facing financial turbulence is worrying news not only for football in Cork but right around the country.

~~~~~

Friday 15th May

League of Ireland Premier Division
Turner's Cross, Cork
Cork City 1–0 Derry City

Fair play to the lads. Dan Murray scored the winner from a set piece knock-down by Greg, and Lordy played excellently in the middle of the park. In a dramatic final few minutes, Stevie O'Donnell was sent off and Derry substitute James McClean had an equaliser disallowed for offside, but the lads held on.

League of Ireland Premier Division table, 15th May 2009

	Pld	W	D	L	Pts
Bohemians	11	7	2	2	23
Cork City	**11**	**7**	**2**	**2**	**23**
Derry City	11	6	3	2	21
Shamrock R	11	5	3	3	18
Galway Utd	11	4	3	4	15
Dundalk	11	4	1	6	13
St Patrick's A.	11	4	0	7	12
Bray Wand.	11	2	5	4	11
Sligo Rovers	11	2	4	5	10
Drogheda Utd	11	1	3	7	6

Friday 22nd May

League of Ireland Premier Division
Carlisle Grounds, Bray
Bray Wanderers 0–2 Cork City

Ding Dong scored again tonight – this time from a free kick – and Healy finished things off. The lads have won six games on the spin. We're now top of the table, and only the Revenue could end our good run on Monday.

Monday 25th May

There was double good news today: first it was announced that the club has until the 15th of June to pay €100,000 and should therefore at least be OK until that date. Then it was announced that we're to play Roy Keane's Ipswich Town in a friendly in June in an effort to bring in some money.

Wednesday 27th May

We were supposed to be paid today but there's no sign of the money in my account.

Thursday 28th May

This morning Doolo asked if I'd been paid and I told him I hadn't. I wasn't the only one. Doolo said he'd been onto Coughlan, who told him all the players had now been paid. 'So when you go home later, check your accounts and ring me if there's a problem,' Doolo told us.

I came home and checked, and the money is in my account – provisionally at least.

Friday 29th May

League of Ireland Premier Division
Turner's Cross, Cork
Cork City 0–1 Bohemians

A very disappointing result, followed by another resignation from the staff as Jerry Kelly – our quirky and dedicated groundsman – has decided to hand in his notice. He aired his frustrations on Facebook, saying: 'But while we're watching the ball on the pitch, there's an awful lot going on behind our backs. That's what's worrying. That's what's really worrying.'

Chapter 3

June to 8th July 2009

Unfortunately the loss against Bohs was to start the lads off on a bad run of form. First they lost to Drogheda away, then they drew with Rovers at home before getting knocked out of the FAI Cup by Sligo Rovers after a replay. A 2–1 loss at home to Dundalk on 19th June rounded off a bad month, and everyone was happy to see the mid-season break on 20th June. I didn't keep my diary for that period as I was too busy organising my testimonial, which took place on 20th June.

Alan Mathews had first suggested the possibility of holding a testimonial for me back in 2008 as a plan for 2009. It was something that my father, who had by this time passed away, had always said I should accept as a high honour if ever the offer transpired. And so the plan was set, and even after Mathews' departure, Tom Coughlan and Doolo were quite supportive of it.

Rather than the usual invitation to an English club to play against City, I decided on a reunion of sorts. The game would feature a Cork City 'Legends and Exiles' side versus the current team. The 'legends' to be involved that day were the likes of Dave Barry, Patsy Freyne, Stephen Napier, Declan Daly, Pat Morley, John Caulfield, Fergie O'Donovan and Anthony Buckley from Cork City's earlier days – combined somewhat with the 98/99 side that had been managed by Dave Barry including the likes of Mark Herrick, Kelvin Flanagan, Derek Coughlan, Dave Hill, Noel Hartigan, Noel Mooney and Colin O'Brien. The 'exiles' included guys coming home for the summer from professional clubs in the UK, such as John O'Flynn, 'crazy' Daz Murphy, Leon McSweeney, Alan Bennett and Brian Barry-Murphy. Despite his ongoing dispute with the club over unpaid wages, Gareth Farrelly also travelled form the UK and, thankfully, had recovered enough from his near-fatal aneurysm to play in the game. However, the premium-level players that would have guaranteed a full Turner's Cross, such as Kevin Doyle, Shane Long, Damien Delaney, Roy O'Donovan and David Meyler, were unfortunately – for various reasons – unable to attend.

Perhaps in an effort to mitigate these absences, my testimonial committee pulled off something of a coup in organising former world athletics champion Sonia O'Sullivan to be our main guest speaker at a lunch (where Dave Barry and Rico would also speak) and to take a penalty on 'Super Keeper' Mick Devine at half-time in the game. Sonia's father, John, had previously been involved with Cobh Ramblers as a goalkeeper, coach and chairman respectively, and so Sonia had an appreciation of the League of Ireland, which was helpful. Another notable attendee at Turners Cross that day was Pat Dolan – which can't have been easy for him, considering the manner of his departure from the club back in 2004. Later on Dolan and Brian Lennox shook hands in a moment that, to me at least, seemed to make the whole event worthwhile. Another positive factor, and a sign of things to come, was the assistance of fans group FORAS, who helped out by volunteering to organise the match day.

While overall it was a success, I did find the whole thing quite embarrassing. It felt somewhat like a wedding where I was marrying myself. But some good was done, I felt, in staging a reunion for the players – something that rarely happens. I also announced in the run-up to the match that I'd be retiring at the end of the season to start my professional training course to become a solicitor. That announcement felt like a weight off my back, though I knew it would confirm to Doolo what he had probably been thinking all along: that my mind was set on getting out.

Following the testimonial we were off on our mid-season break from 21st until 28th June – a time I spent trying to get back to full fitness. I knew that I needed to push for a place in the team on my return, especially with Doolo now being aware of my intention to retire at the end of the season. But more importantly, now that the first eleven were on a bad run, I sensed an opportunity to get back in.

Monday 29th June

First day back training after the break and it turns out nobody's been paid for the month besides Healers, Denis and Murph, who all contacted Coughlan directly to ask for their wages. So we weren't a happy bunch. There was some talk of not training, or of pulling out of the upcoming friendly against Ipswich.

Doolin said it's the same old story, that he was onto Coughlan over the weekend and that he hasn't been paid himself. He reckons it's not helpful that three players have been paid. 'It would be better if we were all paid or nobody at all.'

'It's not f**king good enough,' said Gamble.

'What can I say, Joe?' Doolin replied. 'You're right, but what can I do? I said it to him over the weekend, I'm saying it to him again today.'

Joe wasn't appeased. 'We f**king need to do something about it. It's been happening every month now.'

'Well lads,' Doolin addressed the group, 'what do youse want to do? Do you want to go public about it? Youse could if yee wanted. You should probably go to the PFAI [the players' union] to be honest. Coughlan's been onto me about Páirc Uí Chaoimh, about how I should have went down there and seen the strength conditioning of the GAA guys, and they're not getting paid.' He said this half-laughingly.

Murph replied, 'I already got onto the PFAI and they said all we can do is send a letter to the League, but that'll only end up with us getting points deducted, so f**k that.'

'OK,' said Doolin. 'Let's look and see what he comes up with when I meet him later in the week and we can take it from there.'

In the afternoon we had fitness tests to see who'd enjoyed themselves too much during the mid-season break.

Tuesday 30th June

Lashing rain again today, which was unfortunate as there was a double training session. I had to leave between the sessions though, to present awards to kids at a school in Knocknaheeny, as promised to a friend who works up there. When I approached Doolo in his office about this he was unimpressed by my late notice but he agreed to let me go, and injured Latvian international Robert Mežeckis agreed to go with me too.

Back in the dressing room, goalkeeper Dan Connor announced that he's created a 'fine sheet'. Among the things we're not allowed do, according to his list, and for which we'll get fined, is laughing on the bus. Even worse, it's like the Gulags – you actually get rewarded for ratting someone else up. To be fair to Dan, a fine sheet is something that often helps create a bit of crack among the group, and he tried to make it mildly amusing but I wasn't impressed. The busy b*****d.

While the lads were discussing the list, Doolo was holding one-to-one meetings in his office in relation to our fitness test results. When my turn came he told me that while I did well in the fitness tests, I was 'too nice, Neilly fella.'

He's been saying this to me ever since he got here. Today I didn't accept it.

'Are you talking about on the field, or off of it?' I asked.

'Both,' he replied.

I objected: 'I don't think off the field is relevant.'

'Ya, well,' he partially conceded. 'But maybe but you need to get stronger and nastier on the pitch.'

He might be right about the strengthening; lately I haven't been in the gym as much as in previous years. But I'm not going to change my personality for him. I probably should've confronted him about it sooner.

As usual, Doolo's training was really good, but I noticed my timing was off when making tackles, which was frustrating. I'm hoping it'll come back gradually, but I hacked a few lads down this morning.

After the morning session I ate quickly, grabbed Robert and drove off to Knocknaheeny using directions (written on a napkin) from northsider Alan O'Connor. Robert's a good guy and a very good player, but he's been injured since the third game of the season. His injury, combined with our bad weather, payment problems and the distance from his home in Latvia, means he's been having a fairly rough time of it lately.

In the car on the way there he took a phone-call and was speaking Latvian. It was the first time I've heard him speak properly in his own language, and it was nice to hear. Afterwards he told me the call had been from another Latvian player who'd been offered a contract with another League of Ireland club a few weeks ago after a trial, and who had gone home to Latvia to get his car and bring over his girlfriend. On return to Ireland the contract wasn't forthcoming due to financial problems at the club, but having spent all his money getting back to Ireland, the guy couldn't go home. So he and his girlfriend are now living in the team manager's house.

We shuddered to think how awkward it would be to live with any manager – especially Doolo.

The kids up in Knocknaheeny were brilliant and the whole experience was a pleasant relief for us. On the journey back to training we discussed how much we hate pro football – or at least this version of it.

When we got back there was still no sign of money in anyone's accounts. Doolin said he'd called an official from the club who said the money would be paid today, but we weren't very confident of that happening.

In the afternoon session, Tommy took the warm-up before we played three games of 8 minutes on a large pitch. The name of this particular game is keeping your shape, and due to the large area, the team with the best shape will win. Muzza and I were at the back in our team; after years of playing together we're fairly comfortable, and our team (the yellows) beat the whites convincingly over three games, which was deeply satisfying – especially for me, given my personal battle back towards full fitness.

Afterwards I met Alex, the physio, and he told me that Dan Connor had been looking for me, at which point Dan came around the corner, beaming from ear to ear.

'First fine, Hoggie: five euros for leaving your training top outside.'

With clear delight he presented a little notebook and pointed to my name, which he'd written at the top of the page.

'But YOU brought it in!' I protested. 'Surely players aren't ratting up other players, are they?!'

'That's what the fines are for,' said Dan.

'I don't like that philosophy,' I said.

Lordy, who was walking by, backed me up: 'That's what they're like in Dublin – cut-throat, kill or be killed.'

Kerryman Billy Dennehy entered the conversation, insisting that 'it should only be the coaching staff that can be the rats.'

But Connor replied, 'That fiver would buy you a pint at the end of season, Bill.'

'Sure Hoggie'll buy me a pint anyway, wouldn't you, Hogs?'

'Course I would Bill, and I'd get you a few chips too.'

'Well, rules are rules,' said Dan.

'We haven't been paid in five weeks for f*** sake, and you've created a fine list,' I retorted with disgust.

'Ah, sure it's just a bit of crack,' he answered, laughing.

Wednesday 1ˢᵗ July

As I arrived at training this morning I met Doolin at the door and he asked whether I'd been paid.

'Not by last night, Paul, but I didn't check this morning' I replied.

'You can go in and check on my computer if you like Neilly.'

I checked my account but there was still no sign of the payment.

It felt weird being on Doolo's computer all alone, like being in the schoolmaster's room and going through his stuff.

When Doolo came in to get his phone I told him the money hadn't been paid.

'What bank you with?' he asked. When I told him he said, 'Ya, I'm with them too, and I haven't been paid either.'

We went down the long hall back to the dressing room. Other players were arriving in, but most were already there. Doolo started asking who'd been paid and who hadn't. Some had been paid fully, some partially, but most hadn't been paid at all – especially those with the same bank as Doolo and I.

It transpired that Coughlan's excuse to the lads who'd contacted him over the holidays was that he hadn't realised it was the end of the month last weekend and he thought we were to be paid this week instead.

Pat Sullivan announced that he's had enough of it all and has requested a move back to Dublin. Doolo said he rang the club office yesterday and was told we were all supposed to be paid today. With players now requesting to leave, he's on the warpath.

He called a meeting and asked us what we wanted to do. I suggested calling Coughlan in to see us before doing anything drastic; that way at least we'd cover ourselves. Gamble backed me up, but Doolo wasn't having it.

'But sure he'll only spout the same things he's been saying all along – and that's not worth a bollix.'

I reiterated that we should give Coughlan an opportunity to explain himself, but Doolin said he did that four or five months ago and 'it'll be no different now'.

Tommy said, 'I see what you mean Hog, going through the right process and all that, but it won't matter a f**k if he comes in and then just tells us the same sh*t as the last times.'

I felt they were missing the point. I wanted the players to be covered, if we go public, from the argument that we shouldn't be airing our dirty laundry.

Denis, on the other hand, suggested we should go to the press straight away and pull out of the Ipswich match, and some of the others were swayed by this, but Murph and Gamble agreed with my suggestion.

Gamble asked Doolo, 'Will you ring him?'

'I doubt I'll be able to get him Joe, but I'll try anyway.'

Doolo left the room to make the call. Tommy followed, and the players continued to discuss the situation while they were gone. Some players seemed keen to strike but Colin Healy wanted clarification: 'So what we want is our wages paid by a certain date, and if they're not we go on strike – is that it? Is that what we're talking about?'

Nobody really committed to an answer.

Lordy reiterated that striking for the Ipswich match would damage us more than it would damage Coughlan. 'Sure, he could play under-21s and might still get 7,000 people at the ground.'

Doolin and Tommy returned to the room having failed to reach Coughlan.

Nults announced that from the start of season himself and Gamble have been of the opinion that if we don't win anything this year then the club's f**ked and we'll be going back part-time.

'But we only have the league left since the Setanta Cup draw was scrapped,' Doolin pointed out (the Setanta Cup draw was cancelled last week).

'Ya, so we'll have to win the league,' said Nults.

'The only thing I'd say,' offered Doolin, 'is it's not an ideal situation going into Friday against Galway with players still unpaid. How about the rest of the teams, lads – what's happening with them? Have yee been talking to fellas at other clubs? Are they being paid?'

Gamble had heard (from Neale Fenn) that Bohs are being paid alright at the moment, despite their current predicament.

'Pats are OK too,' said Muz (who's being talking to Daz Ryan).

And while Derry players have been paid, Murph had heard from Kearney that there may be some trouble with contracts, and that they (Derry) are thinking of going back part-time.

Doolin tried to sum things up: 'The way I see it, the whole league must've got together at the start of the season with the idea of slashing wages and going part-time.' He stepped outside to try ringing Coughlan again.

There was a sense of chaos in the room. Some of the younger players were joking around at the back, and Murph had a go at them. 'This is f**king serious, lads,' he warned.

Myself, Lordy and Gamble discussed the potential reaction from the fans if we decided to go public and go on strike. We figured some of them would call us money-hungry b*****ds. Coughlan would probably say he's just trying to keep the club afloat and that he's only missed one payment, and the media would jump onboard and back calls for a return to part-time football, and we'd be the bad boys again like we were during examinership. They'll just blame our wages again and we'll be guilty by association.

I suggested that if we do go public we'll have to set out our case very clearly from the start, making it known that the non-payment of wages is only part of problem, and that the endless empty promises that have been made to us are as much to blame as anything else. We'd also have to make it clear that this is the sixth time it's happened, that some lads such as Robert and Guntars are totally reliant on the payments, and that we'd be better off being told there's a problem with our wages than being promised they're on the way and then not receiving them. Most people are aware of the recent history of the Cork hurlers going on strike, and given the current background of so many people being made unemployed, we'd need to be very careful – and very clear – about the message we convey.

Dan Connor pointed out that the strike route would only hurt ourselves and the club, and that it would lead to part-time, but most of us see part-time football as the only possibility at this stage anyway.

We discussed the transfer window, which starts in July in Ireland and August in the UK. We don't want to be caught out by that again like last year.

'What will we do, so?' asked Joey.

Someone asked for a show of hands for a strike if we're not paid by Friday.

Again Healy wanted clarification: 'So if all players are not paid in full by Friday, then we strike – is that it?'

'Yes,' said Joe.

All hands, including my own, went up.

Just as we were lowering our hands, the Gaffer came back in and said, half-laughingly, 'Well I'm not sure you'll believe this, but according to Tom there's nothing to worry about. We're all gonna be paid today. Those who were paid less than usual, it's because of a tax levy issue that just came in last month. There's some other problem with your one though, Lordy. So look, youse'll have to wait until after training to check your accounts and forget about it until then. OK? Now let's go training.'

We followed Doolo out into the rain, which helped us to forget about the uncertainty of our wages for a while.

After training, Dan Connor came into the dressing room with a load of jumpers that had been left out on the pitch. He threw them down on the masseur's bench, took out his notebook and started scribbling down the squad numbers that were on them.

'Busy b*****d,' I muttered, moving across the room. Dan had his back to me, and spotting the opportunity I grabbed his jumper from its hook and threw it over to Robert, who quickly hid it behind his back. He then gave it to Guntars.

'So,' I said to Dan, who was encouraged by my new-found interest, 'we're gonna fine everyone who left their jumper outside, is that it?'

'Ya,' he said. 'And it'll pay for the beers and champers at the end of season.'

While Dan was distracted by me, Guntars put his jumper in amongst the others.

'That's great, Dan,' I said, and the Latvian lads started to giggle.

A few minutes later Dan picked up his own jumper. 'Yees f**kers!' he said, laughing.

To be fair to him, Dan wrote his own name in the notebook... while we hid his flip-flops.

Thursday 2nd July

When I arrived at the ground this morning it emerged that most of the lads – including Doolo – had been paid. However, Guntars, Robert, young Paul Deasy, Sully, Alan O'Connor, Tommy Dunne and myself still hadn't.

Doolo said the money was meant to go in today, according to the new girl in the office, and he couldn't reach Coughlan by phone. It's getting very tiresome now.

Training consisted of the normal 'day before a match' stuff, and for team shape Doolo gave me a yellow bib. I was at right-back. I looked around and saw that he'd given yellow bibs to most of the first team, including Sully who was centre-half. Greg was on the other team wearing a red bib.

Doolo had a go at me during the game about something or other, but I've decided I'm not listening to him too much anymore. If I'm selected tomorrow I'll focus on winning the game, not on keeping him happy.

After training the lads asked me if I thought we should all go on strike tomorrow as I hadn't been paid. It was nice of them to ask, but I told them no.

Sully agreed: 'We'd be only hurting ourselves.'

There was still no sign of the wages in my account when I checked at home.

The news is focussed on the electrician strikes that are about to happen; they're saying the economy's in virtual freefall.

Tonight a friend asked me whether the stuff Roddy Collins has been saying about Paul Doolin is true. I didn't know what he was talking about, so he told me that Collins had said on the radio that Doolin was fed up with the job down here and had thrown his hat at it.

'I don't know anything about that,' I said. 'I know he's pissed off with the payment issues, and that's totally understandable.'

I've also heard a rumour that Doolo could be off to Stockport County, but I don't believe that either.

Friday 3rd July

I arrived onto the bus for our trip to Galway and passed Doolo, who as manager – and according to custom – was sitting at the front.

'Alright Neilly – have you been paid?' he asked.

I told him I hadn't and that I'd checked online a few hours earlier. I asked whether it was still all the boys with the same bank who hadn't been paid and he said, 'No, just you, Guntars, and Paul Deasy now.'

It could be argued we're easy targets. Luckily I'm not stuck for money at the moment, but I'm not sure about Deasy, who's a young lad with a young baby boy, or Guntars who's over here from Latvia. Anyway, Doolo said he'd get onto Coughlan again to get it sorted.

A few hours later we stopped at a shop. On the way in, Doolo asked me to check my bank balance at the ATM to see if I'd been paid, and Deasy was asked to do the same. I was surprised and pleased to see that my wages been paid – albeit a week and a half late (and my first payment in five-and-a-half weeks). It turned out Guntars had been paid too, but Deasy wasn't sure. Still, I was happy that mine was in and that I could focus on the match.

I'd been gearing up to start this game and didn't want to hear that I was on the bench. It seemed Greg would be the fall guy if I was playing, with Sully switching to centre-back. The Gaffer waited until we were in the dressing room before naming the team: I was in, Greg was out.

Right, I thought, *let's go to work.*

Out on the pitch, Muzza (our captain) called everyone into a huddle and said the usual motivational stuff, and then just as were about to break away, Gamble called us back in.

'I want to say something' he announced. 'We have to play for ourselves tonight, lads, for our season – or else we won't get paid – that's the f**king truth, boys.'

We sprinted away and the whistle blew.

League of Ireland Premier Division
Terryland Park, Galway
Galway United 0–2 Cork City

Guntars got a scrappy 'John Caulfield'-style goal; Faz scored a screamer; and Alan O'Connor played his first game since the Setanta Cup final last year (following his one-man strike for the first few months of the season) and did well. I played well enough; our away fans sang a song they occasionally sing about me when things are going well, and I was glad to hear it. It felt great to be back and winning after so long out. Greg congratulated me after the match, as did Lordy, who also didn't play. The two of them will be back in soon.

But I'm most delighted for our Bosnian winger/striker Faz Kuduzović, whose goal was superb. Faz, like many players from the Balkans, is technically excellent, but he's had a love-hate relationship with Doolin so far this year. The turbulent nature of their relationship to date, in my opinion, stems from a fitness test during pre-season. Although Doolo and Faz were at Drogheda together before arriving here at Cork, during this fitness test they had a major falling out.

The test in question, which we've christened the 'Six 150s', is similar to what many will know as a 'bleeper test', but with a few key differences. Carried out in the main sports hall in Limerick University, it involves six successive attempts to cover 150 metres in 30 seconds, with a 30-second break between each attempt. But it's not a straight run: a line is marked at every 5 metres – so there's a line at 5 metres, then at 10 metres, and at 15, 20 and 25 metres – and the person being tested has to run to the 5-metre line then turn and run back to the start, then go to the 10-metre line and back to the start, and so on, until ideally they get to the 25-metre line and back to the start within the allocated 30 seconds. They're marked for each distance completed in each run, and the total distance covered over the six runs is tallied at the end. If they were to complete the full 25 metres and back, they would have completed 150 metres in total; if they were able to do this on each of the six attempts then they would have a tally of 900 metres at the end.

We've been doing the Six 150s since Pat Dolan's days. The first time we did it, we were all surprised how difficult it was. 900 metres should be no problem, right? Wrong. While the first run feels easy, it's the lack of adequate recovery time that kills you. It's not unknown for first-timers to run a great first two runs before collapsing on the track in exhaustion on the third, while the others keep running around them. Over the years it's become a badge of pride to reach a tally of 800.

Dolan took a particular interest in it; he would watch from a tier above us, screaming down randomly at people he thought were not doing enough. 'Come on Kevin! Come on Liam! George... GEOOOORGE! Make the LINE, George!' If you did well he'd be in good form with you for days. If you did badly you could expect disdain from him for weeks or months until the next test.

The test needs proper monitoring to ensure that people don't cheat by turning early before the given line, so there's an invigilator assigned to each runner to mark his score and to check he's 'making the line'. A warning – and sometimes a second warning – could be issued for not reaching the line properly, and in theory you'd be disqualified if you missed it again.

During one particular test in the pre-season, halfway through Faz's six runs, Doolo intervened to say he hadn't made the line for a second time and should be disqualified. Faz disagreed, but Doolo told the invigilator from Limerick University who was marking Faz's scores to stop marking as he hadn't made the line.

Faz continued to run. 'I f**king did make the line,' he protested.

'No, youse didn't make the bleedin' line, Faz!' shouted Doolo.

Faz ignored him and kept running. The invigilator was unsure of what to do.

'Step out, Faz' said Doolo.

'No,' said Faz, running past him, 'I made the line.'

It went on like this, with Faz running up and down past Doolo, and Doolo telling him to 'pull out' for the rest of his test. But Faz completed it anyway.

While it was somewhat entertaining for those of us watching from the sidelines, this altercation seemed to bring an uncertainty to the relationship between Faz and Doolo – an uncertainty that lingered until tonight's goal. While Faz has been doing quite well recently and has scored a few goals for us, Doolo hadn't really been giving him much credit. But after his rocket tonight Doolo was delighted with him, and Faz wore a big smile that was great to see.

The feeling on the bus after a result like the one we got tonight is what I'll miss most about the game when I hang up my boots. The chance to take it all in, relax and keep the atmosphere going, cocooned together in a warm place as we travel through the night. As I write this, Greg sits across the aisle with his headphones on, singing 'Saturday Night at the Movies'. He has a fantastic voice. Some of the other lads are chatting about the game or playing cards. A few others, including Denis, Murph and Tommy, are gobbling popcorn and laughing at the movie that's playing on a screen upfront near the driver.

Tuesday 7th July

We met at 5.45pm at Turner's Cross for the match against St Pats. On the pitch, the lads grilled Denis on the rumour that Hartlepool are interested in himself and Healers.

'They've made an offer of €20,000 for both of us,' he said, 'but it's been turned down.'

He explained that he's been trying to ring Coughlan about it without success, so he hasn't had a word of explanation.

League of Ireland Premier Division
Turner's Cross, Cork
Cork City 0–1 St Pats

I really thought we were going to start off on a good run after our win at Galway. However, today a strong wind and a bright sun made life difficult in the first half, and the pitch – though recently resurfaced and in better condition than usual – was quite sticky, so passing wasn't easy. The game was scrappy and became an unattractive war of attrition due to the difficult conditions. We kept a clean sheet for the first half and things looked good as we turned around with the wind at our backs, playing into the Shed End, but we missed a good few chances and they broke late and scored against the run of play.

Afterwards Doolo confronted Danny Murphy for being out of position for their goal. He also laid blame on Joe Gamble and youngster Shane Duggan for getting ahead of the play. Joe flared up and argued back. I kept my head down and stayed out of it. One thing with Doolo: you'll never win an argument. He's always right.

A bad result, though, and as we went into the Shed End tunnel at the end of the match, fans were booing and shouting at Doolin. And later, when I walked past the Horseshoe bar on the way to my car, a large crowd was gathered as usual and one of the guys shouted, 'Hoggie – get rid of that prick Doolin, would ya?'

I walked on.

We have tomorrow off and we're back in on Thursday. Our video session that morning should be interesting.

Wednesday 8th July

As part of a drive to promote reading in the community, as a Cork City player I was asked to do a book reading in the City Library. Having studied History in college, I chose an extract from *The History of the Decline and Fall of the Roman Empire* by Edward Gibbon.

On the way to the library I met GAA columnist Michael Moynihan, who was also doing a reading. His *Irish Examiner* colleague John Riordan (a League of Ireland journo) was with him, and John beckoned me over. We had a brief chat about last night (he knew I didn't really want to talk about it) and then he asked if I'd heard what happened at the Horseshoe after the match.

'No – what?'

'Apparently Doolin had a glass thrown over him. Just the drink, but it's scandalous no matter how you feel about him, don't you think?'

I agreed.

'And what's worse,' John continued, 'his parents were there with him, down to watch the match.'

Christ almighty.

Chapter 4

9th to 18th July 2009

Thursday 9th July

When I walked into the dressing room this morning people were quiet. It was obvious nobody really wanted to be there. Losing to Pats at home was bad enough, but after having a pint thrown over his head Doolo would be f**king livid. We knew we'd be easy targets for a bit of venting, so we all kept our heads down and moved swiftly around the corridors, anxious not to bump into him one-v-one.

As usual, Dan Connor had the story. A pint of beer was indeed thrown over Doolo, but it was assistant manager Tommy Dunne's parents, not Doolo's, who were with him, and it happened *outside* the Horseshoe rather than inside it. That all made a little more sense: I couldn't see Doolo walking into the Horseshoe after the match – especially with his parents. Still shameful and disgraceful, though.

I asked Faz where he was after the match. 'Do you have an alibi, Faz?' He didn't hear me but Nults gave me a charity laugh.

When Tommy did his usual count of who was training and who was injured, I told him I was doubtful. My knee has swelled up and is very sore.

'Getting old, Hog,' said 18-year-old Paul Deasy.

'You're right, kid.'

Alex said I should get a scan, but I wanted to see if I could get an injection from the doc so that I can play on Sunday if selected, so he organised an appointment for later at his surgery in Cloughduv. Then Tommy told me I was to go inside with the others who'd played against St Pats on Tuesday, while those who hadn't played were to go outside.

I figured Doolo was about to make us watch the whole game, and unfortunately I was right. We sat down in the meeting room and he said, 'Look at yourselves in it, lads. Not great, boys, not great.'

I was nervous like everyone else. The volume was muted and everyone was quiet. I thought, *this is gonna be boring as hell*. But then I watched myself make big a mistake in the first few minutes. I tried telling myself that mistakes happen, that nobody really noticed. That it was bigger in my mind than in reality.

At half-time the players went out to the toilet and we discussed the footage briefly amongst ourselves. Healers pointed out how slow we looked; Gamble and I agreed. Afterwards the Gaffer came back in and said we looked slow.

The second half began. I volleyed a ball across our box by mistake. It looked like I was trying to pass it to one of our boys, who happened to be near where it landed, though. I exhaled. We got to the 90th minute and their goal, and as it played the Gaffer stood up and gave out to Murph for not keeping our shape. He then replayed the goal in slow motion and pointed at the figure of Murph, who was walking (rather than running) back towards our goal just before they scored. 'You're bleeding *walking* back, Danny?' He also gave out to Denis and Guntars for not holding the ball up.

Doolo announced that neither of the teams we'd just watched would win the league. 'Youse have it ingrained in yis the way we are at the back,' he said. 'Bet yee've been conceding goals like this for years and nobody's said f**k-all to yee.'

He pointed out, again, that every team since 1986 that's won the league has had the best defence, 'bar a year or two'.

'Only so much you can do in six months,' he said, 'but I'm telling youse it has to be better or I'll be getting pints thrown over me every week. OK, that's it. Ice baths for everyone. Back training tomorrow.'

Afterwards Murph told us Doolo had gone into the dressing room straight after the match and whispered to him that he was at fault for every goal this season. That was very harsh in my opinion.

Murph said, 'Even that goal against Dundalk when you went missing, Dan [Connor] – my f**king fault too, was it?' But Dan laughed it off.

Sean Kelly, who's on loan to Galway at moment, texted me on my way home asking whether everyone's been paid, because he still hasn't. So I called Jerry Harris, who told me he himself and Davin O'Neill also haven't been paid. I then called Seany and offered to tell Doolo about it tomorrow; he said he wasn't sure but would get back to me. Doolo has proven to be effective at chasing down Coughlan, to be fair to him.

Later at my appointment, the doc told me my knee is definitely a cartilage problem but it's not too badly damaged. He said he doesn't want to inject me for fear of infection, and he gave me anti-inflammatories instead. He also organised a scan and I'm happy with that.

I later received a call from the doc's office. My MRI scan is at 9.45am tomorrow and it'll cost €410. It's going to be hard to get the club to pay at the moment.

Sunday 12th July

League of Ireland Premier Division
The Showgrounds, Sligo
Sligo Rovers 0–3 Cork City

While my knee wasn't the best, I managed to get through 90 minutes. We won handily enough with goals from Murph, Faz and Sully.

~~~~

City could go bust in two weeks (www.rte.ie, 13th July 2009)

Cork City FC have been given two weeks to raise €400,000 due to the Revenue Commissioners or the club will face a winding up order.

It is understood that cheques paid by Cork to the Revenue recently could not be cashed and a High Court judge has now insisted that the outstanding monies be paid within a two-week period.

A statement released this afternoon by the club said: 'Cork City FC wish to confirm that the case under the Companies Act at the High Court today has been adjourned for two weeks.

'The club has made determined efforts in the past ten days to reach a settlement with Revenue, but to date has been unable to agree a settlement. Cork City will continue its attempts to resolve the issue fully over the coming fortnight.

'At this time it is imperative that our loyal supporters and the people of Cork get behind the club, as this support will be crucial to the future of the club and League of Ireland football in Cork.

'Cork City's upcoming friendly match against Ipswich Town on Sunday, July 19th will offer the club the opportunity to raise much needed funds, and we urge the people of Cork to support the club by attending the match.'

~~~~

Wednesday 15th July

The Gaffer was putting the week's training schedule up on the noticeboard as I got in this morning. He'd scheduled a double session for today, as expected after two days off, meaning a session with fitness guy Mark McManus in the morning and then out on the pitch in the afternoon.

First off, Mark took our body fat readings. (Mine was down a good bit; I've been doing more fitness work at home lately.) Then he put us through a body weights session. As we did this, Denis told us he'd heard that Coughlan doesn't have to pay all the money back in two weeks after all. Apparently he has to pay €200,000 rather than the €400,000, and there's an agreement on how to pay back the rest in instalments.

We finished the weights session and went back into a group meeting with Doolo and Mark. Doolo announced he was unhappy with our recent fitness tests, and also with our body fat tests. He was backed up by Mark, who said nobody's body fat score should be over 11. He called them all out and mine and Greg's were very high. Only Stevie's and Guntars' were worse. But these results were an average from the last three or four tests (including those taken while I was injured) and they didn't include today's results, so I'm hoping I'm less now – especially as I came third in the fitness test.

After Mark had left the room, Doolo asked us whether the club's situation was weighing on our minds.

'Of course it is,' said Gamble. 'Coughlan should be in here explaining the situation.'

After lunch, the players sat and chatted for a while before going out again for the afternoon session. Most of the lads seem optimistic that things will be sorted; the general consensus is that Coughlan will pay the €200,000 and agree to pay the rest, and that he'll sell Healers and Denis if necessary.

Later I spotted our local reporter, Noel 'Spillachi' Spillane, who'd come in for the latest scoop. He was chatting to Denis. Afterwards Denis came in and said, laughing, 'You'll never believe what Spillachi said to me.'

'Go on Denis,' we said.

'Well, he was talking to Coughlan and Coughlan says, "Noel, you have contacts up in Dublin, don't you?" "Ya," says Spillachi. "That's good, so could you find out if we could get Real Madrid flown down [from Dublin where they would soon play Shamrock Rovers in a friendly] for a few hours to play a game and they can fly off again after that?"'

Unbelievable. He's using Spillachi to contact Real Madrid.

Thursday 16th July

In the dressing room this morning the lads were wondering whether Hartlepool have agreed a deal with the club for Denis and Healers. We quizzed Healers as he came in from the gym, and he confirmed that a deal looked likely. He said he doesn't really want to move, but as the club's in trouble he feels he has no choice.

As Healy was talking, Denis came in and sat in his usual place next to Murph.

'I'll miss you Denis, ya pr*ck', Murph told him. 'The crack will never be the same.'

Nulty jumped in: 'Ah, course it will Murph – we'll have Greg doing impressions of Denis. It'll be even better than the real thing!'

Someone asked Healers whether he'll be rooming with Denis over in Hartlepool.

'At the start, I suppose... maybe,' he answered, half-heartedly.

'Best of luck with that,' said Nults.

'Wait until I have the medical,' said Healers. 'They'll be running from me.'

Someone else asked whether the deal had been agreed.

Denis said, 'Well Doolo rang me, and guess what he said, the b*****d?'

The boys quietened down in anticipation of a good laugh.

'He says, "Hello Denis, how are ya?" And I says, "Hello Gaffer, what's up?" I was playing dumb, see. Then he says, "Believe it or not, Hartlepool have come in for you and the club have agreed a fee." Believe it or not! He's some bollix, isn't he? I'm gonna call him Ripleys from now on.'

The lads were in hysterics.

Denis broke into Doolo's Dublin accent as he said it again: 'Bleedin' believe it or not! The bollix!'

There was an elevated atmosphere in the room: the lads are moving on, and this can only be a good thing for them, even though they'll be missed.

We went outside to a field full of cones and Doolo and Tommy, who beckoned us around them. Doolo said he'd spoken to Coughlan and they don't have the €400,000, but they're hoping they can get €100,000 from the lads moving, and from money that'll come from the Ipswich match. They can then agree with the Revenue to pay some back later.

Muzza said, 'I suppose it's not really helpful that we've recently given bounced cheques to the Revenue, then?'

'Ya, Dan,' said Doolo. 'They'll be asking where the money's gonna come from and whether the club's sustainable going forward. They were stung after the club went into examinership. But there's nothing we can do except get on with it.' He looked around at us all. 'What do youse think? Will the club survive?'

Gamble answered for the group: 'From our point of view, we might get paid now but we'll probably be left short again in August, September, October… and then we won't get paid at all − and then we'll be screwed when the transfer windows have closed and can't move.'

'I don't know Joe,' said Doolo. 'They're trying to put a plan together; the club accountant's coming in with Tom on Monday.'

'So do you think it's likely to be cutbacks and a return to part-time they'll be talking about, Gaffer?' asked Gamble.

'Ya, well, I don't know,' said Doolo. 'But something's gonna happen. I doubt they have a Scooby what they're doing at the moment, to be honest. They're probably hoping they'll know more after the Ipswich match and after the two boys have been sold.'

Gamble retorted, 'I wouldn't believe a f**king thing at this stage, to be honest.'

Our spirits had dropped and morale was low as we started training. Doolo and Tommy got us going though, and we ended up doing a very tough session, which brought some relief from the stress and uncertainty.

We played full-sided games at the end of the session, and in preparation for the match against Derry next week, Doolo put Kevin Long next to me at centre-back with Timmy Kiely on the right wing in front of me. These young lads will come in for Greg and Sully, who are suspended after picking up yellow cards, and it'll be very important for me to keep talking to them in the game against Derry. There'll be other changes too, with Lordy coming in to replace his fellow Ballincollig man Healy in midfield.

I did well in training and Doolo complimented me on a goal I scored. 'That was like Shels in 2005, Oggie!' (I got the winner in that game.) I suppose I'm getting on better with him now that I'm back in the team, and especially when he's giving me compliments. He's even getting closer to getting my name right...

Afterwards, at lunch, someone mentioned that Jerry Harris, Sean Kelly and Davin O'Neill still haven't been paid. I overheard Caen saying that he'd had to stop Jerry from buying stuff for the club out of his own money.

I met Jerry outside on the way back to dressing room.

'How are you, Neal?' he asked.

'Not too bad, Jerry. Yourself?'

'I'm OK, but things are bad aren't they?'

I agreed, then added, 'But if the club can survive with the two boys going, then that's the main thing, isn't it?'

'Ya,' Jerry answered, somewhat reluctantly. 'But where do we go from here?' He walked away down the corridor.

Back in the dressing room, Stevie O'Donnell was taking centre stage and entertaining the lads. 'I'm telling you boys – I need a Carlsberg agent like Denis. D'you think I could look him up on 11811?' He put his hand to his ear, 'Hello? Could you connect me to Denis's Carlsberg agent, please?'

Later, Spillachi's exclusive in the *Evening Echo* announced that the deal transferring Denis and Healy to Hartlepool has been completed.

Friday 17th July

The boys were in chirpy form whilst getting ready for training this morning. Greg was asking Denis to bring him with him, as Denis's interpreter.

'Ersurejasusfucking hell...' Greg mimicked Denis before adopting the Queen's English: 'This means, "Hello, could you pass it to my feet, please."'

Everyone had a good laugh – even Denis, who giggled as he tied his laces.

We'd been told there was a meeting at 10 o'clock. 'Big Tom's due in. This should be interesting,' said Stevie.

'What do you reckon he'll say?' asked Nults.

Murph answered, 'I think he'll just tell us we're f***ked.'

Sully disagreed: 'I reckon he'll say everything's grand.'

At 10 o'clock we made our way into the meeting room, where Coughlan was at the top of the room, waiting with Doolo and Tommy.

'Right,' said Doolo. 'I've asked Tom to come in and speak to youse, to explain what's going on. So Tom...'

Coughlan took his cue: 'Right lads, yeer probably all wondering what's going on in the club at the moment. Well, the situation is that I have to pay €400,000 to the Revenue. This is because I made the mistake of paying yee all back the money yee were owed, as well as bonuses, when I took over.'

This prompted an angry reaction around the room.

Coughlan responded, 'Well yee didn't get that back at Drogheda, did yee Paul?'

'No, we only got a percentage of what we were owed,' said Doolo.

'Anyway,' Coughlan continued, 'I paid yee all back as I figured give some and you get some back. Now the Revenue are up my hole and wondering if the club can be sustainable in the future. I've been on about sustainability ever since I took over, but due to the current economic climate it's been very difficult. The Irish economy is due to detract by 8% this year, despite a previous forecast that it was to grow by 2%. That's a

10% difference, lads, and these unprecedented conditions are causing us – and every business you come across – problems. I've already put hundreds of thousands into the club, and I want to keep it going into the future, but there will have to be decisions made next week when I talk to my accountant.'

We were still a little stunned that we were effectively being blamed for anything, but Coughlan continued, 'If you look at the top four clubs, Bohs and Derry are having similar problems; only Shamrock Rovers are stronger because of the way they came out of examinership recently with the fans owning the club. That's what I think should happen more down here. But I'll be able to tell you more when we talk next week. So that's the situation at the moment, lads – any questions?'

Danny Murphy, with his cockney accent, was first up: 'So, I just wanna ask, right, do you think we'll be staying full-time or going part-time?'

Coughlan leant back and answered, 'Well the intention is to remain a full-time club, but you need a full-time attitude too though, Danny. Take a look at the GAA players down in Páirc Uí Chaoimh, their muscular development. They have a full-time attitude and they're not even getting paid.'

Joe Gamble butted in: 'Sorry now Tom, but that's not relevant. It's a different sport, and…'

'What's not relevant?' Coughlan demanded.

'The comment you just made about the Gaelic players – that's a completely different situation.'

Coughlan began to look angry. 'I didn't make any comment, Joe.'

'Yes, you f**king did,' said Joe. 'Just there, about the Gaelic players.'

'I didn't Joe, what do you mean?'

At this point Tommy Dunne intervened. 'I think we need to get back to the question of whether the club's going to stay full-time and whether it's sustainable. From my point of view,

I think we just need everything to be put on the table. That's all the lads – and all of us – are asking for.'

Coughlan paused, and while he was doing so Doolin re-entered the debate. 'Well, I think it's happening all over Ireland. And not just Ireland: people are losing their jobs all over Europe and the bleedin' world. It seems to me that things went up and crazy for a while and now we're coming back down to earth. We suffered last year with Drogheda, but youse got your money paid back. So yee are only suffering now. I think the previous crowd that owned yee f**ked this club up and we're paying for it. Youse had money dished out to yee left right and centre, and I can tell yee this: only one player in Drogheda was on €1,500 – and none of this 3 or 4 grand. Yeerselves or yeer previous owners and St Pats, with the wages they were offering, f**ked it up for everybody.'

Murph was quick to reply, 'You can't give out to us for accepting what we were offered.'

Doolo's voice hit a high pitch: 'I'm not, Murph. Open your ears – it's the previous owners I'm blaming.'

Muz backed up his teammate: 'No, you're giving out to us for getting the money that was owed to us, and that's not fair.'

'No, I'm not,' said Doolin. 'I'm just saying we weren't paid back and youse were.'

Then Dan Connor stepped in: 'Look, Tom, we just want to know what's going on. It happened to me at Drogheda but they let us know when they were short and it was no problem.'

'Ya, you need to tell us if the money's late,' added Muz. 'And, by the way, what *has* been the problem with the payment of the wages?'

Coughlan became angry again at that one: 'I've paid all the wages.'

'No, you haven't paid Davin.'

'Or Sean Kelly or Jerry Harris,' I added.

Coughlan calmed down a bit before attempting to explain: 'Ya, Seany at Galway is a different situation. Galway owe me money and I couldn't get it until I stopped paying him.

Everyone's been taking from Cork City recently and that's going to stop now, for good.'

Stevie was next to take a pop: 'I'd like to know what your plans for next week are? Are you thinking of pay cuts or selling players or what?'

'I have to work it out with my accountant, but I'll let you know next week. Anyway, yee've all been getting paid. I've paid yee back all yeer money and I need yee to stay professional. And by the way, we had a nutritionist come in and she said she wouldn't have even recognised that yee were footballers from what yee are eating.'

Before anybody could react to this, Coughlan wrapped the meeting up.

'I'll talk to yee again next week. OK lads.'

We were all quiet as he left the room. Doolo went with him and then came back in, alone, after a minute.

'Well, what can I say, lads,' he said. 'You've heard him. I'm not really sure whether the money's there, but it might be sustainable at some stage down the line. Full-time football in this country *can* be sustainable, but only if fellas are on decent rather than crazy wages. And I'm not talking about a few hundred quid either. A decent wage, that's all. Anyway, we'll have to wait and see what he comes back with.'

Sully pointed out that he has a full-time job waiting in Dublin, and that he wants to be let go to play part-time up there and start the job, but the club won't let him leave – and if he goes he'll look like the bad egg anyway.

Stevie said Coughlan signed him only a few months ago and must've known at the time that the club was up sh*t creak. 'It leaves me high and dry now,' he said. 'I had good options back then.'

The two Latvian lads sat quietly at the back. They didn't even attempt to take the stage to explain their respective predicaments.

We moved back solemnly to the dressing room to discuss things amongst ourselves. We were unhappy with Doolin for backing up Coughlan. Personally I felt like we'd just been given out to by both of them for 20 minutes.

'Right lads, yee need to look out for yourselves now,' said Gamble. 'He's full of sh*t. I'd get on the blowers if I were you.'

We went out to train but everyone was dispirited and annoyed. Myself, Murph, Gamble and Muzza were particularly pissed off. Murph and Muzza kicked balls around the place in anger. I reacted to Tommy, telling him to f**k off during a training drill, which is not like me. I apologised afterwards and Tommy, thankfully, was cool about it.

Afterwards, Doolo (wisely) told us to take tomorrow off as we were all looking seriously depressed.

I approached Robert Mežeckis in the dressing room afterwards and said, 'I'm going surfing next Tuesday if you're interested, Rob?'

'That would be great,' he said. Then he told me he's going back to Latvia in August for an operation on his Achilles, and he's not coming back.

'OK then – Tuesday. Let's do it so, and bring Guntars too,' I said.

I also chatted to Healers before leaving. 'When are you off, do you know?' I asked.

'Sunday,' he said. 'I've no choice really. The club here is f**ked, isn't it, and they need the money from my transfer.'

Nults asked, 'If the money was fine here and your contract fulfilled, would you stay?'

'Yes, I would,' said Healers. Then he shook our hands, wished us all the best, and left with his gearbag over his shoulder.

Denis had gone too – and quietly at that. Noticing the sudden absence, Nults said, 'And just like that [clicking his fingers] the banter's gone. Right, nobody's allowed to sit on Denis's seat.'

We all looked at Denis's corner; it seemed lonely already.

'Great guy,' said Gamble, 'but how the hell does he put up with all the winding up? I'd be digging the heads off fellas!'

Billy Dennehy answered, 'I think he has something in his ears that changes what he hears, no matter what it is, into a positive thing. It's probably a useful skill for a centre-forward.'

'Bye-bye Ding Dong Denis,' said Nults. Then he added, 'Jesus, the place is dead quiet now.'

As I was leaving I met Jerry Harris in the corridor. As usual he was running some equipment or gear down the place.

'Did you get paid yet, Jerry?' I asked.

'No,' he said, stopping. 'He [Coughlan] said he'd talk to me tomorrow. He's in over his head. I told him when he started: League of Ireland clubs haemorrhage money. It happened to me with Cork United. I was paying for everything, hoping we'd get the lease of Turner's Cross. We might have got ownership of it at the time but it didn't work out.'

'Why, Jerry?'

'Well, we organised a friendly with Man City, thinking we'd make a fortune from it – but it ended up *costing* us a fortune and we could only pay Man City half of what we said we'd pay them. Then there were moves to get us out of the league, and that's what happened. There was no league team in Cork for two years after that.'

'That's probably what'll happen here too,' I said.

Afterwards I gave Timmy a lift to town. He told me he'd be OK if he was living in Cork like some of the other lads with his mum or whatever, but as he's from Tipperary and paying rent... 'Sure they f**ked me out of one place already. What's gonna happen do you think, Hog?'

'I don't know Tim, I really don't,' I told him.

Tim smiled. 'Good year to be retiring though,' he said.

He's right about that.

Chapter 5

19th to 28th July 2009

Sunday 19th July

When I arrived at the ground for the Ipswich match, the lads were talking about what'll happen on Tuesday when the PFAI come down.

'Let's get them to talk for us,' suggested Gamble, 'rather than causing problems for ourselves with Coughlan and the club.'

Murph told us his agent has linked him with Barnet, but the club will be in a position to prevent a deal from taking place if they engineer it that way.

The dynamic in the dressing room is very different without Healers and Denis.

There was a big enough crowd tonight – mostly to see Roy Keane, who received a royal welcome. Funny, for all he's done for Cork soccer, I'm not sure he's ever been part of a match day at Turner's Cross, either as player (certainly not as an adult) or manager before today.

Friendly: Turner's Cross, Cork
Cork City 2–0 Ipswich Town

It was an entertaining match. The pace was quicker than it is in League of Ireland games. Their movement was a lot better than ours and they were in better physical shape. However, in terms of actual footballing ability, the gap was smaller. It was only a pre-season friendly for them, but we did well to win 2–0. And Keano waited in the tunnel to shake our hands as we came in, which was pleasing.

Another Cork man, Damien Delaney, who had played as a left-back for Cork City at the beginning of the 2000/1 season, also made a return. Delaney, recently signed by Keane at

Ipswich for £750,000, had been part of an impressive Cork City youth team that included Gamble and Alan Bennett and had won an FAI Youth Cup in 1999/2000. After that win Gamble was quickly plucked away by Reading on a free transfer, but Delaney remained to make his way into Cork City's first team and made his league debut on the same day as me. Also around this time, Colin Murphy had a brief tenure as Cork City boss before leaving to become Peter Taylor's assistant manager at Leicester. Impressed with the young, left-footed 6 ft 3" Delaney, he signed Damien from us for a reported €75,000. Delaney has since played in the Premiership, travelled through the divisions and around a few different clubs, including Hull and QPR, and has been capped by our national team on a few occasions. It was nice to play against him after all these years and have a brief chat to him after the game. His physical development since his departure has been remarkable; he looked like a thoroughbred racehorse tonight.

Doolo was happy with us afterwards, and particularly with young Kevin Long, who played well beside me.

Tuesday 21st July
At training we found out that Healer's moving to Ipswich now instead of Hartlepool. We all agreed it would be a better move for him to go to the Championship rather than Division One – and more importantly, he won't have to room with Denis.

Word also went around that our goalkeeper coach has packed it in as he can't give the commitment with the money being so unreliable. He's been travelling down from Dublin all year. Tommy wasn't around today either; someone said he's gone to Finland for a week. I'm wondering whether he's planning to pack it in too.

We had a double session this morning and the boys weren't too happy. Fitness coach Mark McManus took our body fat readings before conducting a body weights circuit. Stevie O'Donnell was disgusted: 'What's he doing coming in? He's not even being paid, the busy f**ker.'

We had lunch before our meeting with the PFAI (the players' union). Ollie Cahill, who's still playing with Shamrock Rovers, was down along with his colleague and PFAI CEO Stephen McGuinness. We asked Ollie about their game last night against Real Madrid; he'd come on for the second half and had got Sneijder's jersey – caught him at half-time.

'Good buzz alright,' he said. 'Benzema was sharp as f**k. Ronaldo didn't give his shirt away though, the bollix.'

We told him the stadium looked good and the atmosphere too. Sky Sports helped, we agreed, to make it look better than usual.

Then McGuinness came in: 'Right lads, I need to talk to youse about the situation down here at the moment.'

He explained that if Coughlan asks for pay cuts then 'that means youse can walk away from yeer contracts. He can't have it both ways.'

He said the main thing is to stick together, as it worked for us and for Drogheda last year. 'Individually youse are weak, but together youse are strong, I'm telling ya.'

Someone – probably Stevie – asked McGuinness what he thinks will happen with the club. 'Is it f**ked or what?'

'No – I think with the money from Denis and Healy, and with the money from the Ipswich match, that the club will pull through. The Healy situation could change things dramatically; he could go for a six-figure sum I hear. Also I think the FAI and John Delaney might step in if the club's in total sh*t. The last thing they want to see is Cork out of the league – we all know that. So I think the club will be OK, but he's going to ask yee to take pay cuts. Our position is that most of yee have taken pay cuts already and we need to say enough is enough. He'll need to sort it out soon, so stick together and work through us.'

Murph asked, 'But could he just wait and not pay us until the transfer window's closed and we can't move, and then offer us pay cuts?'

'Youse need to demand that to get your answers soon,' McGuinness replied. 'He was meant to meet yee today, wasn't he? I heard from the FAI that he's still sorting his sh*t out.'

Gamble spoke for us: 'I suppose if we give him until this Friday, which will be a week from the last time we asked him to explain everything, that should be fine.'

'OK – I'll tell him that if you like,' said McGuinness.

Training was hard in the afternoon and I came home wrecked afterwards.

Wednesday 22nd July

Training was tough again this morning and most players felt it. RTE's *Monday Night Soccer* show was down from Dublin though, doing the 'Hardest Shot' competition with us for their show. It's a real shame Denis is gone as he would've won even with a shot from his weaker left foot.

Denis would demonstrate his freakishly strong shot on our European away trips. The night before the fixture, while training in the main stadium[1], egged on by the rest of us and having orchestrated a sneaky moment away from the Gaffer's gaze, he would attempt to kick a ball out of the stadium. The on-looking home team's officials must have wondered what the hell was going on. But to us, at least, it was a very impressive sight – the ball sailing out over the stadium and disappearing into a car park or whatnot. And to Denis's credit he boasted a 100% record until we reached Red Star Belgrade's famous Maracanã ground with its high stands, which sadly were beyond even Denis's powers to conquer.

This morning, because of this, and because we miss him, one by one the players went up to the TV camera and, instead of saying our names and position before hitting the shot, we said something about Denis.

---

[1] In European club fixtures the away team must be allowed to train on the match pitch the night before the game.

Stevie was first up: 'Denis Behan [pause] beehive,' he said before striking the ball.

Lordy was next: 'Denis Behan [pause] barman.'

Gamble: 'Deny Behan... blacktooth.'

Nulty: 'Deny Behan... I only wear Gasoline bejebas.'

While I was tempted to have a go, I decided against taking a shot as my knee was sore and I always tend to embarrass myself on TV.

It was all pretty childish, but there was real sentiment underlining it. It was a kind of dedication to Denis.

Thursday 23rd July

Apparently Coughlan, who had originally agreed to meet us last Tuesday, can't come see us until Saturday – the day we leave for Derry.

'F**k's sake,' said Sully, who's hoping to move once the pay cuts are announced. 'I bet we won't see him at all until next week, after he's made some agreement with the High Court.' This further delay will give Sully less time to move before the transfer deadline.

The lads are losing all faith now. Surely Coughlan should be telling us what he plans to do with our livelihoods before he puts it by the court?

'If we disagree after the court says it's OK, what then?' asked Murph.

Nobody seemed to know the answer to that one.

Friday 24th July

The boys don't think Coughlan will turn up tomorrow. According to Joe, he's talking about 30% wage cuts.

Yesterday I heard on the radio that Healers has signed a two-year deal with Ipswich. It was also announced that Sean Kelly's move to Galway has been made permanent, and I'm glad for him. It must've been a huge deal for him going from Tralee to Arsenal, training with Fàbregas, Nicklas Bendtner and the rest of that youth team. Then when he came back to Cork he couldn't really get into our team. Tough to take, I'd imagine, for any young fella. But he'll play more regularly now in Galway than he did with us, and I'm hoping he'll bounce back to get a lot of senior football as he's very talented.

Training consisted of a long warm-up followed by passing drills, crossing and shooting, and then some work on defensive shape. Towards the end, Doolo focused on the young centre-half Longy and myself as we were playing together at the back. He told me I have to talk Longy through the game: 'Longy shouldn't have to do anything, Neilly lad.'

Saturday 25th July

To my surprise, Coughlan was at the door as I arrived for training this morning. 'Hello Tom,' I said.

'Hello Neal,' he replied. 'Hey, did you see Denis's article in the *Echo* yesterday? He was on about you in it.'

'No, what did he say?'

'Ah, he was taking the p*ss out of you for being a nice guy and for being a better hurler than a soccer player.'

I laughed and pointed out that he was wrong about that: I'm a poor hurler.

Then I went into the dressing room where the boys were getting ready.

'Coughlan's outside,' I announced.

'We know,' said Muzza, and it was clear the boys were feeling positive. Coughlan showing up seemed like a good sign.

Alan O'Connor, who's only recently returned to the set-up after refusing to train without payment, said to me in disbelief, 'Did ya see ya man outside? He came in here and asked me how I was doing, said things would be sorted. He's a mad b*****d, isn't he?'

I looked out of the window and saw Coughlan in Sully's car, talking to him. Shortly afterwards, Sully came in and lay across the bench. We could tell he was happy. The boys asked him whether he's going.

'Ya, he said I can go,' Sully replied.

Most people seemed wrecked in training. I was feeling particularly tired for some reason. Afterwards Doolo asked us, 'Are youse OK, or is something up? Is it all the stuff that's going on in the background?'

Nobody responded, so he went on: 'The game tomorrow against Derry is a big match, youse know that. And with Bohs and Shamrock Rovers playing on same day, that means we have a chance to sneak up. If Derry lose, then that's them out of it. I know we're down bodies, but we've still got a great chance. If youse can play the same as yee did against Ipswich and Sligo then I feel we'll definitely get a win.'

During the warm-down, Lordy and I discussed the fact that we're down to just 16 in training now, like last year, and with a young team again too. All of a sudden we're without Healers, Denis and Gamble (who's injured).

Afterwards we had a meeting with Coughlan. He sat at the top of the usual meeting room with the Gaffer and Tommy on his right.

He began, 'So, to fill yee in lads: as you all know, attendances are down due to the recession and I'm trying to get the fans involved. I also had a meeting with the Revenue yesterday, half a day in Limerick with them. I think things are coming along nicely and we'll come to an agreement or settlement with them. As part of that, I'm working on a plan with them to make us more sustainable. We're coming up with something that I think is fair and that ye'll be happy with.'

The lads looked around at each other as he said this, no doubt thinking of the 30% cuts that have been rumoured lately.

'So yee've said you want to deal with me through the PFAI, is that true?'

Joe looked around at us and said, 'Ya, I think that's true.'

The rest of us nodded.

'Well, it would be easier for me to deal with one person anyway, so that's fine. I'll talk to them on Tuesday and Wednesday. I need to get Monday and the High Court matter with the Revenue out the way first, though. But anyway, good luck up in Derry and keep up the good work. I know you need to get going so I'll leave it at that.'

We travelled to Derry straight after training, and as we were getting on the bus I asked Lordy, 'Do you think this will be our last trip?'

Lordy said he didn't think so.

We reached the Everglades Hotel in Derry at about 8pm, and over a late dinner Lordy and I chatted about all our trips up here over the years. Lordy told me about his first trip to Derry with City, when he roomed with the then-veteran player Stephen Napier (Naps), and how Naps talked about football all night. 'The young fellas today wouldn't talk about it for five minutes,' he said.

Sunday 25th July

League of Ireland Premier Division
The Brandywell, Derry
Derry City 1–1 Cork City

Cork City: Connor, Horgan, Long, Murray, Murphy; Kiely (O'Neill, 61), Lordan, O'Donnell (Duggan, 46), Dennehy; Silagailis (Cambridge, 70), Kuduzović

We played well, considering all the recent changes to the team. Young Shane Duggan scored a lovely goal and Doolo was happy enough, but he says we need more if we're going to challenge for the League.

We arrived home around 4am on Monday morning.

Monday 27th July

I woke at 3pm to the sound of texts bleeping on my phone. One of them was from Lordy: *Where does that leave us? The other fella telling us everything was alright?*

At 3.30pm – while I was still trying to figure out what had happened – local side Douglas Hall's manager texted me, joking that he wants me to sign for them.

3.35pm: a journalist from the *Echo* called me but I didn't answer.

3.40pm: superkeeper Mick Devine texted to abuse me for not telling him 'that the club was f**ked.'

I turned on the radio and caught Billy Barry on 96FM: '...so the club has five days to lodge an appeal. The club is staring down the barrel of a shotgun at the moment. Despite selling our best players –13 players across the water now; it's at least a good club for talent spotting – everything is up in the air. It asks questions of where the FAI are in all of this. Do we need some kind of vetting process for people or investors who are buying clubs, like they've introduced in England? Cork City have a hard core of 2,500 fans whose hearts will be broken today. Considering the club won the league in 2005, the FAI Cup in 2007 and the Setanta Cup last year, it's hard to see how things went so wrong. Of course, the club came out of examinership a few months back, apparently on more stable footing. This news breaking today... it's absolute lunacy.'

The presenter asked, 'Is there anything that can save Cork City, Billy?

Billy replied, 'We need someone with big pockets. The whole thing doesn't bear thinking about really.'

'What's next then?'

'There are still a lot of good players at the club, even though it's been on the slide since Arkaga took over. Tom Coughlan came to the rescue, but things haven't been good. The club wasn't paying its PAYE bill and the Revenue finally caught up and passed them out. I'm absolutely devastated. Tom Coughlan has five days to pull a rabbit out of the hat. I'm afraid it's a sad day for soccer in Cork and the country, and it begs the question: what have the FAI done with the League of Ireland, and what have they done to help Cork City FC? The players put on an excellent display last night up in Derry and this is the thanks they wake up to today.'

At 3.55pm, Ken Tobin on 96FM said, 'I can't confirm this, but I'm hearing that the League of Ireland game on Friday against Bray will not go ahead now. Very sad news.'

At 4pm, Ruairi O'Hagan on RedFM announced, '…€440,000 is owing and the club is insolvent; therefore the court had no choice but to wind up the company where there are 42 or 43 people employed. Meanwhile, club chairman Tom Coughlan remains adamant that he can get the money together for a last-minute settlement with Revenue.'

On the Six O'Clock News on RTE One, Tony O'Donoghue said, 'It's been a bad day for Cork City fans today as the company behind the firm has been ordered to be wound up in the High Court by Judge Laffoy. The club has been in trouble since Arkaga pulled their funds, but then they entered examinership and new owner Tom Coughlan came in. The club now has a three- or four-day window to lodge an appeal.

'The news comes as somewhat of a surprise, with many of the view that Cork would have received enough money lately. They sold players such as Colin Healy, Denis Behan and Dave Mooney, and were due to receive some money from Kevin Doyle's transfer. The club also benefitted from a friendly with Roy Keane's Ipswich Town, with Ipswich foregoing their costs.

'It's a huge blow to the league. Very successful domestically, with the highest gates in the country. If they're in trouble, what future is there for full-time pro football in this country?'

~~~~~

High Court orders Cork City FC to be wound-up
(www.rte.ie, 27th July 2009)

The High Court has ruled that Cork City Football Club must be wound up because of debts of €440,000 owed to the Revenue Commissioners.

Ms Justice Mary Laffoy this afternoon said the company was insolvent and therefore couldn't pay its debts. She also said the court could not impose a compromise on the Revenue, and that she had no choice but to wind-up the company.

The court had already heard that the club employs 45 people and plays an important social role in the city.

Cork City FC came up with €120,000 and a plan to pay back the rest of the money over a 12 month period, but this was rejected.

Ms Justice Laffoy froze the winding-up order until Friday, during which time the company will decide whether to appeal.

Afterwards Chairman Tom Coughlan was adamant they would try and get money together to pay the debt over the coming days.

"She's made an indication of what she's going to do on Friday, which is very clearly wind up the company," Mr Coughlan said.

"That's unless we can get some last minute settlement with the Revenue, which we will try and do over the next 48 hours."

Cork City Football Club statement, 27th July 2009

Following High Court proceedings today, Cork City FC has been given until Friday to settle its liabilities to the Revenue.

The club is doing everything within its power to settle these liabilities and asks that our supporters and the people of Cork get behind us to help us to save the club. It is the intention of the club to continue trading and we are determined to do everything in our power to overcome this hurdle.

At this time, the support of all is vital to us emerging from this situation and the continuation of League of Ireland football in Cork. As we look ahead to Friday night's game against Bray Wanderers at Turner's Cross, we ask the people of Cork to come out and support the team and buy tickets for the game in advance of Friday through our kiosk in Daunt Square and our club store at 22 Sullivan's Quay.

Tuesday 28th July

The players were feeling a mixture of shock and anger this morning. 96FM was on in the kitchen area and Murph said, 'You want to hear it – they're giving out about players' wages again.'

'We're getting blamed again like last time,' said Lordy.

'Well boys,' Muzza declared, '96FM left a voicemail on my phone this morning asking me to come on, so I might as well,' and he headed off down the corridor to ring them.

The rest of us filed into the kitchen area where the radio is. The kitchen's a tight space under the stadium; only one line of people can stand up properly as its roof goes diagonally upwards to standing height, so we all huddled around, listening to the news like civilians in a bomb bunker.

'Here – he's on now,' said Murph.

Neil Prendeville introduced Muzza as Danny Murphy, but Muz didn't correct him.

Prendeville said, 'So these comments you've made about it being Tom Coughlan's fault…'

Muzza interrupted him this time: 'No – that was Danny Murphy, our little left-back.'

'OK, so he's the one that made the comments,' Prendeville said.

Murph stared at the wall looking pissed off, which made myself and Stevie laugh.

Muzza explained to the listeners that we haven't heard anything from the club. 'We've been left in the dark,' he said.

Prendeville asked about the players' wages and Muz told him that the players took wage-cuts last year.

'So is full-time football sustainable here, do you think?' asked Prendeville.

Muz talked about clubs in England with lower crowds, such as Barnet, who do it.

The interview came to an end; overall Muz did very well.

We filed back into dressing room, wondering whether the match on Friday will go ahead.

Training was a low-key affair: Doolo was up at the Setanta Cup draw in Dublin, so Tommy took the session on his own. Tommy's wife is from Finland and he'd been living over there for the past two years before getting the call from Doolo to come back to Ireland and help him at Cork. Tommy told us he'd been planning to move his family back here from Finland before he found out about the club's financial problems.

'Try telling me little one she's not coming back to school here,' he joked. Then he continued: 'From my perspective, you've been a credit to yourselves how you've performed through all of this. You need to keep yourselves fit, as either the club goes under and you'll need to find a new one, or this debt gets paid and we move on. I'm hoping it's the latter. I know it's not easy, but try to put in a good session.'

There was a photographer nearby, and some video camera people had also arrived. The last time we got so much attention we were in the cup final!

Despite Tommy's best efforts, morale was low in training.

Afterwards the lads were again talking about getting blamed for the club's problems. Danny Murphy said he's had enough and wants to leave. Then Caen came in and told us he'd just heard on the radio that the Revenue are now looking for a total of €440,000 by Friday, and they're not making any more deals with the club.

'So we're f**ked, really?' asked Stevie.

Sometimes humour is the best remedy, and Stevie obliged by picking on young Deasy.

'You should've heard Deasy last night: "I'll be happy to f**k off and train with Ringmahon Rangers twice a week and go work in Boyle Sports!"'

The boys had a good laugh at this. 'He'd last a week,' said Muz.

At least we'll know what's happening for definite on Friday. The worst part of all this has been the uncertainty: week to week, day to day, for the last year. It's been hard to get on with our lives.

On the car journey home Timmy asked me again whether I think the situation will improve.

'It's not looking good,' I told him.

'But we'll still get paid tomorrow, ya?'

'No Tim. I don't think so.'

'But I have to pay my €550 rent – I'm gonna have to pack my bags, I'd say.'

'You might be better off Tim, as it's hard to see the club surviving now.'

~~~~

Countdown to Disaster: Cork City Timeline (Neil Ahern, www.independent.ie, 28th July 2009)

August 19 2008 – Kieran McCarthy is appointed examiner of Cork City Football Club after Arkaga group cease funding the company. €1.3m of debts had accumulated with €360,000 owed to the Revenue.

October 16 – McCarthy brings the club successfully through examinership, signing over the ownership to Cork property developer, Tom Coughlan.

December 9 – Alan Mathews is sacked, with a statement saying that the club "needs to bring the salary structures to sustainable levels to ensure (its) long-term survival".

December 12 – Midfielder Liam Kearney admits he may leave the club after issues with backlogged wages. He eventually moves to Derry City.

December – Reports emerge that former Cork Gaelic football boss Billy Morgan and former Ireland international boss Brian Kerr have been approached to succeed Mathews.

January 13 2009 – Former Drogheda United manager Paul Doolin is officially announced as Cork City's new manager.

January/February – The club announce several signings, including former Bohs midfielder Stephen O'Donnell, and former Drogheda United players Fahrudin Kuduzovic and Dan Connor.

March 25 – Danny Murphy is the only player left without any payments for March – he soon accepts a pay-cut.

April 7 – Cork City lets all fans in for free for their home League match against Drogheda United as part of a 'Recession Buster' promotion.

April 19 – Supporters trust FORAS holds an emergency meeting as fears grow over the future of the club, but they move to reassure their members after a meeting with Coughlan, saying in a statement: "Tom Coughlan has repeatedly reassured us that he's not worried. We're going to take his word on that so we're not worried either."

May 13 – The Revenue files a petition to wind up Cork City Investment FC Ltd, the club's holding company.

May 25 – The extent of Cork City's problems are laid bare in their first High Court hearing, with Revenue debts of €289,425 said to have accumulated. The case is deferred as clarification of figures is sought by Cork City's representative Olann Kelleher.

June 15 – The club enters the High Court for a second time but the case is adjourned for four weeks.

July 13 – Ms Justice Laffoy gives a final adjournment in order to facilitate a deal between Cork City Investment FC Ltd and the Revenue, giving them two weeks to thrash out a settlement.

July 16–24 – The club plays a friendly against Roy Keane's Ipswich Town, and sells players Colin Healy and Denis Behan to Ipswich Town and Hartlepool.

July 27 – Cork City Football Club is wound up

Cough up or rebels will die; financial ruin Cork City face race against time to stay alive
(Paul O'Hehir, *Daily Mirror*, 28th July 2009)

WHY did Tom Coughlan buy Cork City last October if he couldn't afford to keep it alive? While a minuscule chance remains that he'll pull off an escape, why has it come to this? These questions kept irate Cork players and fans awake last night as they digested news that the club is set to fold.

Asked yesterday if he felt responsible for the mess, Coughlan ducked the question.

"I'm not interested in that," he said.

"I have a job to do by Friday and we can talk about that afterwards."

The Rebels are on their deathbed and the life support machine will be unplugged on Friday unless Coughlan pulls a rabbit from the hat.

Last night the FAI expressed its concern about Cork's predicament. That's all well and good, but those Cork players and fans will want answers from Abbotstown too.

These problems must have been flagged when Cork's accounts were submitted on a regular basis. Yet the Cork players could be out of a job this weekend.

Those FAI officials have been reluctant to comment throughout this court case - and understandably so as it runs its course. But that safety net will be lifted on Friday and the time for talking begins.

Justice Mary Laffoy granted the winding up order sought by the taxman in the High Court yesterday.

She said that "in reality the company is insolvent." And even though she acknowledged the club's role in the community, she had "no option but to make an order winding up the company." A stay was put on the verdict until Friday, but the club will be liquidated within 21 days unless a miracle cure is found.

Coughlan won't appeal the decision to the Supreme Court as that's a costly business. Instead, he's now relying on favours and unearthing hard cash.

The favour? That the taxman suddenly has second thoughts and accepts Cork's settlement offer which falls short of expectations.

But the fact the Revenue's tough stance hasn't budged since day one of this sorry mess means that won't happen.

Both Cork City and the taxman's legal teams disputed at length the figures owed in court yesterday. The Revenue said the club now owes EUR439,658 in tax. In March - when this case first went before the court - that figure was EUR239,416.

The taxman will settle for 50 percent of the EUR439k up front and the remainder paid over four monthly instalments.

Cork offered EUR120k yesterday - (up from EUR65k a fortnight ago) and offered to pay the balance in 12 monthly EUR24,476 payments. They emailed this proposal to the Revenue last Friday but it was rejected.

The taxman questioned Cork's ability to honour that scheme of arrangement - and told the judge that an earlier EUR15,000 cheque issued by the club had bounced.

Barristers for the Revenue reminded the judge that the court shouldn't give preferential treatment to one taxpayer over the other.

"There are other football clubs out there who pay their taxes and keep their ship in order," said Dermot Cahill Bl.

Coughlan admitted being "a bit surprised" by the winding up order.

"She (Justice Laffoy) has indicated what she wants to do so we're right into extra-time now," he added.

"The Revenue haven't shown us any will that they want to negotiate so we have to go in and get more cash, and fast by Friday.

"Let's see what happens. That's where we are and that's how it stands. We have until Friday to try and do something."

Asked for a ball park figure on what the club might need, Coughlan said: "I don't want to be guessing on it.

"They're talking about 50 per cent so let's try and get that and see what happens. Friday is certainly d-day.

"We'll see what we can do. It's no messing stuff, you know what I mean, this is it."

An FAI statement read: "Following a week which has seen so many positive developments on the pitch for the League of Ireland, the FAI is disappointed that Cork City has failed to meet its obligations to the Revenue Commissioners.

"Despite numerous assurances from Cork City that matters with the Revenue Commissioners would be resolved, the FAI is disappointed and concerned that the club finds itself in this situation.

"The FAI will meet with representatives of Cork City and will continue to monitor the situation ahead of Friday's deadline."

Chapter 6

29th July to 4th August 2009

Wednesday 29th July

After yesterday's events I found it hard to sleep last night. Things were running around inside my head. So at 7.30 this morning I decided to draft a statement on behalf of the players, attempting to outline all the efforts we've made to keep the club afloat. I felt that we needed defending.

Next thing I knew it was 9.42am. I had three minutes to get to training. My gear was ready, so I grabbed my bag, jumped into my car and flew down the link road. I caught a few green lights in a row and although I arrived late, I figured I still had a chance of getting in unnoticed by Doolo – unless any of the lads had noticed my absence and alerted him.

While Dan Connor is to be avoided because of the fines, getting caught by Doolo is much more serious. If he got annoyed I'd have to be on my toes all week at training, and if my performance wasn't up to scratch in the next game he'd be dying to slate me in front of the lads for being late and unprofessional.

I entered the building at a frenetic walking pace. There were a few doors that needed to be passed on the way to the laundry room (where our training gear is kept): the first, to my left, was the meeting room. Doolo hangs around there sometimes, putting stuff on the noticeboard (which is located next to the door), or just looking to see if anyone's late.

I was fly-walking past this door when Nulty's head peeked out and he roared, 'HERE HE IS, BOOOOYS!' to an unseen audience. 'HOGGY'S HERE!'

I then saw the lads' faces – and Doolo's – looking out at me.

Christ. There was an early meeting.

Nulty then backtracked and tried to help me out of it. While blocking the door, he said quietly, 'There are others late too,

Hogs – two of the young boys. You have a few minutes. Hurry though.'

I sprinted to the laundry room and back to the dressing room, then I got dressed into my training gear and was walking back to the meeting room within 45 seconds.

Muzza howled as I entered, 'How the hell did you get changed so quickly?'

The boys laughed – and so did Doolo, albeit not quite as heartily as the rest. He then asked, 'Are you alright Nealy?'

'I'm grand, Paul,' I answered. 'I was just writing up a player statement for the lads.'

He laughed properly at this: 'Oh ya, the solicitor. I forgot. Did you bring in the Bible for us to be sworn in yet?'

Two of the young lads – Kevin Long and Craig Duggan – arrived minutes later, saying Craigy's car had broken down on the link road. Nobody believed them but Craigy and Longy stuck to their guns. And more importantly, they took the spotlight away from me.

Doolo asked us to hush before he began.

'Well,' he said, 'I met Tom and he told me everything's OK. The game's going ahead, so even with everything that's gone on, youse still have a chance of doing something this year.'

We all hope Coughlan is just playing cat and mouse with the Revenue, but as the club's getting so much bad publicity, nobody's sure. FORAS (Friends of the Rebel Army Society: the supporters' trust) apparently offered Coughlan €20,000 before the Ipswich match in order to get involved – with some shares being transferred to them as part of the offer – but he refused. There's another rumour that a business consortium asked him to step aside and he refused that too.

Thursday 30th July
This morning I made sure to arrive nice and early. The lads were talking about a FORAS meeting that took place last night, which Murph had attended.

'The offers from the consortium and FORAS were refused again,' said Murph.

Nulty saw this as a good sign: 'That must mean he has the money, surely?'

While we were in the gym the radio was playing, and suddenly one of the lads asked everyone to hush as the club was being discussed. Billy Barry was on air on 96FM, saying Billy Dennehy has been linked with Sporting Fingal in Dublin, Faz with Dundalk, and how other players are moving too... 'but the players have been fantastic for allowing the deferment of their wages.'

He mentioned the issue of the club requiring the FAI's permission to allow fans in for free, and the other offers made to Coughlan, before revealing that 'Tom Coughlan will be on after the break.'

'So that could have been our last game up in Derry, Hogs?' young Shane Duggan asked me.

'Ya, Duggy – you might have scored the last ever goal for CCFC.'

Shane laughed. 'I'll go down in the annals, then,' he said, before telling me he'd had a call from Limerick FC offering him a contract.

Then Coughlan came on the radio and talked primarily about all the money he had spent since he became chairman.

Stevie O'Donnell walked away from the radio saying, 'From the way Coughlan was talking there, it looks like the club's screwed.' At this point Sully (who has at last been cleared to leave the club and agreed to join Shamrock Rovers up in Dublin) came in, shook everyone's hand and said goodbye. He'll be a big loss too.

There were some news crews with their video cameras out on the pitch again, and Doolo told us, 'I know it's hard to stay focussed but youse need to get on with things and train properly.'

Muzza added, 'Ya, lads – we could go joint second tomorrow.'

But as we'll have a lot of young lads coming in, I reckon anything could happen.

We were all a bit dejected during training – including Tommy, who asked me what I thought about the club's future.

'I don't know, Tom. Yesterday I thought we were gonna be OK, but after listening to the radio today I think it might be gone.'

After we'd finished training, Doolo joked about the timing of my retirement at the end of the year.

'Timing is everything,' I replied, laughing with him.

Later in the evening our PFAI representative, Stephen McGuinness, met us again and was asked how he sees things turning out.

'Well, I don't see Cork being thrown out of the league; they're too important. But [John] Delaney can't step in as other clubs wouldn't be too happy. The Revenue are the one creditor that can wind you up. You owe less money than other clubs, but it seems like the Revenue are coming down hard. They have their reasons, though, with examinership and bounced checks etc. But the game *is* going ahead on Friday, so youse need to try and focus on that. Youse are insured, and so you might have to view it as a trial match to see if youse can get moves. I just met Tom and he assured me it will all be OK, but I'm not sure whether to believe him or not. He said he'll have €300,000 for the Revenue by Friday but we'll have to wait and see. In the meantime I want him to commit to allowing players to move until mid-August if he doesn't pay you by next Wednesday.'

We asked him whether we had the highest wages in the league as Coughlan had been saying on the radio.

'If you include just playing staff and players, then no, but if you include all the staff, then yes. Youse all know that Cork players have always been paid far less than players at Dublin clubs, except for the year when Arkaga took over.'

He told us we were all free to go as of today, like Sully was doing, because they haven't paid us. 'But for those of youse who want to stay, youse'll just need the club to get through tomorrow.'

McGuinness also confirmed that our wages have been deferred until next Wednesday '…if the club survives that long, that is.'

Later I took Robert and Guntars surfing. While my borrowed wetsuits were very tight on the lads, it was great to see them smiling again as they got thrown around by the waves in East Cork.

~~~~

Coughlan rejects bid, as City's last chance saloon appears out of reach (from www.extratime.ie, 30th July 2009)

Tom Coughlan has rejected a bid from a four-man consortium led by the infamous Danny Drew. That's according to Cork City supporters trust FORAS.

At an emotional public meeting last night, FORAS, who are now set to focus on a new club post-winding up order, explained that Drew is the face of a consortium which has had an offer entirely ignored by financially stricken Coughlan.

Drew has also made contact with FORAS in an attempt to speak to Coughlan but the property developer seems uninterested. It seems Drew would not be part of any day-to-day running of the club and was just the leading face in their pursuit to take the club from Coughlan.

Over 200 supporters met in Cork city centre to air their feelings at a highly charged meeting which also saw Dan Murray, Danny Murphy and former chairman Brian Lennox in attendance.

Fans spoke of their desire to save the club, with a mixture of sadness, annoyance and desperation intertwined inside the tiny Telecom Club on MacCurtain Street. Tears were shed as supporters remembered happier days for the club, though most remained defiant that Cork City FC will continue to live on in one form or another.

FORAS also admitted that they approached Coughlan on more than one occasion with funds, only to be rejected. They met with the former-PD election candidate a fortnight ago, where progress looked like a strong possibility. However, Coughlan's demands proved too much and the trust was given a resounding no to any offers.

The supporters have now decided to flood the local and national airwaves later today to spread the word about the Drew consortium. When quizzed on the future of the club after Friday, FORAS were keen to express that they've got plans beyond the end of the week and they urged supporters to invest heavily in the trust if Cork City FC is to live on for many years to come.

[...]

Friday 31st July

While having my usual snooze after my pre-match meal, I was awoken by texts from friends and family saying that the club had been saved.

Somehow Coughlan has pulled it off. F**king brilliant.

~~~~

Club statement, 31st July 2009

On behalf of Cork City FC, we wish to confirm our decision to appeal the decision made by the revenue commissioners not to accept the proposal put forward in the High Court this morning.

It is our intention to seek a stay on the order for leave to appeal to the Supreme Court. During this period we will settle our outstanding liability in full.

We believe that our proposal demonstrates not just our commitment but also our ability to settle our liability in full in the short term. In addition to this, under the guidance of the Quintas Group we now have a sustainable business model which will protect jobs and ensure that a similar situation will not arise going forward.

We have a big match tonight against Bray Wanderers at Turner's Cross, so we are looking forward to getting back to football and hope to see the Rebel Army there in big numbers.

It is appropriate that we take this opportunity to thank all of those who have rallied behind the cause and demonstrated their support in recent times. In particular we would like to thank our manager and players for their loyalty and continuing hard work to deliver success on the pitch. Also, Dermot Desmond and Celtic FC for their commitment to come to Cork, John Delaney and the FAI who have been very helpful and supportive behind the scenes and of course, Jim McCarthy of Quintas for lending us their considerable expertise and advice. Also, we would like to thank Olann Kelleher and Mark Riordan.

Cork City given Revenue lifeline (www.rte.ie, 31st July 2009)

Cork City have been given a last-gasp lifeline at the High Court this afternoon after a deal was agreed with the Revenue Commission to settle outstanding monies owed.

Lawyers for the Revenue Commissioners said that the football club's company had agreed to pay half of its debt today and the balance by 4.30pm next Wednesday.

Ms Justice Mary Laffoy put a stay on the winding up order until next Thursday, saying that if the debt is paid by then the order will be lifted.

Cork City owner Tom Coughlan said: 'We are thrilled to have secured the future of the club and are looking forward to celebrating at Turner's Cross tonight when we host Bray Wanderers in the league.'

But Cork City must still raise the additional €219,000 owing by next Wednesday's deadline.

Tonight's game between Cork City and Bray Wanderers will definitely take place at Turner's Cross, kick-off 7.45pm.

Cork City v Bray Wanderers (Adrian Russell, www.the42.ie (formerly www.thescore.ie), 31st July 2009)

Cruelly, the last song the great Louis Armstrong recorded before he died was 'We have all the time in the world'. Cork City FC is alive and kicking, despite the John Grisham courtroom drama that's unfolded this week, but they're certainly not singing from the rooftops.

It seems like a normal matchday here at Turner's Cross; volunteers are sweeping a sodden pitch, fans are funnelling through the turnstiles while the press box is filling up as normal. This game however is very much the full stop in a week that started with a creditable 1-1 draw in Derry on Sunday before the story shifted to the Four Courts on Monday.

Despite winding up orders and failed compromises with the Revenue, the match tonight will go ahead. Who will take to the field in City colours however is another matter. A trivial one in the life-or-death circumstances, perhaps.

The Seagulls will field a relatively settled side as usual, but the hosts have midfield talisman Joe Gamble rated as a major doubt. We're still waiting on the team sheet here but one thing is certain, Colin Healy, Denis Behan and Pat Sullivan will not line out. The trio have exited Leeside in a bid to raise funds to square the tax bill and to lighten a creaking wage bill.

However, it's progress, at least, that we're dealing in points tonight rather than pounds. As Satchmo sang 'What a wonderful world'; League of Ireland fans are the only judge and jury at Turner's Cross this evening.

~~~~

On arriving into the dressing room at about 6 o'clock, I was told that the Revenue's proceedings hadn't gone away; they'd only been adjourned until next Wednesday. Apparently Coughlan had proof of money coming from a bank in London on the strength of a promise by Glasgow Celtic to play a friendly against us in Cork in the near future. Adding further to the absurdity of it all, it was Micky Harris (Jerry's brother) who'd contacted Celtic, as Jerry was in a position to confirm.

It was bucketing with rain outside and the pitch was very bad in a few spots. Stevie O'Donnell paced around the dressing room asking everyone whether the match was going ahead or not.

'The pitch is in ribbons, Jerry – the match must be off, right?'

'No, I'd say it'll go ahead,' Jerry answered calmly. 'The ref's arriving soon to take a look at the pitch.'

'They'll do everything to play it tonight,' added Muz, to Stevie's clear disappointment.

I've often felt the same before matches: if a doubt's raised a few hours before a game, my mind tends to leap and cling to the hope that it can be liberated from the trauma of pre-match nerves. However, by the time I've warmed up, everything's changed and I'll be counting down the seconds for the game to begin. I suppose it's the waiting around before the warm-up that I've always found the difficult part.

As we emerged from the dressing room tonight there was an unusually large crowd already present. There were also a lot of FORAS people on the pitch, helping to push the water off. The going was quite heavy and the ball was stopping in places as we knocked it about.

There was pressure on us to win tonight, to play our part in the club's good day. Thankfully we won one-nil, with young Gareth Cambridge and Kevin Long doing well and Faz scoring a penalty.

League of Ireland Premier Division

Doolo was happy with us afterwards and let Stephen McGuinness into the dressing room to meet us while he and all the other staff departed. As they were leaving, the fans directly above us in the Shed were singing a song calling our chairman 'a horse's ass.' Noticing the amusement of the lads, Guntars whispered to me, 'What they say?' and then broke out laughing when I told him.

McGuinness announced, 'Youse need to stand up now. It's great that the club is fine and whatever, but youse need to be paid… this week. Some can take another week; some can't. So youse need to sit down on Thursday and sort it out with Tom.'

Saturday 1ˢᵗ August
It was clear this morning that Doolin is becoming increasingly frustrated. He told us in a meeting before training, 'Youse need to do something this week. We're coming to work every day and the mental side of it is the worst. Youse need to do something and I can tell youse one thing: it can't go on like this.'

Dan Connor repeated what he'd said before: 'In any other job there's no way we'd put up with this. But if we strike, we only hurt ourselves.'

We're due to play Bohemians on Friday in Dublin and then Shamrock Rovers at home the following Tuesday. Doolo and Tommy both suggested that we shouldn't wait until the Rovers game, while others – including Greg and myself – said that the Rovers home game would be a better threat as the home gates are important to the club.

In the end we decided to get Gamble, who's injured, to ring McGuinness while we were training and ask whether we need to send the club a statement saying that if the players aren't paid by Friday then we won't be travelling to Dublin.

Before we went out, Jerry came in and told us, 'You all need to bring your own training kit home with you afterwards and wash it yourselves, as Caen isn't here tomorrow. And it looks a lot like you'll be washing your own kit from now on.'

Muzza and I agreed that this was the first step back towards part-time football.

At this point Doolo and Tommy left us alone in the dressing room to discuss our options.

I asked what happens if they can't pay us by Friday and someone answered, 'He will pay us. He'll get the money from somewhere once we push him, just like the Revenue have done.'

We agreed that we need to stick together and get everyone paid, and that if we don't get paid we'll strike.

'Otherwise they'll pick on Deasy and the lads like last time,' said Nults.

'Are we sure we're not in breach of our contracts if we strike?' asked Lordy.

'No, he's already breached our contract by not paying us,' answered Dan Connor.

We agreed that we need to be very careful and do this correctly; otherwise we could be blamed for the death of the club.

In training, those of us who played last night merely did a gentle jog around the pitch and a few stretches, while the lads who didn't play were made to run.

Gamble informed us when we came back inside that he'd spoken to McGuinness, and that we need to give five days' notice to strike. Therefore we'll have to play Friday and do something next Tuesday instead (if we're not paid by then).

When Gamble had finished speaking, Robert stood up and said goodbye to everyone with a stern handshake. I could tell he was glad to be getting away from this madness.

~~~~

Great Escape, Russian Roulette, and going down in Sofia: A week in Irish football (www.touchlineviews.com, 1st August 2009)

It has been a rollercoaster week in Irish football, a week of spectacular highs and incredible lows. But yesterday Cork City FC lived up to their nickname of the 'rebels' by winning their battle against the Revenue Commission to avoid a winding up order, which would have relegated the club from the League of Ireland after a 25 year existence.

The final whistle had well and truly blown, but in extra-time the club managed to come up with the required amount of €220,000, half of the €439,658 that they owed to the Revenue Commission. The remaining €219,000 will be made before 4.30pm on Wednesday, therefore saving the club from extinction. Thus, Cork have now avoided becoming the first team to exit the league in mid-season since Dublin City in 2006.

If yesterday's courtroom battle wasn't enough, there was football to be played last night, at Turner's Cross which saw Cork grab their second victory in the space of 5 hours, beating Bray Wanderers 1-0 in front of just over 3,000 loyal supporters.

Cork might not be out of the woods just yet as the staff and players who agreed to a deferral of their wages for a week have to be paid in full by Wednesday.

PFAI chief Stephen McGuinness warned trouble is still brewing – 'If they aren't paid on Wednesday that will be a breach of the wage deferral they agreed this week," he said, "There's people 'high-fiving' on the stairs there but it's early yet."

All will become clear in the coming days, but for now it looks like the Leesiders have performed the greatest escape since Charles Bronson and Steve McQueen.

[...]

At the opposite end of the spectrum, St. Patrick's Athletic enjoyed victory in their Europa League third qualifying round game against Russian heavyweights Krylya Sovetov…

[…]

Elsewhere, in Bulgaria, Derry City battled bravely but went down 1-0 to CSKA Sofia, leaving them with an uphill battle in the return leg at the Brandywell.

[…]

As all three clubs prepare to ride the emotional rollercoaster for another week, it will be survival of the fittest, but one thing is for sure, no club will be going down without a fight. Passion and belief will be key.

~~~~~

Monday 3rd August

There was no sign of fitness coach Mark McManus this morning, 'and only one session onboard at that,' said Stevie with delight.

Doolo did tell us on Saturday that this week would be a 'down week' – the idea being that we have a 'down week' every 5/6 weeks to recoup. But we all know that a 'down week' really means an 'up week'. It means less time spent training, but training with more intensity.

As such, our session this morning was short but hard. After a tough warm-up we did some reaction sprints; we were divided into twos and I was paired with Guntars, who was standing 5ft away on my right. If Tommy shouted 'Right!' then we all had to run to the right and I had to chase Guntars; if he shouted 'Left!' then we all had to run left and Guntars chased me.

I gave Guntars a wink and the Latvian understood.

'I'm wrecked already,' said Muz, 'I bloody peaked in the warm-up.' Which was unfortunate as he had sprint demon Billy Dennehy chasing him.

Tommy announced that if anyone got caught by their partner they'd be brought over to the bushes and beaten up.

'LEFT!'

I tore off towards the fence with Guntars hot on my heels, but Muzza flew past me with Billy behind him closing fast.

After the reaction sprints we played four games: two 3 v 3s (with one a spare man), where you score by stopping the ball on the line, and two games of 4 v 4 with keepers (so 5 v 5 really) and proper goals. I went over on my ankle tackling Billy Dennehy during a 5 v 5 game, but I didn't pull out of the training as I was enjoying it.

In between each set of games we did sets of 80-metre sprints. After we'd finished on the pitch, Lordy and I went to do some strength work sets in the gym. Greg was in there too, telling the lads about all the former Cork City players that are in the UK at the moment.

'There's guys in every division,' he said. 'Sure we could pick a full squad.'

The conversation moved onto trialists. Greg has always kept an eye out for the unusual trialists at the club over the years.

He recounted the story of a young Nigerian guy – a trialist from a few years ago – who'd asked Greg to assist him when filling out his immigration papers. A few weeks later he'd called Greg with a further query, and Greg, unable to help him this time, had given him Jerry Harris's number. Unfortunately for the Nigerian lad, on answering the phone Jerry was convinced it was just Greg putting on an accent (Greg is brilliant at impressions), and he told him: 'F**k off Greg and leave me alone,' before hanging up.

After finishing up I met Timmy in the dressing room, and he told me that he's had to leave his apartment because he couldn't pay the rent on time 'for the second time'. He's moved back home to Tipperary and is getting the bus up to training every morning now.

Tuesday 4th August

I saw our physio Alex before training this morning and told him that my knee's still sore. He said as it's swollen then the best thing would be to rest today – or at least do gym work and go on the bike rather than training outside. I told Tommy, who was taking the list of people training, and he told me to go and tell the Gaffer.

Doolo was in the gym when I found him. He asked about my injury and seemed to accept what I was saying before walking off. This is the way he reacts to injuries. Other managers have been worse over the years; very few of them were ever overly nice about it.

Gamble took the gym session this morning. 'That must mean Mark is definitely gone,' I told Stevie, who looked hopeful.

Gamble's doing a course on physical development, and so he was delighted to use us as guinea pigs for the day. He put us through core exercises first, and then a weights circuit, during which Tommy came in to check on us a few times. There was no messing though; Gamble made it into a difficult session, throwing in all kinds of exercises that we hadn't done before.

Everything was going smoothly until I heard a loud bang and crash form the other side of the room. As I looked over, Faz appeared to be running from falling glass. It turned out that Nulty had reached up with a medicine ball and smashed the light above himself and Faz.

While the boys were all laughing, Gamble looked fairly relieved as he helped take pieces of glass out of Faz's hair.

Later, Lordy and I chatted about how the employees at the Thomas Cook travel agency are to be removed from their sit-in/strike at work by the Gardaí today. Things seem to be very bad around the place. We agreed that it doesn't bode well for us.

Doolo brought the lads out onto the pitch afterwards for more training, while I stayed in the gym.

'Throw the old sore knee one, did you Hog?' joked young Deasy as he left.

Later, Muz, Lordy, Murph, Dan Connor, Gamble (who was 10 minutes late) and I went to meet Ollie Cahill and McGuinness at Rochestown Park to discuss a plan in respect of our wages. McGuinness told us that Coughlan's talking about paying us 50% of our wages on Wednesday and 50% the Wednesday after that. He also said that until the matter in the High Court has been resolved, he wouldn't advise us to take strike action after all.

'It won't help youse get paid and it'll only end up causing bad will at the moment. Maybe down the line, though. Maybe draft a notice that if youse are not paid by next Friday, then the players will be looking at all avenues available to them. Send that to the club so as to give notice of unhappiness.'

We agreed.

McGuinness told us that Coughlan is still trying to get the money ready for tomorrow, but even that isn't certain at this stage.

Murph responded for us: 'So all this talk could be of no use as the club isn't even out of the winding-up situation yet? Ah, I'm f**king depressed again now.'

'We all thought that was pretty much sorted,' explained Muz.

'Not from what he just told me,' said McGuinness.

Apparently Coughlan is to meet McGuinness again on Thursday to talk about a plan for the future.

McGuinness then told us he wanted us to meet with a guy named Jim McCarthy of Quintas, who wants to get involved and help the club. We agreed, and McGuinness rang McCarthy – who, it appeared, was waiting in the lobby.

McCarthy explained that the Quintas group are involved in the reorganisation of companies that are in financial distress, in order to keep them running if possible. He said that he rang FAI chief executive John Delaney with a view to getting involved, and that Delaney told him to ring Coughlan, which he did, and that's why he was there.

He said he'd looked at the club's financial situation and noticed that there's only one main creditor: the Revenue.

'The total of all other liabilities amount to only about half of what's owed to the Revenue, and so if the club are able to deal with the Revenue tomorrow then it might not be in a terrible position going forward. It'd be a real shame if the club went under. There's a strong support for the club outside of the people who go to the games; the support for the club is much wider than that, as some of you will know. I'd have some ideas going forward; I'm talking about lower wages based solely on attendances and sponsorship. I'd be looking at the Shamrock Rovers model, and a member-run club.'

When he told us this, we knew it would mean a return to part-time football.

McCarthy went on to say that Coughlan needs to come out publicly and ask for help, as he could get it if he did, but he hasn't done that yet. We told him that our trust in Coughlan has reached a very low ebb.

'Maybe it'd be better if we deal with you rather than him,' suggested one of the players. McCarthy answered that this might happen at some stage in the future, but praised Coughlan for the money he's already put in, as well as for the fact that he'd said he'd be willing to step aside for the sake of the club if the time comes.

'So wait to see if the club survives or goes under tomorrow, and we take it from there.'

As we left the meeting we decided that we had two options: the club goes under and we search for new jobs elsewhere, or the club survives and we go part-time.

Dan Connor summed it up as we left: 'Seems like we're f**ked either way.'

Chapter 7

Interview with Robert Mežeckis – 24th May 2016

Some seven years after his forced departure, I called up my Latvian friend Robert. I was aware that after he'd left us he'd had the operation on his Achilles back in Latvia, and that his injury hadn't healed properly, forcing him to retire from the game shortly afterwards. I was also aware that over the last few years he had made his way into the Latvian national team's coaching set-up and that he was now the head of the national team's department. And so, as well as catching up with a good friend, I was very interested to get his views on his time at Cork City FC and the League of Ireland, and how it might compare to things in Latvia.

When I called him he had just pulled into his driveway after a day fishing, but he was happy to talk about old times.

~~~~

Neal Horgan: So, Robert, looking back now, how did you find playing in Ireland?

Robert Mežeckis: Well, Neal, to be honest, I really enjoyed my time in Ireland.

NH: Despite all the money problems?

RM: Yes, I had a great time. I remember surfing with you – that was great fun. And as you know, we had a great team of players – some funny guys – and I was really excited to be there. I remember how the league was really progressing at the time too, or so it seemed. The money issues didn't bother me too much to be honest. What *was* tough, though, was the fact that I got injured so early, so I was not as involved as I wanted to be. I couldn't help or play for the club like I wanted. I had come to play football; this was the most frustrating thing for me. I remember the physio would rub my Achilles every day–

it was very painful. And that rowing machine out in Bishopstown... I still have nightmares about it today.

NH: And you never really recovered from your injury after that?

RM: No, I didn't. I had an operation back in Riga, and then it wasn't better. They said I would have to have another operation, but I said 'No more'.

NH: But you're still involved in football today?

RM: Yes, I am, and delighted to be. I help out with the national team – so I am very lucky.

NH: And how is football in Latvia doing?

RM: Things are getting better. We are trying very hard to improve things...

NH: With the national team or with the national league?

RM: Well, both really. The national team is run by the federation over here and the federation administers the game; however, the federation also oversees sporting and disciplinary matters and the running of our national league in close co-operation with the Union of the Latvian Football Higher League (representing the national league clubs), who are responsible for marketing development and selling TV rights.

NH: Are there full-time professionals in the national league?

RM: Yes: the league is made up of eight clubs, and most of them are fully professional.

NH: I know that you were a full-time professional during your time at Cork City – as well as before that during your time with Skonto Riga, amongst other clubs. Do you know that our league has now gone back part-time?

RM: Do you mean Cork City or the whole league?

NH: Well, the whole league really. But with the top four or five clubs the players are full-time for the season but not paid in the off-season.

RM: In Latvia the full-time players are paid in the off-season.

NH: But you have less than half of the population of Ireland, right?

RM: Yes, we have a population of about 2 million people. It is surprising that you do not have full-time anymore.

NH: How about your neighbours Lithuania – do they have full-time players?

RM: Yes, they do.

NH: And how have your clubs done recently?

RM: Well, everything seems to be moving in the right direction. We've had two new clubs enter the league this year with strong financial backing, so that is good.

NH: How have Latvian clubs done in Europe?

RM: Every club won their first fixture last year [season 2015/16] in the UEFA Europa league and got through to the next round, but they were all eliminated in the second round. And last year [the Latvian top league season, just like the League of Ireland, runs from March to November] Latvian champions FK Ventspils started the UEFA Champions League competition from the second round and were eliminated by the Finnish champions. However, our clubs are improving as the structures have improved.

NH: Well, that's a lot better than our league's record last year. How would you compare yourselves against the Lithuanian club teams – are they better or worse?

RM: The Lithuanian clubs are stronger at the moment, but they have a greater population. I also think people follow soccer more predominantly in Lithuania than in Latvia. Over here we have ice hockey and basketball, which are very strong – although, of course, we have more participants playing soccer than any other sport. But you know, if we were to qualify for the European Championships or whatever, everyone would follow us.

NH: You mentioned the structures improving; has there been a change recently?

RM: Well yes, actually. About three or four years ago we decided to change things – to finance the academies and to link these academies to the clubs.

NH: Who finances the academies?

RM: Partly the federation. Up until we changed it, the clubs were trying to do it on their own, but the federation is more powerful and decided it would help. We also made other decisions: we created a regulation that said every national club would need to be linked with an academy.

NH: You mean the academies that the federation was financing?

RM: Yes. Some academies are owned by the clubs themselves; with others there was a link-up between an existing academy and a national club.

NH: Was there resistance to this?

RM: No. Anyone who knows anything about football knows that this makes sense. It made sense to the clubs and to the academy. And in the long term to the national team.

NH: And how's it going? Have things improved?

RM: Yes, things are better – more aligned – but as you know, these things take time.

NH: But what brought about the change? Did something happen?

RM: No, not really. Although we did notice that Iceland, for example, with a population of about 300,000, had changed their structure and nearly qualified for a major tournament – before finally qualifying for Euro 2016 this time out. Their underage national teams are also doing very well now. We knew we couldn't just sit back and do nothing and expect players to develop for the national team; we wanted to improve. So we started financing the academies and linking them to the national league clubs. As I said, it will take time, but we are certainly on the right path.

NH: And before this, the federation didn't finance the academies?

RM: No, we are on better footing in Latvia now. The academies are financed according to the amount of players in the academy: the more players, the more finance from the federation. It makes sense.

NH: And what happens to your best players – do they leave the academies to go abroad?

RM: Well, we look at it from a player development point of view. Wherever can help the player to develop is best for him. If that means a player moves from one academy to another, within Latvia – from a smaller academy to a bigger one – then that can happen.

NH: But when your players leave Latvia, where do they go?

RM: We seem to have good links with German football now. Just recently two players left our academy at under-19 for Bayer Leverkusen and Koln respectively. And one of our top national players was at Hamburg for four seasons, but next year he will play with 1.FC Koln. But you know what players are like – they'll move wherever they feel is right for them to go. Another national player just signed for Reading in the English Championship. But it would be rare that we would have a player play in Spain or Italy.

NH: I feel in Ireland we may need to take a leaf from your book in Latvia to get our federation to support the academies, or the league clubs in general. Our association – the FAI – have recently been making efforts in that direction, but not enough in my opinion.

RM: Well, you know, Neal, what works for Latvia may not work for Ireland. You need to find your own way in Ireland; find out what is the best for you and keep the good football people involved. Speaking of good football people, I actually met Paul Doolin quite a lot afterwards as he was involved with your underage national team and I would see him at various UEFA events. It was good to see him and speak about old days.

NH: Different when he's not your manager, I'd say! Do you remember the time I brought you up to that school up in Knocknaheeney?

RM: Yes! Actually our national league players and clubs have recently done more work with schools too – they give speeches to the kids about how to live right and so on, like we were doing then in Cork.

NH: Yes, that's good, but do you remember how depressed we were coming back to Bishopstown afterwards with Doolo waiting for us?

RM: Well, I suppose he needed to be hard on us as a coach at times. But he was very good; he really knew the game.

Not long after that I left Robert go. Of everything we discussed I was most interested in the fact that the Latvian Federation had chosen to financially support the academies that were linked to the national league clubs. This is something that could be done here – and could work perfectly with the plans for under-15 and under-13 national leagues. So the question needs to be asked: if the Latvian Federation, for the benefit of Latvian football overall, are happy to fund the academies that link in with their national league clubs, could the FAI do something similar in Ireland?

Chapter 8

5th to 19th August 2009

Wednesday 5th August

'We getting paid, Hog?' Shane Duggan asked me this morning.

'Not yet Shane,' I answered. 'It seems like the club's still having problems collecting the money for the Revenue today – let alone paying us.'

As the other players came in, those of us who were at last night's meeting told them what had happened.

Then Doolo called a meeting in the TV room.

'I could do without watching this, this morning,' Lordy whispered, much to my agreement. But before the DVD of the Bray match was turned on, Doolo asked about yesterday.

'So, what did they tell youse?'

'Basically, that he's struggling to pay today's bill, that he's paid the other €200,000 already, and that we can't do anything until we know the story tomorrow,' Murph answered.

'And how do youse feel about it?' asked Doolo.

'It's like examinership, only worse,' said Muz, 'as we don't know what's gonna happen. Actually, we're more in the dark now than ever.'

Doolin, clearly agitated, replied: 'Well youse can't go on working and not getting paid, and that's being bleedin' honest with youse. We'll have to play Friday either way, but after that who knows? I suppose we can't do anything until tomorrow anyway. Having said that, if we can get a result on Friday and on Tuesday then we'll stay within 6 or 8 points of the leaders going into the last round of matches, and then we're in with a chance. It's not gonna be easy with the players we've lost, but still…'

He turned on the Bray DVD, but for once he wasn't too critical about our performance. Lordy and I agreed that that's probably a good idea at this stage – we've been on the end of enough criticism from outside our camp lately.

During training, my knee felt fine again and that gave me a boost. In the dressing room afterwards we discussed a piece that a local journalist published yesterday, saying that the players at Cork City FC think they have a divine right to be paid. Another local journalist also made a comment about the GAA players not getting paid and being fitter than us.

'They're all having a go at us, the b*****ds,' said Gamble.

'It's just fellas who know nothing about it having a go in the papers – that's all that is,' said Muzza.

While the papers are happy to have a go at us, we'll have to listen to the radio later to see if we still have jobs tomorrow.

Just after 4pm I got a text from my girlfriend Caroline: *Heard ye'll be OK.*

~~~~

Club statement, 5th August 2009

CORK CITY FC is pleased to confirm that, as per the commitment made in the High Court on Friday last, it has settled its outstanding tax liability with the Revenue Commissioners in full. The club will issue a more detailed statement in due course.

~~~~

This has to be good news, but where do we go from here?

Thursday 6th August

This morning we weren't all that concerned with what happened to save the club yesterday; we were more interested in what's going to happen to us in the coming weeks and months. We knew that Jim McCarthy from Quintas was coming in to tell us what to expect, and we were looking forward to hearing what he had to say. The lads also discussed something that Billy Barry said on the radio yesterday, which they're not happy with but which I couldn't quite make out.

Then Doolo arrived in and appeared to be on edge. He ordered us out onto the pitch before giving out to us for not appearing to be properly motivated for training. Then he took a deep breath before calming down and saying, 'Just get a result tomorrow night and we're in with a chance. It's gonna be a tight game, youse all know what Bohs are like. One mistake will probable decide it. And take no bleedin' notice of what Billy bleedin' Barry or anyone else is saying, 'cause they don't know what it's like.'

When Jim McCarthy appeared after training he repeated much of what he'd said last time, telling it straight: 'The plan is to go back to part-time with reduced wages. You'll be paid 40% of your wages tomorrow, and if the crowd's up then maybe we can pay more.'

Stevie asked, 'Can I ask you what kind of pay cuts you're talking about eventually? I accepted a contract here even though I had other offers at the time, and now I can't move. So what'll happen if I want to hold out and stay?'

McCarthy seemed reluctant to commit to an answer. 'I can't go into that now, but you'll know soon enough. It'll depend on the gates and sponsorship. We're doing a full audit of the club and you should know everything, hopefully, by Friday week.'

Dan Connor, who was standing up alongside Jim McCarthy (à la Mick Devine) asked, 'So who came up with the money yesterday?'

McCarthy again held these cards close to his chest: 'I don't want to get into that, but it's sorted now and that's the main thing.'

Gamble asked, 'So you see yourselves getting more involved in the club?'

'Ya, we'd like to. We want to come in and take control of the club. We want to sign every cheque and take that decision-making away from Tom. There could be some money coming in from sponsorship soon too, and so if the attendances are big, then your wages will be better. I can't tell yee what'll happen; good results may mean big crowds and then we honour yeer current contracts. We're looking at performance-based incentives to fill the gap in your wages if possible. However, in the long term we're talking about going back part-time.'

After McCarthy had left, Doolo asked us, 'Well, what will youse do? He's talking about part-time football. Do youse still want to be here for that?' He went on, 'I have to say, it's not ideal preparation for Friday's match, finding out on Thursday that there are pay cuts coming down the line when youse really need to get a result tomorrow...'

There was an overriding sense of dejection as we contemplated the spectre of pay cuts. How much would they be cutting? We still didn't know.

'I'll have to resign,' said kitman Caen. 'I'm on minimum wages already nearly; I can't take a pay cut. It's just not worth it for the work I'm doing.'

Some of the lads started talking about moving to other full-time clubs.

Kevin Long asked me whether I thought he might be able to go on trial. I told him I didn't know.

On the way home, Timmy and I discussed the possibility of him playing in Finland. I feel I'm in a fortunate position in that I've gone through college and got an apprenticeship to become a solicitor waiting for me when I finish up later in the year. Timmy, having left to play with Glasgow Celtic's underage set-up when he was 16, might have a more difficult time ahead of him should he decide to transition out of the footballing world. A trip to Finland would definitely be an opportunity for him, but nothing to rely upon at the same time.

~~~~

Irish soccer - Clubs need realistic expectations (Irish Examiner, 6th August 2009)

When a death is expected newspapers will usually have the obituary ready. So it was with Cork City Football Club yesterday. At mid-afternoon, the prospects for the survival of the club did not sound great, which made the outcome all the more welcome.

The club owed €439,000. Although it made various offers to pay the debt in instalments, it was unable to come to accommodation with the tax people. In the light of all the recent publicity about the businesses being in trouble over owing not just millions but billions of euro, it seemed almost ludicrous that Cork City would be wound up over a debt of less than half a million.

The club looked like becoming another victim of the Celtic Tiger economy and the unrealistic expectations it spawned. Cork City FC got a stay of execution last week on the understanding that it would pay €220,000 immediately and the other €219,000 by close of business yesterday. It duly came up with the money before the deadline.

Sometimes, such a crisis can highlight a bright side by providing a tangible demonstration of the commitment of its friends and supporters. People like Roy Keane and Dermot Desmond came up with valuable help. Roy Keane bought one of the Cork City players on behalf of Ipswich Town and had his team play a money-spinning game with the club. Dermot Desmond also agreed to have Celtic play a friendly with Cork City.

A number of clubs in the League of Ireland have been in deep financial trouble in recent years. They include some of the most famous clubs like Shamrock Rovers, which survived examinership, Shelbourne and Bohemians, as well as Drogheda United. Too many clubs had unrealistic expectations.

There will have to be some imaginative thinking on what route Irish soccer will take. In recent years rugby has gone professional and has been thriving. There is no reason that soccer should not do so as well, if it adopted a more practical approach in the financial climate.

Irish soccer supporters with the international team have proved to be among the best and most effective ambassadors that this country ever sent abroad. They impressed people everywhere by following their team to World Cups in the true spirit of sport. None of the Irish team at those times was playing with any club in this country, but most of them were nurtured in the League of Ireland.

The supporters, who distinguished themselves in Europe, America and Asia, have demonstrated that there is a magnificent basis of support in this country. This should be exploited with a practical approach and realistic expectations.

Friday 7th August

While I was sitting on the bus this morning, waiting to set off to Dublin for the Bohs game, I spotted Jerry Harris shuffling gear from his van in and under the bus. He looked terrible and Caen explained that he was sick. 'He should just go home to bed, for f**k's sake,' he said.

I've heard that Jerry paid for the footballs for the Ipswich match out of his own pocket. The guy would do anything for the club, and has given everything for Cork football over the years. He looked wrecked this morning though, and it captured the way the rest of us feel.

I'm sick to death of being asked about the whole thing. Everybody's asking about it: money this, money that. Greg told me he's sick of talking about it too.

Gamble, as PFAI rep, had to go around asking who'd been paid.

'Mine's in, Gamble,' I told him, 'but it hasn't cleared yet.'

'So you can't touch it yet?'

'No, I can't.'

'Then you haven't been paid if you can't touch it,' Joe confirmed.

By the time Gamble had finished his rounds it was clear that those with accounts at one particular bank had been paid while those with accounts at other banks hadn't. Gamble rang McGuinness to let him know the situation and McGuinness advised that we should do something to highlight our woes to the public at the Rovers game on Tuesday.

'What can we do, though?' Gamble asked.

'Own goal from kick-off?' someone suggested, to much derision from the lads.

A few hours later we reached Dalymount Park. As we walked into the centre circle in our tracksuits, Tommy and Doolo recounted their early memories of 'Dalyer,' when the Irish national team used to play there.

'Do you remember the game against the Soviets, Paul?' said Tommy.

'I was a ball boy over there... but there were bleedin' 15,000 fans on the pitch,' Doolo replied, and they both started laughing.

League of Ireland Premier Division
Dalymount Park, Dublin
Bohemians 1–0 Cork City

As the game progressed we were slowly ground down by a physically superior Bohs side, who certainly know how to win ugly. Unfortunately, the goal came from my area of the pitch, and so I know I'm going to have to defend myself in the video session next week.

After the match Doolo had a go at Stevie for reacting to being substituted. He also had a go at him for his positioning just before their goal.

'You weren't organised quickly enough getting back, and so you gave away the free kick that they scored from.'

We got changed in the slow, languid way that players do when beaten, pulling our socks off wearily and keeping our heads down.

On the way out, Muzza met McGuinness (the PFAI are based in Dublin), who wanted to know exactly how we're planning to protest on Tuesday. There was some discussion on the journey home about getting the ball from the kick-off, running up to the end line and then running back and putting the ball on the spot. (McGuinness may have come up with this one.)

Muzza asked me my thoughts on it.

'I don't know what that would achieve, Muz, but I do feel we need to make some kind of protest.'

Nults asked, 'Are we definitely getting paid on Thursday?'

'Depends on the crowd at the Rovers match on Tuesday,' answered Muz.

We discussed the news that Stevie may be off to Shamrock Rovers, and that young Kevin Long has been linked to a cross-channel move.

Monday 10th August
Everyone was majorly depressed coming in today. To make matters worse, when passing Doolo's office, Stevie had heard Doolo talking to Tommy about doing a video session on the Bohs match. I couldn't think of anything less appealing.

The mood lightened a bit as the lads discussed Gamble's interview in this morning's paper, in which he was asked about people blaming the players' wages for the club's current plight.

'They can go f**k themselves,' was Gamble's quote.

Tommy arrived in, asking, 'Are we all alright for training?'

Gamble answered, 'Ya, we're alright, Tommy, but everyone's depressed out of their heads.'

Tommy wasn't overly sympathetic: 'Well youse need to get on with things, cause we have a game again tomorrow. Now in for the meeting, yez c*nts.'

We must've been the gloomiest-looking footballers ever, trudging down the hallway with slumped shoulders and weary expressions.

On arrival, Doolo had his back to us at the top of the room, remote control in hand. The footage was paused; I could see it was just before their goal. Predictable enough really from the old Doolo: no messing about – straight for the jugular.

I took a seat towards the right-hand side at the back of the room. Last time I'd sat to left the Gaffer had slated me; perhaps a simple change of seats would make a difference. (As our former manager Damien Richardson used to say: *footballers are superstitious creatures*. They'll choose very carefully where they sit in dressing rooms before games; if they lose a game or play poorly they'll sit somewhere else next time, and if the play well or win they'll stick to the same spot and damn anyone who tries to make them move...)

Stevie, hiding near me at the back, whispered nervously, 'He's gonna have a right go at me here.'

Alarmed, I figured if Doolo had a go at Stevie then he'd easily move onto me.

But it was too late to move as the meeting had started.

Doolo pressed play and we watched the lead-up to the goal, in which Stevie gave away the free kick that allowed Bohs to score. After that, Doolo paused the video and started (indirectly) ripping into him.

'We're lazy because we're not fit enough,' he seethed. 'We're sauntering back...'

Stevie and the rest of us had expected this.

Next Doolo had go at everyone in various ways for what they should and shouldn't have done. He pointed at me with regard to defending the free kick, saying, 'Oggie, you've only picked up [Neale] Fenn at the last second.'

I remember what happened but it's a difficult one to explain. I'd been marking Fenn initially, but then Davin O'Neill, who'd come on as a substitute minutes before, ran over to me and said Tommy had told him to pick up Fenn for set pieces, and that I was spare. Assuming this to be the case, I went looking for any of their players that were unmarked. Joseph N'do was standing on his own so I picked him up, but seconds later, just before they took the free kick, Lordy ran over and told me N'do was his man. I looked around again and spotted that Davin had moved as Dan Connor had brought him out into the two-man wall defending the free kick. Fenn was therefore free again and I ran over to mark him just in time. However, Killian Brennan was left unmarked and scored with a flicked header.

Tommy said Davin should've been marking Brennan, but I pointed out that Davin had said he'd been told to mark Fenn (by Tommy!).

'But this is what it's about,' Doolo intervened. 'Davin's not here today and he's not here half the time cause he's part-time. So we can't get your work done.'

The meeting petered out.

On the way out, Stevie reflected on his grilling: 'He was right, to be fair though, and so I don't mind.'

Later, in training, the Gaffer and Tommy were still in foul form with us. (They probably planned to be this way after the bad result.) During the set-piece routines, Doolo had a go at Murph for chatting to Gamble. 'Wee fella – keep your mouth shut!' he shouted. Murph had a go back and they got into a brief slagging match.

At the end he brought us together and told us, 'Youse need to be sharp tomorrow [against Rovers]. Don't throw away your good work against Sligo, Derry and Galway. Because the only thing I'd say is that youse are going to be paid on Wednesday or Thursday, so that's sorted for the short term and youse can focus on tomorrow's match.'

Five minutes later, in the safety of the changing room with the door closed, Stevie chided Murph: 'You got bitched there, Danny.'

Murph half-laughed, responding, 'I know, mate. I was just standing there doing nothing and he turns and has a go at me. Totally unprovoked.'

I had a look at one of the tabloids, which featured a picture of Doolin with Bohs manager Pat Fenlon. The article was defending full-time football in the country and outlining the advances we've made with it, comparing the performance of our clubs this year with the Northern Ireland and Scottish clubs that got hammered in Europe lately. In the article, Fenlon said that's what we'll be going back to if we go part-time, while Doolin praised Pat's great result in Europe last week.

I'm glad these people have the same beliefs about full-time football as I do; that it's necessary, that it's possible, and that it could yield great nights for Irish football in the future. The opposite sentiment seems to have been prevailing in some quarters lately, with a lot of people blaming our wages and talking about how unsustainable full-time football is. Many seem to think that a return to part time would mean clubs being more sustainable, but I was talking to former City chairman Brian Lennox the other day and he said these people fail to see the taxation issue with part-time players. Clubs have to pay a hell of a lot of tax for part-time players (as those players have already used up their tax credits for their full-time job), whereas they can pay a full-time player a lot more net for the same gross wage. The problem seems to be the off-season when there's a lack of income coming into the club to pay full-time players. There must be way around this, though.

People have also failed to notice that the recent attempt at full-time football in this country has been made by a few clubs on their own. There was no plan from above, like the rugby had when it went full-time. In fact it often seems to me that the FAI would *prefer* that we were part-time and less of a headache for them.

As it stands, it looks like we're going part-time at Cork City. Gamble's on about leaving; Stevie's talking about quitting after we get paid this week, and Dan Connor's off to Exeter next week.

After I'd got changed I saw Alex, the physio, who made an appointment for me to see the specialist for my knee. It's quite sore all the time now after matches and is becoming a problem.

Tuesday 11th August

I probably should have, but I didn't see it coming.

I was named on the bench for the match against Rovers.

Greg was in my position and Kevin Long at centre-half. Doolo had given me no indication in training yesterday, and having trained well I was properly geared up for the match. It was a beautiful day and I was really looking forward to playing in front of the big crowd that we always get against Rovers. Also, with them second in the league and us third, there was much at stake.

The f**ker.

During his pre-match team talk, Doolo said something about Rovers being good at set pieces so that's why he'd picked the team that he had. As he finished his talk and the lads started getting ready, I was aware of eyes looking at me, awaiting a reaction.

I got changed quicker than normal and went outside onto the pitch. Stevie was out there early too as he'd also been dropped. We consoled ourselves with the fact that we could at least have a bit of crack in the dugout.

'Poor old Guntars has been bombed out completely,' said Stevie. 'He hasn't even made the bench. And his Mrs is over from Latvia this week to see him and all.'

Nulty, who was also on the bench, joined us and said he'd noticed Guntars getting dressed as if he was on the bench and wondered whether he even knows or not.

'Someone go tell him, for f**k's sake,' said Stevie, and Nulty toddled over towards the Latvian.

Tommy came out next and beckoned me over. He said he felt that last Friday against Bohs I was over-covering for the centre-half who was playing next to me, and that I'd caused myself problems because of this. I told him I wouldn't usually do that but I feel it's what Doolo wants me to do this year, to stay very tight to the centre-back. Tommy recommended that I should go and speak to Doolo if I feel I have a grievance. Then he told me that in general he thinks I've been doing well, and we left it at that.

I wandered back over to Stevie as the first team came out, and we warmed up separately (as usual) on the other side of the pitch. Stevie reckons he might be off to Finland next week; his agent is recommending it but Stevie doesn't know if he wants to go.

Then I heard my name being called by Tommy from across the pitch. Greg had hurt his ankle during the first team's warm-up game. *Oh f**k.* I ran over and did a few runs while their game was paused. Two minutes later, after receiving some physio treatment, Greg got up and I gave him back the bib without touching the ball before stumbling back to the bomb squad.

The game finally began. In the end we'd decided, with the help of the PFAI, that our protest about the wages would be a message printed on white t-shirts: 'CCFC = Contracts Commitment from Clubs'. The Shamrock Rovers players, in support, wore a shirt saying 'Players Supporting Players.' These white shirts were worn over their jerseys as they walked out onto the pitch. The photographers seemed to like it and snapped away as they hovered around the players, but who knows whether it'll have much effect.

As the game began, half of me wanted us to win and the other half wanted us to concede five goals, and for Doolo to be shown up for dropping me. I knew I'd still have to be ready in case anyone got injured – even though, having been dropped, I wasn't in any mindset to go on. As I was the only defender on the bench I had to be on the lookout for any defender that looked hurt.

Murph went down after 10 minutes… I went for a run. Longy went down after 35… I went for a run…

I returned to the bench and sat next to Stevie and Nults. Doolo was going ballistic at every little mistake the lads made, and Tommy's reactions were similar. That seems to be their way of dealing with the tension, but it's terrible to be around. It makes you feel like you don't want to come on and be shouted at by them. Stevie and Nults had a bit of crack about certain things in the match, while Timmy (who'd also been dropped and was sitting on my other side) was chatting away like a mad hatter about this player and that.

'You'll need ear muffs there, Hog,' chided Stevie.

We continued to watch the game, which was a tight affair with few chances either way.

Half time came and again I felt like a fraud, walking around kicking balls during the break. Nults, Stevie and I played 'keep em ups' and chatted away. Then the lads came out again and we sauntered back onto the bench for the second half.

Twenty minutes in, Timmy was brought on and he jumped wildly into one of their players in the air, giving away a free. 'He was like a kamikaze pilot there, the nutcase,' said Stevie. The whole bench chuckled, trying not to be heard by Doolo, but the Gaffer didn't seem to notice as he was focussed on the game.

Davin took on their full-back, Ollie Cahill, and we heard Doolo commenting to Tommy, 'Ya see – he can't beat him. He can't go past him.' A second later Davin threw a wonderful shimmy and went beautifully past Ollie. Doolo and Tommy remained silent and Stevie elbowed me in the side.

'Good shout there, Doolo,' Stevie whispered (although Ollie Cahill did get back to make a tackle on Davin).

Ollie got booed from the City fans all night. Stevie asked me why this was, as Sully – who was also playing for Rovers tonight – wasn't booed at all.

'It's probably because Ollie played with Shels a few years ago when they were our main rivals,' I told him. 'It's not that Ollie wasn't good at City; he was. In fact he was very good.'

After about 65 minutes Longy went down again and Doolo told me to warm up. I ran out a few times before heading back to the dugout. Longy was OK.

Lordy had a really good game in the middle of the park, and I was delighted when he was named man of the match. He's been an unsung hero for many a year.

League of Ireland Premier Division
Turner's Cross, Cork
Cork City 0–0 Shamrock Rovers

Afterwards I returned to the changing room and quickly got dressed. Doolo announced that there'll be proper training tomorrow morning in Bishopstown for the bomb squad, while the guys who played will just have recovery. I exited swiftly, and on my drive home I couldn't help being annoyed that the last 24 hours felt like a complete waste of my time.

Wednesday 12th August
Doolo was on his mobile in the corridor as I arrived this morning. I walked past him to the dressing room, where one of the lads told me that Jerry Harris's wages had been paid by cheque but it had bounced. Nults added, 'Doolo's raging.'

We wondered whether Doolo and Tommy would see it out until the end of the year.

The bomb squad were shocked this morning as there was no sign of Tommy, which meant Doolo would be training us on his own. With small numbers he could closely scrutinise every one of us.

'He'll run us,' I said, but Stevie didn't think so.

Then Doolo came in and told us that the whole squad was to go to Leisureworld. The lads who'd played last night would just use the swimming pool, whereas the bomb squad would go to the gym. We were all delighted with that.

Doolo went on to say that we'll be paid the rest of the money that's owed to us by Friday, and that if anyone's going on trial they should make sure to get permission from the club. 'I'm not sure that you'll be insured if you go on trial without permission and get injured,' he said.

It's a strange situation for a manager to be in.

Dan Connor, who normally sits next to me, has gone to Exeter on trial. Young Kevin Long was also missing and someone said he could be gone to Millwall. Timmy was in, and the boys quizzed him and Stevie about Finland. Billy Dennehy is being linked with Hereford but he said he doesn't really want to go back to England. Having spent a few years at Sunderland in his teens, he now prefers being closer to home. Nults has been calling him 'Sporting Dingle' lately, as Sporting Fingal have been interested in him and Billy's from Kerry. I tell the boys I'm going to the Barrs (my local GAA team) on trial for the week and this gets a few laughs.

There's also some talk about Dave 'Moons' Mooney, who scored twice for Reading last night in a league cup game. This is great to hear.

I then met Guntars in the hallway and he looked totally pissed off. I don't blame him: apparently, on top of being dropped yesterday with his Mrs over from Latvia, he wasn't paid the 40% like the rest of us. Yesterday he told us there was nothing in his account; I decided not to ask him about it today.

I drove to Leisureworld with Timmy, who doesn't know whether to leave the club or not. He'd prefer to stay, despite his accommodation issues.

After returning from Leisureworld I called the Doc and got an appointment to see a specialist on 26th August. My knee's feeling sore again.

Friday 14th August

There's no game this weekend, for a change, and numbers were noticeably down this morning as fellas were making the most of the chance to get away.

'Stevie's gone to Motherwell on trial,' said Nulty, which explained why the place was so quiet. Someone else said that Kevin Long had gone on trial at Millwall, but just as they said it he walked in with his buddy Craigy.

'What's the story, bud?' Nulty asked him.

Longy explained that he was scheduled to go to Millwall on Wednesday and that his flights were booked and he was just waiting on the Millwall secretary to ring our secretary (Jerry Harris) to confirm. Next thing Longy received a call from Doolo telling him that he can't leave as his wages have been paid in full. 'I told him I'd only had 40% like the rest of the lads,' Longy said. But Doolo told him to go check his account and when he did he found that his wages had been paid in full earlier that day.

'Can't be stopping a young fella going to help his career,' said Nults.

I agreed, adding: 'It'd be different if they were planning to offer you a full-time contract here, but they've made it clear enough that we're all going part time.'

While we were on the topic, Muzza said he'd been talking to McGuinness and apparently we're going to be paid our remaining 60% next Wednesday. 'But the guy from Quintas isn't coming in to talk to us today after all,' he added.

'I thought he was gonna talk to us today and tell us what to expect going forward,' I said.

'Sure he won't know anything more,' said Murph. 'They're still waiting on money to come in to pay the Revenue off.'

Fed up with the money talk, I headed off towards the boot room. As I did so I saw Jerry Harris, Caen and Alex (who's getting married on Monday) in the corridor, talking about how terrible it is that we're not being told what's going on.

'I just want to know what's happening before I hand in my notice,' said Caen. Jerry seemed to be at the end of his tether too.

I put on my boots and walked out onto the pitch early. Coming out under the small tunnel that leads from the corridor under the decrepit stadium, I hit the fresh air and started into a run across the open pitch. I felt the comforting grip of my studs as I paced in one direction and then another. Then, grabbing a football out of a ball bag, I volleyed it softly into the air above my head using the instep of my right foot. I watched it climb and spin into the blue sky before plummeting back towards me at pace. I felt the weight of it on my inner step as I controlled it before driving it, with spin, back up into the sky with my left instep. It felt therapeutic to be alone again with a just football and the elements.

A few minutes later the lads arrived out with all their noise and movement, and Tommy took us on a good hard session (Doolo wasn't around). My knee wasn't feeling great, but as I didn't want to lose fitness or have to wait around the dressing room thinking about things, I trained nonetheless. However, afterwards it was clear that my knee had deteriorated and I showed Tommy the swelling. He said I need to start looking after it, so I rang the Doc to see if could get an earlier appointment with the consultant and he said he'd see what he could do.

In the afternoon I checked my account and noticed that the remaining 60% of my wages was there, and while it hasn't cleared yet I was still surprised and delighted to see it on the screen.

Monday 17th August
Stevie O'Donnell was back from Motherwell this morning, but Dan Connor was still away so I had loads of legroom in the dressing room and didn't have to worry about any fines. We discussed the fact that Denis Behan had been awarded Man of the Match over the weekend for Hartlepool, where he's

apparently been christened 'The Beast.' Healy got a game for Ipswich too, which was good to hear.

Other former League of Ireland players in the UK were also mentioned.

'Did you see [Keith] Fahey for Birmingham against [Manchester] United?' asked Nults, before answering his own question: 'He did well in fairness to him.'

'Young Jay O'Shea from Galway United made his debut for Birmingham too,' said Murph.

Then Tommy came in and asked us, 'How are yee all, all OK for training?'

Everyone seemed to be OK.

He asked me how my knee was and I told him it was still sore and a little swollen.

'Well if it's sore you shouldn't train; there's no use being brave now and then not being available for the game on Friday.'

'Tommy, do you have any idea when we're getting paid?' Nulty asked.

'You should all be paid by Wednesday if not before,' said Tommy.

As Tommy left I told Nults that I got paid and he said, 'Ya, Stevie did too I think.'

'Ya, I got paid alright,' Stevie confirmed.

At that point Tommy's head popped back around the door. 'Right, meeting down the hallway and make it snappy, yee f**kers.'

We followed him out to the meeting room.

Doolo was standing facing us at the top of the room with one foot on the seat of a chair, as is his usual style. Leaning forward, he asked, 'Is that everyone Tommy?' A few young boys hurried in and sat down, and the door was closed.

'First and foremost, has anyone been paid?'

I put my hand up. 'Ya, I have Paul.'

Stevie's hand also went up. 'Ya, I've been paid too I think.'

I clarified that I was paid on Friday but it hasn't cleared yet, and Stevie said the same.

'So,' said Doolo, 'the two of youse and Kevin [Long] are the only ones. How come youse were paid? Did youse ring him or something?'

Perhaps it's poetic justice for dropping us, you pr**k, I thought, before answering, 'No, I don't know why.'

Stevie didn't know either.

'Well ye'll all be paid by Wednesday, apparently. He's also told me that he's gonna come in on Wednesday and give you two options; one will be to take a pay cut, and I'm not sure what the other will be. Some kind of reorganising of the contracts or sometin.'

Murph was prepared for this. 'Right Paul, he's saying we have only two options and we have to take one or the other, but he's in no position to say that. He has to pay us all our wages by the end of the season or the club won't get a licence next year.'

Doolo was somewhat defensive in his response: 'I don't know Murph, let's see what he says on Wednesday.'

'We should just let McGuinness deal with him,' said Gamble, 'otherwise it'll just turn into a slagging match like the last time.'

Doolo nodded, appearing to agree before continuing, 'Also, Mark [McManus – our fitness coach] hasn't got paid since the day he walked into the club, so he won't be coming in here again, and he told me we can't use the Leisureworld gym or pool anymore so ye'll have to pay to go in there. He left a voicemail on my phone and I can't blame the guy really. So Joey's gonna be taking the gym this morning.'

On hearing this the boys moaned sarcastically.

'Just upper body though Joe,' Tommy said hastily (the last session Joey took had played hell with our gluteal muscles), 'and stay away from the bleedin' lights. Faz nearly got decapitated last time.'

But Doolo wasn't finished: 'Also, the camera guy hasn't been paid – is that right, Tommy? – or maybe he had some arrangement with FORAS or something, and as FORAS don't want to be part of the plans anymore he's not going to be videoing the matches for us anymore, or sometin' like that. So no more video analysis from now on anyway, which isn't great to be honest with youse.'

'Yee'll probably be delighted with that, yees c*nts.' Tommy bellowed with laughter and a few of the boys sniggered.

Doolo continued: 'Anyway boys, if we all get paid that means we can all be right for Friday's match. First place is looking difficult now, but I think second place is still there for us. So we need to be right for the game.'

We left the meeting room, headed back into our dressing room and shut the door.

Stevie's voice rose in disgust: 'How about the f**king video guy? He had to wait until after the f***king Bohs game when I got crucified ? The pr**k.' He was being half-serious, but as the rest of the lads laughed he joined in.

We were all trying to guess what option 'B' might be on Wednesday. Some of the lads think Coughlan will offer to pay out the rest of the contract (or at least part of it) if we leave; others think he'll just say we can leave.

'I couldn't see them offering any money to leave, to be honest,' I said – although someone pointed out that it would make financial sense for them to fork out and pay off some of the lads on bigger contracts. Anyway, we'll see what happens on Wednesday.

Tommy came back in and asked us, 'So do youse want to do the gym work and then have lunch and go outside this afternoon, or do youse want to go straight outside after gym work?'

The lads were unanimous: straight out after gym work.

'OK,' said Tommy, 'but be careful with them, Joe.'

'Ah, it won't be that hard anyway this time,' said Gamble, and we went off to do weights and a core session in the gym.

Afterwards my knee was still sore, so I told Tommy I wouldn't be training outside today. Then I went to see our stand-in physio (Alex got married yesterday), and then I watched training from the stand as Doolo ran the lads hard.

By the end of the session the lads are spent. In the dressing room afterwards, some reckoned it was the hardest session since pre-season.

Doolo put his head around the door and told everyone to have ice baths, then he turned to spot me in corner behind the door, where I always sit.

'Oggie, I want to talk to you. Come down here a sec,' he said before walking off at high pace. We went down the corridor and I followed him into his office.

'Right, take a seat.'

Doolo sat behind his desk and faced me with fire in his eyes.

'So your knee's sore, is it? But how come you're not training today though, when you were available for selection on Friday? Did you go running on Saturday or Sunday?'

I'd been thinking on the way down the corridor that he might give me a grilling.

'No,' I said, 'I was giving my leg a complete rest so I did nothing Saturday or Sunday.'

'How come, then, you were available for selection on Friday and now you're not?' he asked sternly. His head was moving around a lot as he spoke, as if he was ready for a confrontation. But then I realised that he'd got it wrong.

'I was available for selection on *Tuesday*,' I said.

Doolo's expression changed. He said nothing and allowed me to explain.

'My knee had been sore since the Bohs match last Friday, where I wore long studs. I was then available for selection on Tuesday against Rovers, and would have played even though it was sore. Of course I *was* disappointed that I didn't play, and I know you might think I'm sulking or something, but that's not the case. My leg's getting worse and that's the issue. I trained on Wednesday and Friday anyway, but it got sore again when I trained with Tommy.'

'Oh, right,' said Doolo, obviously realising he'd got it wrong. 'So what's the story now?'

I told him about my appointment for 26th August and how the Doc's trying to get me in sooner.

'So is it swollen or what?'

I showed him my knee. 'It's not swollen that much now but it's sore and getting worse. I feel the problem now is that I won't be 100% for the matches and I'm no good to you if that's the case.'

'Right,' he said. Then he stood up and led me back towards the dressing room, saying, 'You know we're down on numbers as it is; we'll need everyone available to us.'

'I know,' I said, 'but I need to be right for both our sakes.'

'Sure Alex will be back tomorrow,' said Doolo, and we left it at that.

Back in the dressing room, I thought about what had just happened. Obviously Doolo had got things wrong and shouldn't have assumed I was trying to get an easy day, but to be fair to him most managers are like this; they hate people being injured. Many wouldn't even talk to you if you were injured, as you were of no use to them. And God help you if whatever scan they send you for doesn't show anything up: then it's definitely in your head and they're likely to run you for longer than everyone else and hold a grudge against you.

So I know it's not just Paul Doolin that's like this. And in truth I respect him for bringing me into a room and attempting to grill me one-on-one rather than saying nothing and holding it against me for the week. It's not like Doolo to get these things wrong, though; maybe the situation is affecting him also.

Tuesday 18th August

I checked my bank this morning and the 60% had cleared through into my account. Great stuff.

I was the first of the players to arrive at training, and Caen, who was carrying a big basket of gear towards the laundry room, congratulated me.

'Is Alex here?' I asked.

'No – Emma [the girl covering for the physio] is still here,' Caen replied. 'Alex was allowed one day off for his honeymoon: that's the kind of place we're working in,' he quipped as he walked off down the corridor.

The lads arrived in dribs and drabs, coming in from the incessant drizzly rain and grey skies that sometimes sit over this part of Ireland.

In the dressing room we talked about Seany Kelly scoring 'Goal of the Month' on *Monday Night Soccer* for Galway United. We're all glad for him.

Then, inevitably, the issue of wages came up.

Some of the lads have been paid like myself – including Muzza and one or two others – but everyone else is still waiting. Muzza said he was talking to McGuinness last night, who'd told him Coughlan won't be coming to see us tomorrow after all. He also said the pay cuts are going to be 25%, and Stevie reacted to this with obvious frustration: 'We need to know what's going on, for f**k's sake!'

Then Murph walked in, and on hearing the boys chatting about it he said, 'No – it's not gonna be 25%. I was talking to McGuinness and he told me 30%, and that the club want us to take the first pay cut for this month – as in for the last three weeks.

'No f**king chance – f**k that.' Muzza read my thoughts exactly.

Then young Paul Deasy piped up from the corner: 'I was talking to Sully, and McGuinness told *him* that the pay cuts would be 40%.'

Nulty, to my right, was working out in his head how much a 40% wage cut would be for his wages. He looked at the ceiling, then he looked down and said in a somewhat startled voice: 'No f**king way'.

Greg, Lordy, Faz and I wondered what Gamble (who is always in the know) had been told. I reckoned 50%. Then Gamble arrived (last one in, as usual) and said, 'No – Coughlan didn't tell me about wage cuts as he says he doesn't know yet. He has to talk to that guy from Quintas about it, but he's away on holidays. He did say that some players won't have any pay cuts if they're on minimum wage, but all the others will though.'

'Whatever happened to us being happy with the pay cuts on offer?' said Lordy, and we all laughed.

Gamble continued: 'He did say that he wants the club to remain full time, though.'

'Ya, but on 100 euro a week,' said Lordy.

'And he'll want us in every day for double sessions at that,' I added.

Stevie seemed more despondent than the rest of us. 'What about the McCarthy guy and his model – that's right out the door now is it?'

The lads didn't know for certain, but some suspected Quintas were out of the equation now.

Longy said that the girl in the office is leaving too.

'She must've realised what a hellhole this place is to work in now,' said Muzza.

Then Lordy told us that Caen had handed his notice in too. (Caen later told me he's going to work as security guard with his brother.)

Dan Connor was still away; Timmy was missing too, and Davin was at work.

I decided to train, as my knee seemed to have settled down a little and I wanted to see what it was like. During the warm-up and passing drills it was as though there were needles going through it – but then we did some work on team shape and it began to feel alright again.

Doolo and Tommy had to stand in as players as we were down numbers. This is never a good thing.

During the shape routine, Doolo put Billy Dennehy on my side. He's a fit and fast b*****d and seemed to be getting the ball every time and running at me with it. I did OK, but it was hard as they had two-on-one on me every time. However, it's a drill that's *meant* to be hard for full-backs, overloading us with pressure. There's a lot of running involved: I had to get out to Billy as he got the ball, turn him back if possible, then sprint back inside next to my centre-back as the ball was transferred to the other side, in order to remain tight as a back four. When the defenders won the ball back we had to play it straight to the person on the halfway line, who would give it to one of their wingers and they'd come running at us again.

After what seemed like forever, Doolo finally ended the routine and we gathered around him.

He told us he's never had a situation where players have gone away to other clubs on trial and then come back wanting to play. 'It's not good for team morale, to be honest with youse,' he said. 'And the way things are at the moment, we need to be a tight group. Third place is great for all the crap that's gone on, but to win this league you need one of either two things. Do youse know what those things are?'

We made a few wrong guesses before he told us, 'You either need to buy all the best players, or you need to be at a club for three years and work with what you've got. Neither of those things are bleedin' possible here at the moment. The administrative side of things here is letting us down, and youse've been great but youse need to keep it up now.'

Doolo's clearly pissed off with how things have gone since he's come in, but to be honest – and no offence to him – I'm sick of hearing about it all and my mind started to wonder.

'OK, that's it,' he said finally, and we picked up a few pieces of equipment and headed inside.

We got changed and then we headed to the meeting room to have our lunch (which, to be fair, has arrived every day without fail). Perhaps sensing that we needed a lift, while we were eating, Greg told us a story about Denis buying a remote controlled helicopter at a stall in Thailand when the duo were on holiday there. While packing for the flight home, Denis had put the remote control for the helicopter into his carry-on bag and decided to carry the helicopter onto the plane also.

'Then, in the back of the cab at two in the morning, Denis suddenly shouts, "Ah, f**k it!" and when I ask him what's wrong he says, "Ah, Greg. Amen't I after leaving me helicopter back at the hotel!" He then grabs my phone and rings Mo – the guy who runs the hotel. "Ah Mo, I left me helicopter in the hotel!" But Mo doesn't have much English and he's saying, "wha helicopter?" Denis tries to explain a few more times and I'm in stitches in the taxi. Then Denis hangs up and is totally pissed off. He tries to forget about it… but didn't he forget all about the remote control in his carry-on? So as he goes through the security gate he gets stopped and tries to explain to the girl from security what the remote control in his carry-on bag is for. "Love, I left me helicopter in the hotel." "Wha helicopter?" she says. Then finally, when he was unpacking at home after a 10-hour flight, his fiancée asked him what the remote control was for. "Ah love, I don't wanna talk about it."'

Greg performed it all in an exaggerated Denis voice and we were all made up.

'What must they think of him over in Hartlepool?' asked Stevie.

Chapter 9

20th to 31st August 2009

Thursday 20th August

This morning came the dreaded news of more bounced cheques. At least this time there'd been some communication: both Muzza and Greg had received phone calls from the club before training to inform them of the situation.

'Some girl rang me this morning and when I picked up she said she was ringing to tell me not to worry about the bounced cheque,' explained Muz, 'and that the money would be in my account this afternoon. I didn't even know the cheque had bounced until she rang me!'

It turned out a lot of other cheques had bounced too, including Stevie's, and he seemed mightily pissed off about it.

As mine was paid by cheque I began to worry. I found Doolo, who was prowling the corridors, and asked whether I could use his computer again to check. He asked me what bank I'm with, and when I told him he said, 'No, that means your money has been taken out too, but you'll be fine again by this afternoon.'

I returned to the dressing room no clearer about the situation.

Others were worse off, though: Alan O'Connor, young Deasy and Guntars still had no sign of the 60% in their accounts – that is, there hasn't even been an attempt to pay them.

Muz said, 'The reason the girl gave for the money being taken out of our accounts is that the club didn't want some players getting paid on Friday before others. They want all players to be paid at the same time from now on.'

I found this incredible. 'So the club's saying that the cheques didn't bounce at all but that it was their *decision* to take the money out... for fairness purposes... even though they're three weeks late?'

'I know,' said Muz. 'Doesn't really add up, does it?'

Doolo came in and started walking around telling everyone that they should be paid by the end of the day. Then Faz came in looking bothered.

'Lads,' he said, 'I just met a strange bloke out there in the corridor looking for Timmy [Timmy was out sick today]. He told me he's Timmy's landlord and he's looking for his key back.'

The boys laughed at this but apparently it was true.

'He was in the other day too,' said Nults.

At that point Davin arrived in, dressed in his work clothes, and got a big cheer. Doolo had called him in to watch our last video session, which the lads also thought was funny but Davin wasn't impressed.

As we walked in to watch the video session, Stevie whispered to me, 'At least you and me can get our cigars out today as we didn't play.'

Doolo turned on the DVD and proceeded, as expected, to cane most people – and in particular Davin. Much-needed relief came when the DVD began to malfunction and Tommy struggled to fix it. Doolo started ordering Tommy around: 'No Tommy, that's not it, try the other channel. Put it in again and see... no, the other channel!'

Unfortunately, Tommy fixed it after a few minutes, allowing Doolo to return to caning the lads. After getting abused by Doolo for about 20 minutes, Davin said, 'See yee lads,' and headed back to work.

We went outside and trained. Dan Connor was back, but Nults has moved into top spot for the goalkeeping position, and Doolo used him rather than Dan as the main goalkeeper while we practiced our set pieces.

I, on the other hand, remain firmly rooted in the bomb squad – a group whose defined role during set-piece routines is to be cannon fodder for the first team.

As we finished up, some of the lads said they saw Coughlan's car coming in and out while we were training, and Caen said, 'He's playing games with us now.'

Later I checked my account and it turned out my payment hadn't bounced; nor had it been removed and put back in again for 'fairness' purposes.

Friday 21st August

As our bus left Silversprings Hotel at 11.45am this morning for Drogheda, I took my usual seat at the back, just across from Greg. A few seats up, Murph was talking about wages. He'd heard from McGuinness that from now on Coughlan's going to pay us fortnightly – or in two instalments per month at least – instead of monthly. But he's actually going to pay us *everything we're owed* until the end of the season (at least that's what he's saying). Then at the end of the season he's going to sit down and talk with the lads who've got longer contracts.

The lads found this hard to believe. After all the talk of pay cuts over the last few months, they've now decided we're to get fully paid until the end of the season? We were about to grill Murph when Muz interjected: 'Ya, McGuinness told me the same; it's some turn up for the books if it's true.'

'Why would he do this when we were already resigned to the idea of taking pay-cuts?' I asked.

The someone said, 'Jesus – here he is lads.'

I looked out the back window and there indeed was Coughlan, walking towards the door of the bus.

Tommy hadn't arrived yet, and with Doolo awaiting us in Drogheda, Coughlan had us all to himself. He climbed onto the bus and made his way slowly down the aisle. We hushed down and the atmosphere felt fairly tense as he approached.

He stopped halfway and began: 'OK lads, I just want to say a few words to yee there before yee leave. I know it's been a while since I last talked to you, and a lot has happened since, but I suppose I just want to apologise for what's gone on over the last few weeks. You've all been reading the papers, but it's not all our fault what's happened. You see, everyone's feeling it at the moment. But I'm here again to tell you that I'm not a quitter, and we're still here, aren't we?

'Anyway, some of you might've been onto the two Dannys, and you may know our plan for the future already. Well, we *are* going to honour the commitments we've made until the end of the season. And we'll sit down with people after that. So I'll be meeting Stephen McGuinness on Tuesday with regard to arranging the payments, but I'm sure you'll all be happy with them.

'And lads, before I leave I just want to say that we're going to move on from this now, and even though some of our sponsors have let us down lately we're going to move on from them too. So that's it, lads. Thanks for your efforts lately; yee have been great. And good luck tonight. Alright,' he said, before turning and getting off the bus.

The second he stepped off the bus, Gamble said, 'Well I don't know about yee, but I don't believe a word of it.'

As the bus pulled off we wondered how Coughlan could say those things and then walk off while Deasy and Guntars, at the top of the bus, still haven't been paid for last month.

Approaching Dublin, the traffic was bad and we moved very slowly towards our hotel in Drogheda where Doolo was waiting. On arrival we devoured our pre-match meal, relaxed for a few minutes, and then Doolo called us back into the dining room for a team meeting.

He started glibly: 'Well, youse all know there won't be any football played in the match tonight. It'll just be a battle.'

Like most self-respecting players, I'm inclined to dislike the manager when I'm in the bomb squad, and perhaps because of this I found Doolo's team talk particularly depressing tonight.

The team and subs were named. Nulty was playing instead of Dan Connor; Stevie and myself were on the bench. My instant reaction was relief – my knee could do with the rest –

but on the bus on the way to the ground I felt a little disappointed with myself that I didn't really want to be playing.

After waiting around the dressing room for what seemed a lifetime, the game began and the ball was battered high in the air from one end to the other. While my opinion may not have been entirely objective, I truly considered it the worst game of football I've ever watched. It didn't help that the instructions from the line for both sides were, in the main, limited to 'Put it in the corner!'

While this can be an effective strategy, and the other team were also committed to it tonight, it was completely at odds with what Doolo and Tommy have had us doing every day in training over the last few months with all our passing drills. I can understand Doolo's point of view – that he's judged by results, and even if we win ugly, everyone's happy – but watching this type of game from the bench is totally demoralising. In the end we triumphed one-nil, with one of their lads scoring an OG.

League of Ireland Premier Division
Hunky Dorys Park, Drogheda
Drogheda United 0–1 Cork City

On the bus afterwards the lads who'd played discussed how many times they'd headed the ball. 'I don't think I've ever headed a ball in a match so much in my life,' said centre-half Muzza.

What's the point of it all? I wondered, sunk into my seat at the back of the bus.

Monday 24th August
On arrival this morning we discovered we were in for double sessions both today and tomorrow. It wasn't welcome news.

The lads weren't sure whether Coughlan's going to turn up tomorrow to meet us, or whether he's meeting McGuinness tomorrow either. Doolo came into the dressing room and asked the question (now routine) of who's been paid and who hasn't. Alan O'Connor, Guntars and Deasy still haven't.

My fellow full-back Danny Murphy mentioned to me that he's suspended in a few weeks for our game against Dundalk, as he's picked up too many yellow cards. 'That means Doolo will want you to be available, Hog, to play left back.'

My knee was sore during training today so Doolo advised me to rest it tomorrow and just do some upper body stuff in the gym.

Later the doc called me to let me know that I have an appointment with the specialist tomorrow at 8.30am.

Tuesday 25th August
'You're in big trouble here, fella,' the specialist said as he looked at the scan of my knee. 'There's a hell of a lot of wear and tear, and on top of that you're missing some of the lining on your cartilage.' He showed me a tear in the cartilage on the scan.

We discussed my options and decided that keyhole would be best, and we scheduled it in for next Monday.

'It won't fix it completely, but it'll get rid of a lot of the junk that's floating around in there.'

He said the reason I was feeling OK in games, after warming up, was because of adrenalin.

I drove to training happy that something was being done about my situation, although I wasn't looking forward to telling Doolo.

I met Alex (the physio) when I arrived and asked how he was doing, knowing that he was in the process of emigrating to Canada.

'Ya, I'm pretty busy, and it's going fine apart from the fact that my cheque just bounced.'

'What?' I asked. 'Which cheque?'

'The 60% cheque. And some of the lads' ones have bounced too. It really is beyond a joke now. And sure what chance have I got of ever seeing that money now that I'm leaving the country?'

When their training ended, some of the boys joined me in the gym.

Guntars was first: 'How are you, Hogs?

'Good,' I said, 'and you?'

'I'm fine, but training was very tough today. *Very* tough.'

Then Stevie arrived in. 'Alright Hogs, did your cheque bounce?'

'I don't know Stevie, I don't think so.'

'Well mine did, and it's the second one that's bounced twice now. It's a f**king joke, isn't it?'

'Isn't Coughlan meant to be coming in at 2 o'clock today?' I asked.

'Ya he is, but I don't think he'll show his face,' said Stevie in disgust.

Later, in the dressing room, it emerged that cheques have bounced with loads of the lads – including Lordy, Nulty and Faz.

Nults complained, 'I wouldn't mind but I've spent money on the strength of it being in my account.'

Lordy added, 'Ya, and I've paid off debts on my credit card using it too.'

'Doolo's screwing,' said Murph. 'Nobody will want to play for us next season – that's what I'm worried about. Sure it's *costing* Faz and Stevie and others to be playing with us at the moment.'

We headed into the meeting room when lunch arrived. Doolo joined us, and on seeing me he said quite jovially, 'Ah, Hoggie – there you are. How did you get on, fella?'

I explained that I was scheduled for keyhole on Monday.

'Monday? Sure we can't afford to lose ya,' he uttered.

I laughed.

'I'm serious,' he said.

Tommy, who was walking past, joked, 'Sure the whole place will probably be shut down by Monday anyway Paul.'

'Ya, you could be right there Tommo,' Doolo conceded. 'The only bleedin' solution would be to put my head in the oven, forget about the whole bleedin' thing.'

Tommy and the boys nearby laughed.

During lunch we learned that Coughlan wasn't coming in to see us at 2 o'clock, but that he was due to meet McGuinness tonight. We were also told that the money owing to the lads whose cheques had bounced would be paid in cash into their accounts in the afternoon.

In the gym later, I chatted with Jerry Harris while he was in doing exercises to help his hips. He's 67 and in good nick, doing a jog every day. He asked about my knee and said he'd had several keyholes himself over the years, but that 'somehow it's still hanging together'. He also told me that the club still hadn't paid him the 60%, and that a good few of the coaching staff are in the same predicament.

'It's terrible what's going on; it's no way to run a business. Just the other day a cheque bounced for UCC for the use of the Farm [training pitches], and so we can't use the facilities over there now for the underage teams.'

I finished my session and left Jerry to his hip manoeuvres.

Afterwards I chatted to Alan O'Connor, who was outside sitting in his car. He'd just arrived. It was about 1.30pm. He explained his lateness before I even asked: 'I was actually here this morning Hogs, but whatever the lads are thinking, whether they'll go on strike or not, I'm not gonna train until I get paid. F**k that.'

Then he asked, 'So is Coughlan coming in at 2 like they said?'

'No, he's not coming in now Al. A load of the boys' cheques have bounced. Did your cheque bounce?' I asked.

He laughed as he answered, 'No, they haven't even attempted to pay me yet. Myself and Deasy were saying earlier that we'd love to have the dignity of a bounced cheque.'

Wednesday 26th August

Pay day for the monthly wage for August. No sign of it in my account; no surprises there.

Thursday 27th August

When I walked into the dressing room this morning I met Stevie, who asked whether I'd been paid the 60% for July.

'Ya,' I answered. 'It didn't bounce since it went in that Friday about a week-and-a half ago. How about you?'

'Well the third cheque has gone in, but I can't get at the money yet and if you ask me it's likely to bounce – so NO, I didn't get paid,' he said, looking downcast. Then his face brightened: '…but did you hear about Dan Connor?'

'No?'

He explained that Dan Connor had been on a list of names that Coughlan said he'd paid on Tuesday afternoon, but in fact Dan didn't get anything while the rest of the people on the list all received payment (albeit by cheque). '…so Dan got onto the Gaffer and the Gaffer called Coughlan, who said they'd put Dan's wages into someone else's f**king account by mistake!' Stevie laughed. 'And so some random punter has Dan Connor's wages in their account today!'

'That's karma for the fines list,' I suggested, and we both laughed.

When the rest of the boys arrived we worked out there are eight people that haven't been paid at all – that is they haven't even had cheques lodged into their accounts – the payment being the 60% from July. They include renegade striker Alan O'Connor, the unfortunate Guntars, Lordy, part-timer Davin O'Neill, Timmy Kiely of no fixed abode, and young players Deasy, Craigy and Gareth Cambridge. It seems to me that some of the people on this list might be deemed easier targets than the likes of cockney rebel Danny Murphy or the fiery Joe Gamble.

In any event, we discussed the fact that Coughlan had a list of players to pay (the list that included Dan Connor) and wondered why the others weren't on that list. We all agreed that it wasn't fair.

'It's the people who they think won't cause any sh*t that they haven't paid, the f**kers,' said Murph.

Nobody knows what to do about it. Muz, Murph and Gamble said they'd met Coughlan and McGuinness on Wednesday, and Coughlan had apparently worked out some way of paying us all in instalments (more than we're currently being paid) for the rest of the season.

'The bottom line is that the club's skint,' said Muz, 'and from the sound of it the guy from Quintas will want to take the club apart and go part-time.'

'So what do we want?' I asked. 'Do we want the current situation, where we're getting messed about but are still being promised our wages until the end of season, or do we want Quintas, who'll make us go part-time with cutbacks?'

Nulty piped up: 'For f**k's sake! I've just realised that means those lads' wages are a month late – a whole f**king month! That's unreal! We have to do something…'

'We shouldn't go on strike though,' Murph pointed out, 'as you have to give notice, and McGuinness said that once you've used up your strike for a game you can't really use it again – therefore wouldn't we be better off using it in a big game at home rather than this Saturday [against Cliftonville in the Setanta Cup, where only a small crowd is expected]?'

'Ya, I know what you mean Murph, but we have to do something if the lads don't get paid tomorrow,' said Nults.

Stevie, who was looking increasingly dejected, added, 'I feel like just packing it in, walking away and collecting my wages that I'm owed later.'

Gamble advised him, 'You'll be waiting until January if you do that. Sully [now at Rovers] is still owed money, and he's been told it won't be paid until January as that's the deadline the club's been given in order to get a license for next year. Everybody has to have been paid before that; the UEFA club licensing regulations are the only bargaining tool we've got.'

'That's the reason we got the money we were owed from last season too, because of those regulations,' I explained to Stevie.

Someone suggested that Healers and Denis are also owed money by the club.

'No,' said Nults, 'Denis got paid. He was cute about it; he told Coughlan he wouldn't sign the contract with Hartlepool until he got paid what was owed to him. As the club couldn't get the transfer money until he signed the contract, Denis got what he was owed. Apparently the club had offered to pay him back what he was owed in instalments over a longer period, but Denis insisted on the whole lot upfront.'

Fair play to him, we all agreed.

'Denis was always a cute whore,' said Muz. 'But anyway, how about we tell the Gaffer that if we don't get paid tomorrow we're gonna do something on Saturday? Whether that's delaying the match or not playing, I don't know...'

'It's amazing,' said Nults, 'we haven't even mentioned that our August wages are due.'

Davin agreed, 'Ya, sure this is the same problem we'll have next month also: getting the money currently owed to us for August.'

We remained in the dressing room for another 15 minutes, talking about the ins and outs of the situation without coming to any fixed plan. Everyone was depressed and looking to 'bomb off' training when physio Alex's head popped around the door and he announced, 'All the best lads – I'm not hanging around as I haven't been paid and my last two cheques have bounced. Good luck to yee all and I hope yee all get paid.'

We all shook his hand and then he left.

'He's dead right,' someone said.

A few minutes later Alan O'Connor walked out, stating he wasn't coming back until he was paid. I wondered whether he would ever come back.

There was talk of gathering our bills for bounced checks and sending them to the club.

'I'm owed a tenner for the last two,' Stevie said.

'How much?' They only charged me €3 at my bank,' said Faz.

Someone else said their bank is charging €6. At least we'll have learnt one thing from all of this: which bank is the most competitive for bounced cheque charges!

At 10.25 we went out into the rain, which was now accompanied by a fresh chill. The Gaffer quickly called us together and told us he was aware of the situation, and that he thinks it's a disgrace.

'How many haven't been paid yet?' he asked.

Ten of the lads (including those, like Stevie, who've had cheques lodged into their accounts that haven't cleared) put up their hands.

Gamble said, 'Well Gaffer, if the boys aren't paid tomorrow then we're thinking that we're not gonna play on Saturday.'

The Gaffer went quiet for a few seconds before replying, slowly, 'Well if that's what youse've decided to do, I can understand.'

Tommy brought us off for a warm-up, and while we were running around a few of us wondered whether Doolo would chase Coughlan again. Shortly afterwards the Gaffer went inside and was spotted using his phone.

Later, during a fast feet drill, the Gaffer called me as I was running past him. 'Oggie, can you get that appointment cancelled? Murph's suspended Friday week.'

'But my knee isn't right,' I said.

'Well you'll have to chance it; we've got nobody else.'

I kept running and didn't reply.

We then had possession games with three goals, and I noticed that the Gaffer was being nicer to me than usual. I couldn't help thinking it was because he wants something from me. *He's wasting his time*, I thought to myself. I don't want my appointment moved around.

We finished with a shooting drill, following which the Gaffer called us in together again.

'I know it's been tough, lads. I just rang Tom there and gave out to him, telling him it's a bleedin' disgrace the way the club's being run– and it is. But we have to think about what we wanted from the start of the year. To be up there with a chance of Europe, and that's where we are. It'd be great to finish in third – maybe second – but at the moment we could still finish sixth, so yee have to decide what yees want. We'll need everyone, as we're down to bare bones as it is.'

During lunch Doolo called me to his office. 'Oggie, can you ask to get that appointment cancelled? We're struggling for numbers.'

'I'll ask' I said.

When I got home I rang the specialist's office. The secretary answered and said she wasn't sure whether the appointment could be changed. 'I'll get back to you later today, or more likely tomorrow,' she said.

Friday 28th August

The specialist's secretary called me this morning before training. 'I'm afraid you'll be waiting three weeks or more for another appointment if you cancel Monday's,' she said.

'In that case I'll go for Monday so,' I confirmed.

I drove to training and met the Gaffer in the hall. When I told him, he initially misunderstood what I was saying.

'Ah sure, three or four weeks away might be OK,' he said.

'No,' I said, 'I'm not waiting that long. I'm having it on Monday.'

'Right. So how long until the Dundalk match that Danny's suspended for? Let me think... it's on September 11th or 12th – and when's your op?'

'Monday, 31st August.'

'OK, so maybe you'll be back in time?'

'Ya, I might be. Nults said he was back running within three days when he had it done, so there's a chance.'

In the dressing room it emerged that Deasy, Lordy and Timmy got paid by cheque yesterday, while Guntars didn't get paid anything and Stevie still can't get near his. Billy Dennehy revealed that it was his account that the club had put Dan Connor's money into. 'I was gonna take it as this month's overdue payment, but that'd be bad on Dan and I couldn't do that, so he has it now.'

We grilled Guntars: 'Are you sure you didn't get paid – even by cheque?'

'No, nothing. I check this morning,' he said firmly.

'OK, so Guntars hasn't been paid... what are we gonna do?' asked Muzza.

Alan O'Connor wasn't around and neither was Davin or young Craigy, so we didn't know if they'd been paid.

We were then called into the meeting room, and once we'd all settled down the Gaffer asked us who still hasn't been paid.

Stevie put his hand up and explained, 'Mine hasn't cleared, so I haven't been paid.'

Guntars and Deasy also raised their hands.

'OK,' said Doolo, 'so it's the three of youse, plus maybe Davin, Craigy and Alan O'Connor. And Coughlan told me he's paid everyone. It's a f**king joke. But what I will say is that he's talking about a plan – isn't he Muzza? Have you told the lads that yet?'

Muzza replied, 'All I know is that Coughlan's coming to meet McGuinness on Monday to agree on a way of paying us until the end of season in six instalments. And McGuinness is talking about putting something into the agreement to make sure that if he's late with any of the instalments we go on strike or something like that.'

'Ya, that sounds fine Muz,' said Doolin, 'but that the fact is we already have it in black and white in our contracts that we're meant to get paid, and that isn't making too much of a difference at the moment. Anyway, what it really means is that he's offering to pay us in full until the end of the season, and from what I've heard the Quintas guy is talking about 50% pay cuts, so basically yee have no option.'

Assistant manager Tommy Dunne wanted further confirmation about who's still unpaid: 'So you've received none of the 60% July payment yet, Guntars?'

'No, nothing Tommy,' Guntars replied grimly.

'That's a f**king disgrace,' said Tommy.

'Well I don't know what youse can do lads in regard to Guntars and the others,' Doolo continued, 'but messing around with the match could get you in trouble. They're not the only ones that haven't been paid – there's also Jerry Harris, Caen… so youse need to get onto McGuinness and get it sorted somehow.'

The Gaffer and Tommy headed out and we bowled back into the dressing room to discuss our options, which seemed to come down to: a) strike now and don't train; or b) do the warm-up for training only and then come back inside so as to get Doolo on Coughlan's back.

As we discussed our options Joey rang Coughlan directly. Coughlan answered and said he'd definitely paid Guntars. So Guntars went out and checked again on the computer in Doolo's room, but when he came back in he said, 'Still no pay.'

We felt totally powerless.

We figured Doolo must have gotten onto Coughlan to get Alex paid yesterday, and it obviously worked as Alex received his money and was back in today. We wondered if we should use the same tactic; refuse to train and get Doolo to put pressure on him this way. But some of the boys said they'd just heard Doolo giving out to Coughlan on the phone, so it'd probably make no difference.

In the end everyone filed outside for our normal pre-match training. It was very windy in the exposed Bishopstown training ground, and our crossing and finishing drills were ruined. At the end the Gaffer went through our strategy for the Cliftonville game.

During lunch the boys were on about Bohs' situation. A developer guy, Liam Carroll, had pledged €40 million and a new stadium at Dalymount, but had got out of it over some legal problem (a separate interest over the land).

'Bohs have spent €4.2 million on the strength of this money, so now it seems like they're f**ked,' said Dan Connor.

'We're in a much better position than them so, are we?' I asked.

'Ya, but we have no assets; they still have Dalyers,' said Connor.

'Thank f**k we have no assets,' said Caen, 'otherwise we would've gotten into serious sh*t by now.'

Saturday 29th August

As I knew I wasn't starting the match, and was unlikely to be involved at any stage, I had a strong temptation to go surfing this morning. Despite this, I decided to do my normal home match routine. I can't drop below the professional standard; I'd be leaving myself open to attack from others and I'd also be letting myself down. I only have to think of former senior pros like Woodsy, Colin T, Stephen Napier, Fergy O'Donoghue, Decky Daly, Johnny Glynn, Derek Coughlan... guys who never let their standards drop, even when they weren't in the first 11. They left me with a good impression of what a senior pro should be like at all times, and particularly when not involved. Maybe I could leave the same kind of impression with the younger lads; there's some good in that.

During my post-meal walk I came across a junior game being played. I sat and watched, jealous of those guys who can just show up for the game 45 minutes beforehand, enjoy it and then be free for rest of weekend. I know I have a lot going for me but I miss that side of the amateur game – the freedom of it. Money brings chains. At least I don't have too long to go before I'll be playing at a level like that and enjoying the game again. I can't wait for that.

I continued with my day's routine and arrived at Turner's Cross for 5.15pm, an hour and 45 minutes before kick-off.

There was a new physio in, learning the ropes from Alex.

'Last day, Alex' I said.

'I know, I'm gonna cry,' he replied sarcastically.

I walked onto the pitch. Some of the lads were out there already, chatting as the surface was being watered around them. It looked in good nick.

'Did you see what Coughlan said in *The Sun*?' Nults asked. 'He said he's gonna defer all our wages until January.'

The boys laughed in disbelief.

'F**k that,' said Gamble, 'he came onto the bus last week and said he'd pay us in instalments and on time. We should hold him to that.'

Our disbelieving smiles masked a sense of fear: we all know there's no smoke without fire.

Guntars arrived out onto the pitch and was asked whether he'd been paid.

'Yes, I paid, but not cleared yet,' he said.

'How has it not cleared if you're with the same bank that the club's with?'

Guntars just shook his head.

Then the Gaffer came out and asked very sternly, 'Guntars – has it cleared yet?'

'No, not cleared Paul.'

The Gaffer walked away with his phone in his hand and came back with Coughlan on the line.

'So Tom, you're saying the money should be cleared into his account, and Guntars, you're saying it hasn't cleared?'

Guntars looked under pressure but he answered clearly, 'It has not cleared.'

'You're saying it has cleared, Tom, but he's saying it's not there...' the Gaffer stopped speaking while he listened to Coughlan, and then he turned back to Guntars: 'He's saying it could be a problem with your account. Did you have this problem before, fella?'

'No problem before,' said Guntars.

'Well he says the money's gone in, fella.' At this point the Gaffer walked away, still on the phone to Coughlan.

Stevie summarised: 'So what we're saying is it's all your fault, Guntars, for having an account with that particular bank. No problem with the other boys who have accounts at that same bank, though.'

The lads laughed despite themselves.

Afterwards, in the dressing room, the team talk commenced...

'Same team that started last week, lads,' said Doolo.

So I was definitely on the bench.

'Yous've had your difficulties lately, but youse need to start well in this tournament [which instead of being cancelled, as rumoured, is being played over two seasons] if youse want to go on and win it like youse did last year. Youse've all been paid – nearly all of youse anyway – and he's promised to pay the rest and honour the contracts, so youse need to do the business and not let yourselves down.'

He went on to talk about tactics before finishing up and we went back outside for the warm-up. When the first team went off to do more intensive work, us subs headed in the other direction to chill out and pass the ball around.

I was having a kickabout with Guntars when I heard 'Hoggie!' called out from the first team area. I looked over to see Tommy beckoning me, with young centre-back Kevin Long lying on the ground having his knee checked by Alex. I thought to myself, *Please don't be injured Longy!* As I passed them I saw Longy clutching his knee and looking particularly distressed; I felt like telling him he'd be alright, but I didn't want to pressurise him into playing injured and so I said nothing.

Tommy asked me to join in the first team warm-up game, which I did, but my head was all over the place and I wasn't at the same concentration level as the other lads.

During a break between games I went looking for Longy. Alex had him walking on haunches (i.e. putting pressure on his knee) and was asking him how it felt. Longy said it felt sore alright, at which stage I tried to do the same exercise myself, unseen by Alex, and I nearly ruptured my knee. *No way could I do that*, I thought, but it was too late to say I couldn't play. Then the Gaffer came out of the dressing room and spoke to Longy, and I saw Longy shake his head. *Oh f**k.*

He went inside with Alex to be assessed further. We were just about to move off to do fast feet work, which is short and intensive, when Alex came back out.

'How's Longy?' I asked.

'He's out: you're playing,' Alex replied.

'Now get your head on it mate,' said Muz.

Setanta Cup (group stages): Turner's Cross, Cork
Cork City 1–0 Cliftonville

Despite my concerns about my knee, the game turned out OK. In fact I enjoyed it as the surface was good and we knocked the ball around a bit. They had a good few chances in the second half but we held on for the win.

Even so, the Gaffer was unhappy afterwards. He approached Murph who was seated in the dressing room, bent low towards him and quietly gave out to him.

Murph's reaction wasn't so quiet: 'F**k that! I'm sick of it!' He took off his shirt and threw it onto the floor. 'I'm sick off yee shouting at me on the pitch every f**king minute! I can't concentrate, can't enjoy the game!'

Tommy butted in: 'Ah grow up Murph – it's a professional game.'

'Ya, course it is, but yee are f**king putting me off by shouting at me all the time.'

The Gaffer took up the battle: 'That's not the problem Murph; it's you and your new f**king boots every week. Blue one week, red the next… a new pair every bleedin' week. It's no wonder!'

Murph argued back: 'What does is matter if I like to buy new f**king boots?'

I felt like backing him up but I was happy enough with my own performance so I didn't really want to ruin the buzz by getting into a fight with the Gaffer.

Gamble changed the subject by giving out to Timmy (who came on as a sub but gave the ball away a few times when we were under pressure): 'For f**k's sake Timmy, you need to be more switched on. You can't be f**king giving the ball way like that.'

Timmy listened, to be fair to him.

'I wouldn't say it to you Timmy if you weren't a good player, but you are and you can do it. You just need to f**king switch on.'

I wish the Gaffer would take a leaf from Gamble's book with regard to getting his message across. Gamble always adds a positive along with the negatives, but that's not Doolo's style at the moment.

He was quick to jump onto Gamble's message.

'Ya, this is what you're dealing with: fellas making the same mistakes over and over again. And you've gotten away with it for years here because the managers said f**k-all about it and now this is the way we are.'

I thought about sticking up for Timmy by pointing out that he's only been around for a year or so, but then I realised Doolo was really getting at Murph – and probably me too – so I kept my head down.

The boys moved slowly away and into showers. It felt like we'd lost the game.

We had to go to the Beer Garden (a local pub) afterwards as they'd sponsored the game. When I got there the place was full of City fans, and Coughlan was at the bar.

'Well done tonight,' he said. 'Do you want a drink?'

'Thanks but I'm OK,' I replied, and wandered off to find the rest of the lads.

Monday 31st August
Operation day: St Mary's Orthopaedic Hospital, Gurranabraher. Before knocking me out to perform the surgery, the specialist said he was hoping to be able to shave off the tear but if he couldn't do that he'd just take out the bits that are causing the problems.

Chapter 10

1st to 15th September 2009

Tuesday 1st September

I got a call from Spillachi this morning on my mobile.

'Alright Hoggie?'

'Noel, how are you?'

'Good thanks. Listen,' Spillachi went on in a low voice, 'I was wondering whether you were at the meeting with Tom Coughlan yesterday?'

'No,' I said, and told him about my operation.

'Oh, I didn't know that.' He took the details of what was wrong with me, what I'd had done, the specialist's name, how long I'll be out etc, saying he might run a piece.

He then told me, 'Anyway, apparently Coughlan came up with a scheme of delaying the players' payments until January 2010. The players weren't too happy with it; McGuinness was down and they've threatened to go on all-out strike if it's not agreed to be paid by December.'

'Well that's news to me, Noel. Christ! Did anything else happen?'

'No – I was just wondering if you knew anything. I'll ring Gamble or Muzza instead,' he said.

'Ya, do that. And thanks for the update.'

Spillachi laughed: 'No bother – and good luck with the leg.'

'Thanks Noel.'

Later I went online and found that the club had published a statement on their website:

CCFC statement, 1st September 2009 (from www.corkcityfc.net, 1st September 2009)

Cork City Football Club wish to confirm that we are in negotiation with all staff with a view to paying everybody in full as per their contracts.

While a great many businesses are implementing pay-cuts at this time, CCFC wish to honour all existing obligations to the end of the season. This is only possible by phasing the payments over a slightly extended period. The club has issued a written proposal to the players and we are awaiting their response.

The club appreciates the efforts being made by all stakeholders during these difficult times and firmly believes that these difficulties can be overcome through the continued cooperation of all concerned.

At this time our primary focus is on securing European qualification, starting with Friday night's game against Galway United at Turner's Cross, kick off 7.45.

Later, another statement was released on the club's website:

Following consultation with the club's financial advisers, CCFC has set a target of achieving an attendance of 5,000 fans at each of our remaining six league games this season, as we bid to achieve European qualification.

This will allow us to meet our financial obligations, and we are calling on the people of Cork to get behind us!

I'd be surprised if Cork City, in its entire history, has ever managed to attract a crowd of over 5,000 for six games in a row – and yet the club's saying if it doesn't happen now, they won't be able to meet their financial commitments.

Coughlan Told To Pay Up or Face Cork Player Strike (*Irish Independent* – www.independent.ie – 1st September 2009)

CORK CITY'S players have given club owner Tom Coughlan an ultimatum over the wages they are owed as relations between the two parties become increasingly fractious.

Having rejected the club's offer to pay them their outstanding wages between now and the end of next January, the players are insisting that they be fully reimbursed by the start of December at the very latest.

If there is no agreement reached on the matter, the players are expected to resort to an all-out strike.

Some members of the squad considered taking industrial action before their Setanta Cup tie against Cliftonville last Saturday but were advised against such a course of action by PFAI secretary Stephen McGuinness, who met with the players yesterday.

"No footballer wants to not play, but if it comes to the stage where all avenues of negotiation have been exhausted then industrial action is the only other option," said McGuinness.

"The lads have had enough at this stage. The talking has to end now. It's time for action and, if we can come to agreement over wages, then that must be honoured."

Most of the Cork City players have received just 20pc of the wages owed to them for the month of August, having already taken a substantial pay-cut.

Meanwhile, Derry City chairman Pat McDaid has confirmed that they will be making cuts across the board in the coming weeks.

~~~~

Later, on *Newstalk* radio station, I heard a report stating that supporters' group FORAS have withdrawn their assistance from Tom Coughlan.

None of this makes for good news.

Wednesday 2nd September

This morning the orthopaedic specialist called me to update me on the op: 'We removed a lot of wear and tear alright, and also something that was flapping over the knee. However, it's important to say again that the work we've done is only a temporary measure; it won't fix the underlying problem but it'll hopefully get you to the end of the season.'

At 12.30 I drove to training and met Gamble in the dressing room while all the others were still out on the pitch.

'How are you, Hog? How did the op go?'

I gave him the lowdown on my knee.

'And how are you?' I asked.

'My knee's sore too alright, but I'm good otherwise.'

'So did you get the 20% of the wages?' I asked.

'No – what 20%?'

'They were on about us getting 20% of our August wages in the paper and I was wondering did you get it? Because I didn't.'

'No – I don't think anybody did. They must have it wrong. Coughlan was in alright and we reached an agreement: everyone's to be paid by December in six instalments, equating to roughly 60% of our wages each time, and if he doesn't pay us we're going on strike straight away.'

Young Kevin Long had come in while we were speaking and he added, 'Ya, McGuinness is gonna come in and ballot us for strike action, so if it does happen we'll be ready.'

'So if he's late with any one instalment then we strike?' I asked.

'Ya,' said Gamble, 'that's the agreement. And the first instalment day is the 10th of September... I think'.

I went down the hall to see our new physio, Patrick, who was treating Timmy – who also seems to be having knee/cartilage problems. It seems like a good number of us are having the same problems lately: myself, Gamble, Muz, Lordy, Kevin Long and now Timmy. I reckon it might be down to the training we're doing, every day. It's quite grinding on the bodies and bones; and since Mark McManus has gone we aren't doing any organised weight training to build up the muscles in order to protect our bones.

Then the Gaffer came in looking for our masseur Keith (who it appeared was back after doing an Alex – that is, quitting in order to get paid up).

'Alright Neilly,' said the Gaffer. 'How are you? What's the story?'

I explained again.

'So, stitches out in 10 days. When will you be ready to go?'

Patrick butted in: 'Roughly two weeks from the time of operation.' This matched with what the specialist had said, which was encouraging.

'OK, that's not too bad then,' said Doolo before walking off.

Lordy came in next, also looking to get treatment for his knee.

'Alright Hogs – how's the knee?'

I gave him the spiel.

'Well, you missed some meetings,' he said.

'Ya, I heard about the agreement.'

'Ya, but did you hear about Abraham Lincoln?'

'Did I hear about what?'

'So Coughlan told a story after we'd finished negotiating with him. He took out a piece of paper and said, "Lads would yee mind if I read a story to yee," and then he started reading from the page: "There once was a man from Illinois who started his own business and wanted to be successful, but it didn't work out and he had to close down and everyone laughed at him and called him a failure, so then he went into politics and went for election and failed, and everyone laughed at him again. Then he tried a business again and it didn't work and everyone said he was a failure once more. And do you know who this man was? He was Abraham Lincoln – the greatest leader of the USA."'

I couldn't quite believe what I was hearing. 'Bet that went down well with the lads,' I said.

'You've gotta laugh,' said Lordy.

Before I left, Patrick gave me exercises to build up the muscles around my knee.

'Grand job – thanks,' I said.

On the way out to my car I saw Stevie about to drive off himself. He spotted me, pulled over and rolled down the window.

'How's the knee, Hog?'

After going through the usual routine I told him I'd heard about Coughlan's story. 'That's some funny stuff,' I said.

'Ah ya, but did you hear the best bit from Doolo?'

'No?'

Stevie's face lit up as he told me: 'Well, about halfway through big Tom's story, Doolo started saying, "It's Obama! Ya, it's definitely Obama!" and ya man Tom just kinda looked at him but kept reading, and then he came to the end and said it's Abraham Lincoln, and Doolo goes, "Ah sure, ya, it could've been either one or the other – Lincoln or Obama."'

We chuckled at this for a while before heading off home.

Later I received an email from Stephen McGuinness, outlining the six instalment dates.

Friday 4ᵗʰ September

League of Ireland Premier Division
Turner's Cross, Cork
Cork City 4–2 Galway United

I hobbled down to the ground on crutches to watch the lads play particularly well – and with style. I did think Galway were poor, but maybe that was just my ego trying to find an excuse for City playing well without me.

Either way, it's a great win – particularly as Bohs lost at home to bottom club Bray tonight. There may be life left in the title race after all...

Monday 7th September

This morning we were told that renegade striker Alan O'Connor has gone back to Rockmount. We were also told that Jerry's grandson – kitman Caen – has left. According to Lordy, Caen got paid what he was owed before he left, which was good to hear.

The boys discussed all the former City players who'd scored over the weekend: Leon McSweeney, John O'Flynn and Denis all got goals, while Kearney scored for Derry on his comeback from a broken leg, and Doyler scored for Ireland in the World Cup qualifier away to Cyprus.

According to Faz, Denis's goal was a rocket. 'Honestly mate, a Ronaldo-style free kick,' he told me. 'Top class.'

Meanwhile the Gaffer was sniffing around making sure everyone had 'weighed in'. I tried to hide, but there was no escape and Tommy spotted me. Which was a shame because my weight was up about a kilo.

While my knee was sore and stiff, I was able to do some exercises and so I went home happy that I'm on the mend.

Tuesday 8th September

Some trialists and underage lads were crowding the dressing room this morning. Joey asked Tommy why so many players were there.

'It's because of tomorrow; we need to play a few of them.'

We're due to play the friendly against Glasgow Celtic in the game that was organised to save the club, but I'm not sure what kind of crowd we're likely to get – especially since Celtic's main players are away on international duty.

The boys talked about how McGuinness is apparently having problems getting through to Tom Coughlan in order to get him to sign up to what we agreed.

I told Nults that I don't think there's much chance of us getting our first instalment on Thursday, as tomorrow's money

174

will be going to pay off the bank loan that was used to pay the Revenue.

'No, I think we'll get paid all right,' answered Nults. 'He has to this time.'

'Do you wanna bet?' I said.

Nults smiled and declined.

Then the Gaffer called us (just the main squad) into the meeting room. He asked what we're planning to do, as he'd heard that Coughlan hasn't signed up to that agreement yet.

'Now's the time to do it,' he said. 'Threaten the club with the Celtic match or we'll be messed around for the rest of the season.'

Muz disagreed: 'I'm not sure us refusing to play tomorrow will affect the crowd at all. He could play the under-21s and still get a good crowd against Celtic.'

The Gaffer took this onboard but said it might still cause him trouble, as '…I might not have the time to organise a team for tomorrow, and that could jeopardise the game.'

Gamble broke in: 'The way I see it, if I don't get paid on Thursday then I'm not playing on Saturday [in the league game away to Dundalk]. F**k that.'

Tommy chipped in: 'But yees need to get this sorted soon; why not do it now?'

'I'll tell ye this,' said the Gaffer angrily, 'I got a call from the wife on Friday to say my 60% payment for July had bounced for the second time. Youse mightn't have noticed but I was going mad that day. I f**ked him out of it and told him I'm not gonna have any dealings with him until the end of the season.'

After pausing to collect himself, the Gaffer continued on a different note: 'Anyway. Friday's was a great performance by youse, so you can't use this as an excuse. Shels won the league a few years ago and hadn't been paid for four months. Youse will get yeer money, whether it's from Tom Coughlan, Quintas or Richard Bleedin' Branson. Either that or the club's f**ked.

'That's the situation, so we need to focus on the league as we still have a great chance. I don't care too much about tomorrow, but if we win on Saturday... I was saying earlier that I'd be happy if we were nine points off the leaders with nine games to go; well it could be five points off with nine games to go now – and you can't tell me the league's over if that's the case.

'So we need everyone to be fully committed to the cause for the final eight weeks, OK? Right, that's all. Outside for 10.15.'

After the lads had gone out to the pitch I headed to the gym and heard on the radio that Kevin Doyle has been made captain of Ireland for the friendly against South Africa tonight at Thomond Park. I'm delighted for him. It's just a shame they don't make a bit more of where players come from at the internationals. It wouldn't do the League of Ireland any harm...

Wednesday 9th September
This morning Muzza rang me to say that Coughlan had invited myself, Danny Murphy, Gamble and himself (Muzza) to a fundraising lunch at Rochestown Park Hotel to accompany the Celtic match.

I arrived at 1.30pm, but for some reason the lunch was delayed until 2.45. There were 20 or 30 tables, all looking fairly full, with Coughlan seated at the top table alongside the Lord Mayor and some other local dignitaries.

Muz told us that Gamble had texted him to say he wouldn't be coming – how could we expect anything else from 'No-Show Joe'? – and while the Gaffer's name was also on our table there was no sign of him either.

The event was well organised and the speakers included Coughlan himself, who, happily for me, told the Abraham Lincoln story at the end of his speech. 'There once was a lawyer from Illinois who...'

The other lads weren't so thrilled.

'That's it – I'm calling him 'Abe' from now on,' said Murph.

After the speeches there were some Irish dancers who called Coughlan to the stage. At first he refused, saying he couldn't dance, but after much persuading he got up there. Initially he danced in an awkward kind of way, but then he made a rigorous attempt at an Irish dancing style, hopping and jumping about the place like *Riverdance*.

Everybody at my table found this highly entertaining, and I managed to record a bit of it on my phone to show the rest of the lads later. As we watched him jump up and down on the stage, Muz said to me, 'You've got to hand it to him – he's got some balls.'

I agreed. In fact I thought to myself, *If he's prepared to make a fool of himself for the sake of the club, then fair play to him.* But tomorrow I might feel differently.

Friendly: Turner's Cross, Cork
Cork City 0–1 Celtic FC
Attendance: ≈ 3,700

Thursday 10th September

I checked my account at 3pm: no sign of the money.

Friday 11th September

I checked again this morning and found that the money had been paid into my account. It had cleared and was dated yesterday: great stuff.

At training it turned out most people have been paid, although young Longy hasn't and Guntars and Stevie have been paid in cheques that apparently haven't cleared yet.

'He's broken the agreement already, for f**k's sake,' someone said.

Muzza handed around copies of the agreement, signed by Muzza and a representative of CCFC (not Tom), outlining the instalment dates. Later, two guys in suits came in with our payslips and told us they'll be dealing with our wages for the rest of season, and so if we have any problems we should call them rather than Coughlan. They seem like nice guys, but the boys agreed that only time will tell.

In our usual meeting the Gaffer talked insistently about winning tomorrow. He was totally up for it, analysing Dundalk's last match as well as our own. It's easy to see how he grinds out results as a manager: he allows no let-up, no complacency whatsoever.

After the meeting we heard that Gareth Farrelly has petitioned the club with winding-up proceedings in the High Court in an effort to get the money he's owed.

Saturday 12th September

Glorious weather again today – probably the best day of the year so far. The lads didn't get to enjoy it though; they had to get on the bus first thing in the morning to travel up to Dundalk. But for once I could enjoy the sunshine and I decided to go for my first run. I did a lap and a half around the pitch in Bishopstown and felt great, but then, rather suddenly, I felt pain and had to stop. It left me frustrated and worried about my knee.

I checked Teletext later to discover that we'd lost to a late goal.

League of Ireland Premier Division
Oriel Park, Dundalk
Dundalk 1–0 Cork City

Monday 14th September

When I arrived for training this morning I was surprised to see that there were only two cars in the car park. *Maybe the club has gone under*, I thought, before working out the more likely scenario that because the match was played on Saturday, Doolo had given the boys Monday off instead of Sunday.

I texted a few of the lads but none texted back at first, and I suddenly had the fear that they were off training somewhere else and I'd get in trouble for missing it. But then: *beep, beep*... Text from Muzza: *Yeah mate back in 2moro.*

Great stuff.

I was about to leave when I saw Timmy walking in through the gates of the car park.

'Is training off, Hog?' he asked.

'Yeah, in tomorrow instead – do you want a lift back to town or somewhere?'

'No, I'll do a bit,' he said, and walked past me into the gym. Mainly out of guilt, I followed him in and did a weights circuit with him.

Masseur Keith came in and we asked him about Saturday's match.

'Poor game to be honest,' he said. 'The other team deserved it and we looked tired. But our boys nearly didn't get on the bus at all, as some of their cheques didn't clear and so they were saying Coughlan's broken the agreement already and they weren't gonna travel. Then someone said we'll have to play the game or we're only f**king ourselves up in the league, so they decided they'll do something either way this weekend coming in the Setanta Cup game against Sligo. Whether they actually will or not in the end though, I don't know.'

Timmy and I listened to this and went back to our weights without flinching. We're used to it now.

Tuesday 15th September
Everyone was back in this morning, and Tommy told us we were scheduled to do a run in the woods. The boys weren't sure what to make of this. We did this kind of run in pre-season a few times and sometimes it was hard while other times it was nice and easy, depending on what the Gaffer had planned. The injured lads (Muzza, Timmy, Longy and myself)

would be staying in Bishopstown though, with the physio and the gym.

At 10am, before they set off, the Gaffer called us all in for a meeting. He spoke about the loss last week, how maybe the Celtic match had affected a few of the lads, how they looked tired, how we have to watch the suspensions with such a small squad now.

'But eight points down with nine games to go – I would've taken that at the start of the season,' he said.

Then he changed tack: 'But tell me this, what are yee gonna do on Saturday [for the Setanta Cup against Sligo]?'

The boys were silent.

He continued, 'We need to know so as to plan training for the week. Who still hasn't been paid?'

About five or six hands were raised, all lads who were waiting on cheques to be cleared into their accounts. Greg explained that it shows up on the computer and looks like it's gone through, but he'd called the bank and was told he couldn't touch it yet as it hadn't cleared.

'That's the situation with a few of our accounts,' said Lordy, 'it shows up like it's cleared but in fact it hasn't yet.'

Doolo continued, 'So because some have been paid and some haven't, it creates problems, doesn't it? Maybe some of yee who've been paid are naturally enough not too bothered, while those who haven't been paid have a pain in their backside. Do yee want this to continue?'

'It is only gonna get worse,' said Tommy.

'Ya,' said Doolin. 'If the club can't even meet the first instalment and there's meant to be two instalments next month…'

Tommy added, 'Ya, yee have to do something this Saturday or else it's just gonna keep going on, isn't it?'

Muzza eventually answered for us: 'We know that we have to do something, and we'd *like* to do something; it's just figuring out a way to do it – something that covers us as players also. We need to take a proper ballot like McGuinness was saying.'

'But Coughlan's already broken the agreement,' someone pointed out.

'Ya, but we need a proper ballot and to give a week's notice like McGuinness is saying in order to strike,' said Murph.

We discussed a text from McGuinness that said roughly the following: *PFAI text alert: a representative from the club will attend training on Wednesday and backed by the PFAI he will set up accounts at AIB for players who need the money cleared straight away on the day due as per agreement. Stephen PFAI.*

The club are making out that the delay is down to the fact that we don't all use the same bank, and they're trying to get everyone to join AIB tomorrow (they've told us to bring in a form of ID and a utility bill). But the boys aren't having it.

'It's just another excuse – another delaying tactic,' said Stevie.

The Gaffer was of the same mind: 'Sure Guntars is with AIB, isn't he? And he's had more problems than anyone else, for f**k's sake.'

'Gaffer, do you think those cheques will clear at all?' Stevie asked.

'I don't know, Stevie. And even if they do, they can still be pulled. It happened to me last month. So what are youse gonna do?' he repeated. 'Do youse want this to continue or not?'

Gamble replied, 'Well to be honest Gaffer, I'm sick-sh*t of all this. It comes down to two options: we either force Coughlan out and get that Quintas guy in – meaning a likely 50% wage cut – or we just put up with what's going on.'

I said what was on my mind: 'The one thing I'd say though is… if we do go on strike, then we'll need you two [Doolo and Tommy] to be onboard.'

The Gaffer was quick to respond: 'I've been having fights with him since day one; I've got a pain in my bleedin' backside over it.'

'I know you have,' I said, 'but if we go on strike the media will make it look like the players are causing problems again, and you know what happened last time – the club just came out and said we had the highest wages in the league and that we wouldn't take pay cuts. We need everyone to be in on it, including you and Tommy, if we do go on strike.'

'But everyone will know yee are being messed about,' said the Gaffer.

Joey backed me up: 'No Gaffer – they'll blame the players' wages like they did last time.'

The Gaffer didn't respond to this.

Muzza mentioned the possibility of the Gaffer playing the under-21s for the Setanta Cup game on Saturday, as the league is the important thing and we don't want to f**k with that. Nothing was decided though, and the boys went off running in the woods.

Morale in the gym was low as the injured players went about their individual bits. After doing his weights with Longy, Timmy – probably out of boredom – attempted a John O'Flynn trick: jumping across three gym balls in a row, going flying over one to the next on his chest. It provided a brief moment of entertainment as I ran on the treadmill.

Our captain, Muzza, on the other side of the gym, was barely talking and we all knew to leave him alone. It's fine for me as I'm getting out soon, but I don't know what he's thinking he'll do next. He's settled in Cork at 26, with a house and girlfriend and child. Last thing he'd want to do now is leave.

He lay back on the bench and quietly did his weights.

After the treadmill I went outside and ran five laps, faster than I have so far. I can tell my leg's improving fast.

The lads eventually came back from the woods looking wrecked, and Dan Connor summed the experience up: 'That was a f**king blow'.

To cheer us up, over lunch, Greg entertained us with some brilliant Denis impressions.

Chapter 11

17th to 29th September 2009

Thursday 17th September

This morning the lads were arguing about how we should protest the non-payment of wages. Nults was particularly pissed off that, despite the agreement being broken, there's no way of forcing the club to pay us as promised.

Muzza confirmed this position: 'We'd look like complete assholes; the accounts will say that the club's paid us as per the agreement even if they supply cheques that bounce or that clear a few days later.'

Nults replied, 'There's no way this can go on – we *have* to do something.'

'Ya, but what *can* we do?' asked Gamble. 'We can't go on strike because the media and people around the city will say the players are acting the bollox again, and our only other option is Quintas who'll only pay us 50% of our wages. There's f**k-all we can do.'

Nults had no reply; he just sat there looking thoroughly pissed off.

Later, physio Patrick let me do the warm-up with the lads, and it felt great to get a touch of the ball again. The warm-up was simple enough, just everyone jogging around with a ball each doing step-overs, keepy-uppies, Cruyff turns etc… loads of touches of the ball, which was very pleasing for me.

Then the lads went off to do a shooting drill but I pulled out, with Tommy's approval: 'Well, you'll know yourself; you're the best judge of whether you can do it or not.'

Indoors I found Liam Meaney – one of the two new club officials that we'd met last week – helping people to change their bank accounts if they wanted to.

Friday 18ᵗʰ September

The boys were on about this Sunday's All-Ireland final between Cork and Kerry. Billy Dennehy was pressed for a prediction, but like a cute Kerryman he gave nothing away.

I asked Muz whether he'll watch it and he said he'll be watching the Manchester derby instead.

The lads then got to talking about how Eanna and the club marketing manager, Kev Mull, haven't been paid and are thinking of going on strike. Minutes later, Kev Mull arrived into the dressing room to say hello.

'So when are yee striking mate?' asked Muz.

Kev laughed it off before admitting, 'There's just no money there mate, is there?'

In training I did the warm-up again with the lads, and individual stuff with new physio Pa, and then more running than I've done yet. After that I watched the lads go through team shape for tomorrow's game. From this I could tell it'll be a very young and inexperienced team, with some debuts even. Doolo was being as professional as ever to be fair to him, going through things meticulously with the lads. No shortcuts are being taken, even though things are so bad.

Later on, worryingly, my knee swelled up again.

Saturday 19ᵗʰ September

Due to the swelling I took a day off from my rehab, and received the lads' result via teletext.

Setanta Cup (group stage): The Showgrounds, Sligo
Sligo Rovers 2–2 Cork City

A good result, considering the young team. I texted Lordy who told me we're off until Tuesday, which means I can travel to the All-Ireland final. Brilliant.

Sunday 20th September

I left Cork at 6.30am to beat the traffic. It was still dark as I drove over Bridge Street in the city to bring me towards the tunnel and the motorway to Dublin. I imagined what the atmosphere would be like later at Croke Park, and the excitement the All-Ireland final day brings. The city was still asleep except for a few stragglers and one or two cars full of sleeping passengers on their way to the match. I passed a few buses from West Cork and began to get really excited; I hadn't had the opportunity to travel as a supporter like this for a long time.

To think that supporters in their thousands had travelled from Cork to Dublin like this for *our* games, at least once or twice over the last few years. It was a nice thought. Perhaps during the FAI Cup finals we've reached we might have been responsible for a similar level of excitement and anticipation. I'd never really thought about it like that before, and I felt quite proud about the whole football thing – which was nice for a change.

All-Ireland Final: Croke Park, Dublin
Cork 1-9 v Kerry 0-16

After all the excitement, the result was hard to take.

Monday 21st September

I did some weight training on my own this morning, but I was worried as my knee was still swollen. Afterwards I rang Doolo to tell him I'll be starting my Blackhall course tomorrow. I'd been worrying all weekend about his reaction, but he just said, 'Fair enough, just get your timetable and ring me tomorrow, OK Neilly.'

I was surprised and delighted by his apparent understanding; it was out of keeping with his normal demanding self.

Tuesday 22nd September

Back to college and into a different world. No Doolo giving out about mistakes; none of the lads messing about. At the start I felt like the old man ('Brooks') from *Shawshank Redemption* who couldn't deal with getting out of prison and wanted to get back in. But I settled in after a while and was happy to be progressing with my legal training.

Later, I trained with the reserves and texted Doolo: *I'll be able to make it in the morning and we can chat about my timetable then. Neil Ogden!*

He didn't reply.

My timetable is looking pretty ominous though.

Wednesday 23rd September

I met Doolo and Tommy in the hallway as I arrived in, and they wasted no time in asking about my timetable. I told them it looked quite demanding and involved mostly mornings, but that my assigned mentor was going to try and help me to deal with things on a week-to-week basis.

Tommy said to Doolo, 'How many weeks left, Paul? Eight or nine? Sure we could bring Neal and Davin on their own sessions in the afternoon or evening once in a while?'

Doolo listened but didn't say anything.

I answered for him, 'Well that'd be great Tommy, and I'd be delighted with that, but I don't want to put yee under pressure.'

Doolo interrupted, 'How about tomorrow – can you train?'

'No, I can't make it tomorrow.'

'OK, let's see how it goes,' he said, and walked away.

I completed a full training session for the first time since my operation, but I played terribly. I seemed to be focusing on getting my body and knee to the ball but not on what to do with it afterwards. I made some terrible passes during our training game, and actually hit my foot off the ground a few times after misjudging the ground in relation to my foot. As training finished I walked off feeling depressed and embarrassed about how bad I was.

On the way in I met Spillachi lurking by the doorway with the cassette tape recorder from the 1980s that he always carries. I was late for college already but did a quick piece with him, talking the talk, saying all the right things – how the lads are playing well and how Pats will be well up for it on Friday after losing their manager Jeff Kenna last week; how the knee's progressing and how I was happy with my first full day training.

But privately I felt I'd never get back into the team and that I'd have to pack it in soon. I felt disillusioned, but then I thought to myself, *What do I have to lose? Give it a few more weeks at least...*

I looked at my timetable again and figured I could miss a few lectures to make training tomorrow.

Thursday 24th September
I checked my email this morning before training and saw that McGuinness had sent us a message regarding a request from the club to delay our next instalment, apparently due to the postponement of a forthcoming home game against Derry City.

I wasn't sure whether to believe this excuse or not.

While the Gaffer was surprised when he saw me arrive at training, I was positively shocked when he asked me, 'So are you available for tomorrow's game then?'

I'd thought after yesterday's performance that he'd want rid of me as soon as possible, but that's obviously not the case.

'Ya,' I said, delighted. 'I'm available to travel, Gaffer.'

I trained better, passed the ball more cleanly and felt the old touch coming back. I felt like myself again. I wasn't thinking of my knee when the ball was coming to me – just what I'd do when I got it. So I'm at least starting to get through that stage of recovery.

At the end of the session one of the younger lads, 'Mul' (Stephen Mulcahy), was played at right-back while I was put running around with some of the midfield lads in a drill designed to test the back four. The Gaffer was concentrating on testing Mul at right-back. He asked the attacking lads to give the ball to left-winger Billy Dennehy so he could take Mul on one-v-one. The first time he got the ball, Billy went past Mul easily enough, but after that Mul defended very well.

After about 10 minutes of this the Gaffer called it quits, and as we are walking off Tommy asked me would I be alright for tomorrow. 'Ya' I replied, 'but really only as cover, I'd say.'

'Right Hog, at the moment he'll probably start young Mul, but he might change his mind overnight. Could you play 90 minutes if he asked you?'

'I really don't know about playing a full game, but I'll be there tomorrow anyhow,' I said.

As I was going inside, Doolo called me into his office and asked how I was.

'I felt good Paul. I'm not thinking about the knee, which is great.'

'But how about your movement and turning?'

'It's not there yet, to be honest,' I said.

'OK, but could you give me 30 minutes if I needed you?'

'Ya, I could give you 30 minutes alright.'

'OK. See you tomorrow so Neilly.'

I drove into town to make my 12.30 lecture, delighted that I was still part of Doolo and Tommy's plans.

Friday 25th September
At 11.45am I drove up the hill to our meeting point at Silversprings Hotel and parked next to Muz.

'Alright Hogs, how are you?' he asked as I got out of my car.

I gave him the spiel about the knee getting better. 'How about yourself, Muz?'

'Mate, I'm just out for a day trip with the lads,' he said, devoid of his gearbag (as he was injured) and with a newspaper under his arm.

As I made my way to the back of the bus I spotted an unidentifiable torso lying across the back seats, taking up both mine and Greg's spots. In an effort to identify it I threw my keys (which are of a quite considerable weight) at its belly, which was the only part I could aim for as I approached. A head sprang up, shouting, 'Awww!' It was Greg.

'You're back you f**ker, for f**k's sake!' he laughed, while budging over to the right and allowing me onto my patch at the back left-hand corner of the bus.

Muzza, as usual, sat in the seat directly in front of me, with Guntars to my right in front of Greg. Then Stevie and Murph's seats were in a row with the 'card school' a little further forward. However, also as usual, Stevie wasn't in his seat but was hanging about the place, chatting and generally taking the piss. All good-humoured fun with everyone looking forward to an important game against a good side later on in Dublin.

Then, suddenly, a message carried down from the top of the bus. Someone near the card school heard it and it got relayed to us at the back: 'Christ – they're saying the bus driver won't drive up, and that we have to get off.'

'You're f**king kidding!' exclaimed Muzza.

But Murph answered, 'No Muz, it's true. Tommy's the one saying it. They haven't been paid and are refusing to move until it's resolved.'

There was a mixture of excitement and bewilderment all around.

'What the f**k are we gonna do?' asked Muzza.

As I followed the rest of the lads down towards the front, I passed Joe Gamble who remained seated and was looking up towards the driver. He looked absolutely disgusted but he wasn't moving. Everyone else was getting off the bus. Tommy had already gotten off and I could see him outside talking on his phone. I felt sorry for Tommy, having to deal with this bizarre situation – especially since the Gaffer was already up in Dublin, waiting for us.

Most of the lads exited the bus and were walking about the place, making calls and messing about. I passed the driver on my way out to join them. He didn't seem too bothered about the whole thing. We all knew he was only following instructions and so nobody bothered to ask him anything.

As I looked back, only Gamble (who was holding his head in his hands) and the driver remained on the bus.

'What are we gonna do, Tommy?' demanded young Deasy – always asking questions.

Tommy replied without flinching, 'I'll tell you what we're gonna do: get the bus driver in a headlock, drag him into the bushes, and then tie Billy Dennehy [who's a flier] to the bus so he can run us to Dublin.'

It got the boys laughing, but then Tommy went off to talk to club administrator Eanna, who was making more serious phone calls further away from us.

He came back a few minutes later and told us, 'Eanna called Tom Coughlan and the new club guy Liam…' but I barely caught what he said next due to shuffling among the lads. Apparently neither Coughlan nor Liam Meaney could talk to Eanna because of some meeting they were in, or something like that. I then properly heard Eanna say something about Coughlan being the only one with access to the money, and '…if we leave it until they come out of those meetings we'll miss our pre-match food in Dublin.'

Stevie turned to me: 'This is f**king embarrassing. We're setting a new low. I don't think I've ever heard of any Irish team not being able to travel to a match.'

Myself and Murph suggested driving up.

'OK, how many cars have we got?' asked Tommy, and then he called all the lads into a meeting in front of the bus. We duly gathered around him in a circle.

'OK lads, look,' he said. 'We'll be waiting a few hours at least for Tom or anyone from the club to get this sorted, so…'

Just then Jerry Harris burst in, which was quite uncharacteristic of him, 'Tommy, this is a downright disgrace.' Jerry was red-faced and highly agitated. 'This can't go on – he can't treat us like this.'

'Calm down, Jerry,' someone said, 'it's not Tommy's fault.'

Jerry nodded and walked away to cool off, and Tommy continued: '…so look, some of the lads are saying we might drive up. What do youse think of that?'

Muz answered first, 'No way Tommy, we shouldn't drive up. We'll be driving up every week if we do it now. It's already happening to the under-20s.'

I hadn't thought about it that way.

Just at that moment, 'No-Show' Joe stepped off the bus and, having overheard the discussion, offered his thoughts: 'No f**king way should we drive. No f**king way.'

All the boys agreed, including Murph and myself, who both now saw what a foolish idea it was. The boys walked off into different groups, discussing the possible permutations. Myself and Lordy ended up with Jerry Harris, who was still seething. 'This is the last straw now,' he said. 'There's no way I could bring up all the gear in my van either – I just couldn't do it.'

We were stood near the front of the bus and the driver was looking out at us. It looked as if we were stopping him from driving away, when – of course – the opposite was true. At this point I remembered that I had a camera in my college bag, and I went to get it from my seat at the back of the bus. *These photos could be worth taking*, I thought.

Muzza followed me onto the bus, asking, 'Do you have the number of that girl [Emer O'Hea] from 96FM? I've tried calling RedFM but couldn't get through; I'm gonna try 96 now. People need to know we're being treated like this.'

I gave him the number, and discussed with him briefly whether going on the radio was the right thing to do.

'Well we've tried calling Coughlan and the club…'

I agreed: 'I suppose it might finally show them up a little – let people know what we're dealing with rather than the spin that's usually given out to the media.'

Muz got through to 96FM and started chatting live on the radio about the situation.

I went back outside to where some of the lads were eating their own food that they'd brought with them. Then a photographer arrived and wasted no time in taking photos of us (thus rendering my own photos worthless). As usual the boys acted up for the cameras.

Photos were taken of us all standing around Dan Connor's beaten-up Fiesta, and after Dan shouted, 'How many football players can you get into a Fiesta?' more shots were taken with a few of the lads sitting in the boot of the car.

'We could've picked a nicer car, for f**k's sake,' said Murph, laughing.

Stevie warned: 'We're making fools of ourselves here.'

At this point we heard that 96FM had started an appeal to come up with the money for us to pay the bus company. They'd apparently reached €900 within a few minutes and they'd thought that was the price for the trip to Dublin, but we owed the bus company something like €2,500 so they had to raise the target.

Stevie summed it up nicely: 'We look like we're begging now.'

Then more news, this time via Muz: 'OK lads, they've got the money. It took them about 15 minutes. We're off to Dublin again – get everyone on the bus.'

As we piled back onto the bus, Gamble said to me, 'It says a lot about the people of Cork that they'd give out money for us to get to the game. Fair f**king play.'

As we took our seats and discussed events, one of the lads asked, 'Did you see ya man with the wad of cash?'

Billy Dennehy explained: 'Some random guy turned up in the car park with €900 in cash. He was gonna give it to one of the lads until he was told we didn't need it anymore.'

Later, Muzza said that Coughlan had actually come out of his meeting and paid up the money for the bus company in the end, and that the bus company were going to come onto the radio and say it was all a misunderstanding.

As we were driving towards the tunnel a minibus passed us on our left, slowed down to our speed and beeped its horn. We all turned to see the people on the bus, some waving their hands out of the windows, others with their hands against the windows, all waving what looked like leaflets. I was trying to figure out what the leaflets were, and then I saw... 'they're waving €20 and €50 notes, the b*****ds!'

All the boys enjoyed the humour.

'They must've been listening to the radio and then spotted our crest on the bus,' said Stevie.

They moved past us but then slowed down so that we had to pass them again. Again they waved money at us, and I saw a few of them were drinking bottles of beer and realised they must be Cork City fans going to the game. Just as I was about to tell Stevie, who was standing in the aisle near me, he jumped up on the seat next to the window, turned around and pulled down his pants.

This got a huge reaction from both buses, and Stevie, egged on by the reaction, turned his head, still with his pants down, and gave the other bus a two-fingered salute.

Stevie was delighted with himself until Nults told him, 'That was a f**king fans' bus, ya idiot.'

Stevie stopped grinning and said, very seriously, 'You're f**king kidding.'

He sat down and took some time to take it all in, before laughing and reflecting to the lads, 'And the worst part of it is that I turned my face and gave them holly too.'

After all the drama I went to sleep, only waking as we arrived into the Louis Fitzgerald Hotel car park in Dublin, as arranged, for our pre-match meal.

When we arrived into the lobby we met the Gaffer who, understandably, was not in great form. We ate fast and got to the ground. I was named on the bench, thank God. My knee wasn't ready for anything like 90 minutes.

The game kicked off and we played well to begin with, with Davin scoring a nice goal. Then in the second half Pats attacked and Nulty got blocked coming out for a cross, allowing one of their players to head the ball over him towards the goal. Just as the ball was about to go over the line, Greg dived back and was judged to have handled it to stop it going in.

From where I was sitting it looked like he'd headed it, but the referee saw it perfectly and sent Greg off, awarding a penalty to Pats. They scored, making it one-all and game on. The Pats crowd roared their team and the game was full of action now.

Around this point I was asked to warm up a few times, as usual.

I was warming up with Dan Connor near the corner flag when a City fan of about 17 or 18 years of age approached us and asked us over the barricades, 'Hoggie, Dan, tell us who did the mooney on the bus! Was it Gamble?'

'No,' we answered.

'Was it Stevie? Was it Greg?'

We decided to disengage at that point, running off to continue our warm-ups where he couldn't reach us. But as we ran back past him towards the dugout five minutes later, he called out, 'We know it was you Hoggie that pulled the mooney.'

This pleased Dan Connor greatly.

I thought, *I'm gonna kill Stevie later when I catch him.*

Perhaps because St Pats had a new management team in place, and they were still finding their way, they failed to kill us off. They couldn't break down our 10 men and the lads held on until the end. Of particular note was that young Mul came through the game with flying colours. To make your league debut in the heated cauldron that tonight's game turned into could make or break a guy's career. To be fair to Mul, he showed everyone that he's well able to play at this level.

League of Ireland Premier Division
Richmond Park, Dublin
St Pats 1–1 Cork City

After the match I told the Gaffer that I wouldn't be able train on Monday (we have a league game against Sligo on Tuesday) as I had a tutorial that I needed to attend.

Doolo replied, 'OK Neilly, but is there a reserve game here tomorrow? I think there might be.'

'Yes there is Paul, against Pats reserves. I could stay with my brother who lives up here if that suits?'

'That's fine so,' he said, and I went off to find Jerry Harris (as one does in such moments) to tell him my plans.

Jerry said he'd let the reserve manager Stewart Ashton know. 'Normally we'd put you up, but I know at the moment the club would have a problem with that,' he explained, apologetically.

'Don't worry Jerry,' I said, 'I'm staying with my brother.'

I rang my brother, who lives on the other side of Dublin from Richmond Park, but got no answer.

Then, luckily, I spotted Spillachi and Micky Harris getting a taxi into the city.

'Can I hop in lads?' I asked.

'Do sure,' said Spillachi.

As we travelled towards Dublin I filled them in about the bus situation, but they knew it all already. They also insisted on paying for the fare, which was kind of them.

I arrived at my brother's door and thankfully he was in.

Saturday 26ᵗʰ September
This morning I got a lift back to Richmond Park with Ian Turner – a promising young player who'd travelled up with the first team last night and stayed up with his sister to play the reserve game today.

Under 20s/Reserves league: Richmond Park, Dublin
St Pats Reserves 0–0 Cork City Reserves

I did well to get through 90 minutes. After the game I chatted with former Shelbourne player and Sligo man Alan Cawley about the league in general. We were in agreement about how bad things are.

On the bus home with the reserves it was announced on the radio that Ding Dong Denis had scored again for Hartlepool, which I was delighted to hear.

Sunday 27ᵗʰ September
Today I could barely walk.

Monday 28ᵗʰ September
Spillachi texted me first thing this morning: *How did reserve game go? Are u ok to play Tuesday?* I texted back to say the game went OK but I didn't know about Tuesday's, and he replied: *Good luck if you do play.*

I'll miss Spillachi when I retire; he's a good guy alright.

Tuesday 29ᵗʰ September

FORAS not with Coughlan as fans blame Cork City owner
(*Irish Times*, 29ᵗʰ September 2009)

The relationship between Cork City owner Tom Coughlan and the club's supporters group, Foras, is likely to deteriorate further after the latter described the events of last Friday as the most humiliating in the club's history.

"To hear the captain of Cork City FC live on local radio, essentially begging the people of Cork for the money for a bus to take them to Dublin, so they can fulfil a fixture, is surely the most humiliating episode in the entire history of Cork City FC," said the organisation's board of management in a statement yesterday.

"The blame for these problems lies squarely with Cork City Investments Ltd and its owner, Mr Tom Coughlan."

Foras have called for Coughlan to open the accounts of the club so the full extent of its problems can be assessed by potential investors.

With further legal threats to the club's continued operation looming because of the financial difficulties, Foras have reiterated their willingness to take over the running of City's underage structures. but the prospect of any sort of cooperation with Coughlan looks slim.

Through all of this, Paul Doolin and his players continue to soldier on defiantly, and, after Friday's draw in Inchicore, the City boss is hoping a win over Sligo Rovers this evening might keep his side in the hunt for a place in Europe next season.

Greg O'Halloran is suspended for tonight's game after being sent off at the weekend, but Neal Horgan should be fit to start, while Dan Murray and Stephen O'Donnell both face late tests prior to kick-off. [...]

It was only by chance that I didn't arrive an hour late for the match tonight. I happened to meet a former schoolteacher of mine, Declan Davis, in the city, and he informed me of the early start – which was just as well.

As the players huddled together, chatting before the match, Danny Murphy whispered to me, 'Do you know you're playing tonight?'

'What? My knee's still stiff from the reserve game!'

'Ya well, you'd wanna get loose; the Gaffer told me. Honestly mate.'

The Gaffer confirmed it later.

Happily, my leg felt better after the warm-up.

In his pre-match speech the Gaffer explained, 'There's another bleedin' thing going on tonight that's not helping: the fans are demonstrating. They're not coming into the ground until 10 minutes after the kick-off, which won't help us really. But youse need to keep your bleedin' heads on it.'

League of Ireland Premier Division
Turner's Cross, Cork
Cork City 0–0 Sligo Rovers

While I wasn't great I was very happy to get through the game with a clean sheet.

Chapter 12

30th September to 30th October 2009

Wednesday 30th September and Thursday 1st October

As expected, following my first senior game in a month I've felt very sore all over the last couple of days.

Friday 2nd October

Today before training the lads were discussing a reporter from a local paper who's been writing things we're not happy about. From what he's been saying we're guessing he must be close to Coughlan. He's been comparing us unfavourably with GAA players, just like Coughlan has in the past.

'I bet that reporter will mention Portsmouth not getting paid either soon,' said Murph. 'It'll give Coughlan more stuff to say to us.'

Later, out on the pitch, the Gaffer told us he'd spoken to Liam (Meaney), who'd said we'll definitely be paid next Wednesday.

'How about the following week?' someone asked.

'He didn't say anything about that,' said Doolo, and then he added, 'I don't know what youse think about changing bank accounts?'

'I'm not doing it anyway,' answered Murph.

'Well that's fine Danny, and anyway I've asked for youse to be given bank drafts, which are the next best thing to cash if they can't deal with youse through your own banks.'

The boys were happy enough with this.

'Anyway, let's go on now and finish strongly,' said Doolo before leading us into a run around the pitch.

Towards the end of training, during a shooting drill, I chipped Nults beautifully in goal – but the Gaffer wasn't impressed and he shouted at me, 'Oggie, what did I tell ya! Youse are meant to be *testing* the keepers!'

Despite this, training was very good. The lads were aware that there were some Preston scouts at the ground, and this excited some of them.

Tuesday 6th October

I didn't expect to start the game tonight as a few of the lads are back. I also couldn't make training yesterday as I had a tutorial in college, so I figured it was probable that Doolo would pick the other lads in front of me. But when the Gaffer called out the team and subs in the dressing room, I wasn't in the squad at all, which, I admit, came as a bit of a shock.

As the lads got ready I left the dressing room off and walked towards the main stand. There were supporters piling into the ground now; I could sense they were looking at me but I kept my head down. I made it to the stand and was relieved to find one of the younger lads, Ian Turner, to sit next to. Turner's trying hard to pin down a contract at the moment and so he was bubbling with enthusiasm for everything Cork City FC tonight. He jumped up whenever we came close to scoring and kept talking about how we could do with the win. When we were awarded a soft penalty in the first half he said, 'That's the bit of luck we were due, isn't it Hog?'

I granted him a single nod.

He's right about all that of course, and I commend him for his enthusiasm, but I didn't have any tonight. At times I was nearly cheering on Derry, but in truth I didn't really care either way. However, I kept my negativity hidden in order to avoid contaminating the young lad with it.

In fact he reminded me of myself some 10 years ago – eager and excited to get near the first team. Clearly, 10 or so seasons in the League of Ireland can make a person cynical. Having said that, if I'd been picked to play tonight and we'd won, then I'd be buzzing with adrenalin afterwards. I was aware that much of my negativity was tied in with not being picked.

I watched Liam Kearney's performance in the game. He played well enough for Derry and I was glad for him, that he'd settled well with them after breaking his leg a few months ago. I gave him a brief salute after the game while he was doing an interview but we didn't chat.

League of Ireland Premier Division
Turner's Cross, Cork
Cork City 2–0 Derry City

In order to appease my growing guilt about my negativity, I decided to do a few box-to-box runs after the pitch had cleared of the players. Jerry provided me with some gear in the training room and I headed out into the dying floodlights. There were a few kids having a kickabout on the pitch; some elderly Munster FA officials tried to clear them off but the youngsters proved too quick for the old men, who gave up after a few minutes and left the kids to play on.

I ran past at high speed in the increasing darkness.

The crowd wasn't huge tonight – only 1,700 or so for quite a big match. People are staying away.

Wednesday 7th October

I rang Lordy this morning from college. We were supposed to be paid today but there's no sign of my wages in my account. He answered in a hushed voice, telling me he was in a meeting at Rochestown Park Hotel and that the boys were deciding what to do.

'Nobody's been paid,' he said.

I felt relieved to be somewhat removed from affairs; I knew all too well that the meeting would end up frustrating and depressing all the lads.

Lordy also told me that McGuinness is coming into training tomorrow and that they're trying to get Coughlan to come in too.

I found out later that I have a mandatory tutorial tomorrow morning. Our college lecturers keep telling us that if anyone misses this tutorial they'll fail the course. So I texted Doolo to tell him I can't train but that I'll ring him tomorrow evening to see if he wants me to travel on Friday.

Thursday 8th October

I rang Lordy again today for an update. I was aware that I was semi-pestering him, but he remained helpful.

'Only Murph's been paid,' he said, 'nobody else. Liam [Meaney] was there instead of Coughlan with McGuinness so the boys gave Liam abuse about the wages. Liam said he didn't have them, but that Coughlan had secured money from somewhere for them. The boys weren't satisfied with this. Then Doolo and McGuinness went out of the room to discuss possible strike action. At that point Liam received a text to say everyone would be paid by 4pm today.'

I checked my internet banking (it was now 4.30pm) while talking to Lordy and I hadn't been paid. Lordy said he'd been paid but it was €700 short. He had experienced a tax issue in the past that had caused this kind of reduction, but he thought it had been sorted.

'The Gaffer's asked even the injured players to travel to the Bray game tomorrow as we might be balloting for strike action after the game.'

'OK, I'll ring the Gaffer,' I said. 'Good luck if I don't see you tomorrow.'

'Thanks Hog.'

I tried to call the Gaffer. *He'll be in bloody great form now*, I thought as it rang, but to my surprise he wasn't in such bad form after all. He sounded like he was on the way to Dublin already. He told me that I'd be in the squad tomorrow night as Stevie's out and he asked whether I'd been paid. I told him I hadn't.

'All the lads were meant to be paid by 4pm today,' he said. 'Ring Liam or one of the lads and try to get it sorted.'

'OK,' I said, 'no bother.'

'…and by the way,' he said, 'the reason I left you out the other night was because I wanted someone on the bench who could cover both the centre-half and right-back positions.'

'Ya, OK Paul, that's no bother,' I said. 'See you tomorrow then.'

I then rang Liam, but it sounded like his phone was off.

Friday 9th October

After our pre-match meal in Bray a strike ballot was held. Stephen McGuinness attended and counted the votes. He announced the results afterwards; they supported a strike action.

League of Ireland Premier Division
The Carlisle Ground, Bray, Co. Wicklow
Bray Wanderers 3–2 Cork City

A bad result. I came on towards the end.

Wednesday 14th October

I missed two lectures to get into training this morning. On the way in I met Jerry, who was walking down the corridor bringing out two big bags of balls. He asked me whether I'd been paid.

'No, not yet Jerry.'

'Ok, but did you get the text from Liam? He said he'll be in tomorrow to answer any questions.'

'There's some chance of him answering all our questions,' I said.

'He'll be here all day,' said Jerry, laughing as he wandered off.

In the dressing room the boys were asking each other about pay. Greg and Stevie's wages still hadn't cleared.

'I can't believe they paid you with a cheque again Stevie,' I jibed.

'I know, the f**kers,' he answered wearily.

The boys asked about my lectures at college. Nults declared, 'I couldn't sit down all day and read a book, no way.'

Faz chipped in, 'Well I'd rather be listening to a lecture than sitting here shivering.'

It was a nice morning though, and we walked out together at 10.25. We spotted Doolo and Tommy over the other side of pitch; we feared the worst as there were no cones set out.

'F**king no cones out boys – we're going running,' somebody complained.

But we didn't go running. In fact all we did was a warm-up and some team shape.

Young Kevin Long, who was called up for the Irish under-21s last night, was running late, so we had just four defenders for team shape. The Gaffer put me in as full-back with Mul as centre-half. He then set up the attackers to come at us, and when we won the ball we'd knock it back to midfield and then run out the pitch following the ball. He was trying to get us to move out quicker as a back four; he thinks the goals conceded against Bray last Friday were a result of the back four being too deep, too slow to get out.

When Longy arrived the Gaffer told Mul to step out behind goal for a while. He added more attackers and they came at us, having been instructed to whip the ball into the box as much as possible in order to replicate what we expect from Bohs. The Gaffer explained that Bohs will be very direct with very little build-up from the back. They'll be physically strong up front and in midfield to match that style of play.

This simple style is part of the reason for their recent success, but it also goes some way towards explaining why Irish football isn't progressing as well as it should be.

It's a 'launch it' type of game. Bohs have very good players, no doubt, and they can play some very good football at times, but their main mode is to launch the ball high up the pitch and win the resulting headers. If they don't win the headers, they win the knockdowns. Then they give it wide, cross it into box, attempt to out-muscle defenders and score. A game based as much on physicality as skill.

The football on display for the fans suffers as a result; nobody's expecting anything but a dogged affair on Friday. Winning headers, getting up and out, turning their back four... these are all parts of the game that need to be addressed. But I feel we need to play to our strengths, which over the last few years have been to pass the ball and to keep it. To pass and move, and move again, to keep the ball cleverly and patiently, before striking at the other side. I feel we've grown fairly accomplished at this type of game (at least within our league) and it's what I prefer.

But I don't think Doolin considers us capable of winning with this style. He wants us to replicate what Bohs are doing; to be physical, not to bother too much with passing the ball around.

So standing behind the goal, waiting as the rest of the lads played a restricted type of team shape, I thought: *Just get on with it, there's only a few weeks left.*

Afterwards, still on the pitch, Doolo gave a speech about not letting ourselves down and how coming third would be a great achievement considering everything that's gone on around us.

I have to admit I admire his drive.

In the dressing room after training, young Kevin Long told us Coughlan had called him the day before and left a message on his phone, congratulating him for getting onto the Irish under-21 team. '...and then he called up to my gaff with a bottle of champagne, but I was out so he sat in with my dad for half an hour.'

'All this and he still hasn't paid ya,' said Stevie in disbelief.

After lunch I told the Gaffer I can't make training tomorrow.

He said, 'OK, see you at the usual time Friday.'
I made it back to college for 1.15pm.

Friday 16ᵗʰ October

League of Ireland Premier Division
Turner's Cross, Cork
Cork City FC 0–2 Bohemians FC

To my surprise, Doolo played me after all and I did quite well, but even so we lost 2–0. Maybe he's been right about us recently. Maybe in this league a team needs to be very good before it can hope to win a league playing attractive football. We're not at that level at the moment.

Monday 19ᵗʰ October
Before training this morning the Gaffer said, 'Sorry about the grass being long fellas, but the guy who owns the lawnmower hasn't been paid for it and he's taken it back – so we have no lawnmower now.'

The Gaffer then reverted to his new favourite topic: how we're still wanting to play too much football. 'Some of those Bohs players have seven league titles in their bag, but some of youse are happy to just play football and nothing else. I'm telling youse now, that's not what I'm looking for. Do yee want to finish third or what? Youse have a great chance of rectifying things tomorrow against Rovers, but they'll be up for it as they think they might catch Bohs, so youse'll need to be right.'

I told Doolo afterwards that I'd make my own way to Dublin as I was struggling with college. 'OK Neilly fella,' he said and wandered off.

Later I got a text from McGuinness asking about money, but there was no sign of it in my account. I checked with Lordy and he hadn't received his either.

Then I got a text from Liam, who said the money would be in our accounts by 5pm.

I checked later and there was still no sign of it.

My flatmate has just come in and told me he'd heard on *Newstalk* that we're going on strike.

Tuesday 20th October

On my way to college, at about 9am, I heard Tom Dunne on *Newstalk* saying that 'Cork City players are likely to strike today over pay; they've said they won't get on the bus until they're paid.'

I had a moot court case in college but they allowed me finish early in order to travel to the match. I'd booked a flight to Dublin and an airbike taxi from Dublin airport to Tallaght to make the match on time.

On my way to Cork Airport I rang Lordy, who told me, 'Ya man Liam arrived to the bus at Silversprings with bank drafts for all of us. Jerry must have your one Hog.'

After arriving in from Dublin Airport I asked the guy to leave me off around the corner from the Rovers ground, as the Gaffer wouldn't be too happy to see me on the bike. The bus arrived shortly afterwards and the Gaffer asked, 'Did ya parachute in Hog, did ya?'

'I did, ya.'

On the pitch I asked the lads whether they'd been paid. Most of them had. Jerry had my bank draft too. While young Longy hadn't been paid he was happy enough to play anyway.

In the dressing room before the match, Murph said, 'Someone was on the radio saying that I'd refused get on the bus until we got paid, that I'd dragged the club to the bank or something.'

The boys laughed at this, but poor Murph was annoyed at being singled out unfairly.

The Gaffer named the team and I was on the bench. I was happy enough with this; I was tired and my hamstring's still sore from the Bohs match. But then, during the warm-up, Davin got injured.

I stayed out with the other subs as the players went in, but five minutes later I got a shout from the tunnel – it was Pa, the physio, pointing at me and beckoning me to come in.

'Davin's f**ked,' he said.

Nults gave me a nod, 'All the best, Hog.'

The Gaffer said, 'Right Hoggie – you're marking Dessie Baker or the English guy for corners, alright?'

I needed to get myself right. Needed to bring confidence and good feeling onto the pitch.

Later, when we walked out, the atmosphere was electric.

We conceded early, with Sully scoring against us. Despite this I was enjoying the game. Funnily enough, Doolo and Tommy gave out to me halfway through for not getting the ball from the keeper. I thought, *This is new!* I'd be happy to drop and get the ball from Nults all day long!

We dominated for rest of the half but didn't look like scoring. We were playing good football for a change, though, which suited us. Then we continued this on into the second half and scored two good goals. I made a few boo-boos but did some good things too.

League of Ireland Premier Division
Tallaght Stadium, Dublin
Shamrock Rovers 1–2 Cork City

As I went into the dressing room afterwards the Gaffer said something about me trying to turn them, and Tommy was laughing.

'I was sick of shouting at you, Hog!'

Joining in with the laughter, I agreed with him. 'I crossed the ball in for *them* at one stage, Tom!'

The atmosphere was good and even the Gaffer said, 'Youse were great tonight.'

On the bus home, Muz reminded me that this was my last trip back from Dublin. 'Not a bad one to go out on, son.'

'You're not wrong there, Muz,' I said.

The Gaffer and Tommy stayed up in Dublin, so the atmosphere on the bus was magic and we arrived home at 1.30am. As we were getting off, Jerry Harris half-seriously said to Muzza, 'Muz, will you tell us all to bring miners' torches for training on Thursday?'

'Why?' I asked.

'Oh ya Neal – you weren't there during the week, were you? They've cut off the electricity in Bishopstown so it's very dark around the place.'

Club statement, 20th October 2009

Cork City Football Club wish to confirm that all players have been paid up to date, as of today, October 20th. While there was a brief delay in the payment of wages due to some players, the club has remained in constant contact with the relevant bodies, along with players and management.

[...]

Like a number of other clubs in the League of Ireland, Cork City Football Club is not sustaining itself financially and has required the investment of significant private funds. The current economic climate has led to a significant drop in advertising and ancillary revenues, while credit has not been as readily available from the business or financial communities as would be hoped.

[...]

Despite the difficulties we have encountered, Cork City FC has honoured all players' contracts and has paid all backpay to all of our players resulting from the club entering Examinership under its previous owners.

The club has not, at any point, requested that players take pay-cuts.

While it is regrettable that there have been occasions where players have not been paid on time, paying the players the terms agreed in their contracts remains the priority of Cork City Football Club, and all players are now paid up to date.

We acknowledge the continued support of our sponsors and supporters through these difficult times and this is greatly appreciated by all at the club. With only a matter of weeks to go in the season, Cork City have an excellent chance of qualifying for Europe and we are confident of achieving this and of a successful future for the football club.

Friday 23rd October

It rained all day today, so I knew the pitch would be very heavy against Drogheda later.

In the dressing room at Turner's Cross the boys were on about Bishopstown the day before, where '…there's still no lights, and no showers now, as well as a horrible smell of rat piss,' according to Murph.

They discussed the excuse given by the club for the electricity failure – something to do with maintenance – but Jerry Harris knew better: 'Maintenance my ass; they haven't paid the bill, that's the problem.'

We went outside in our tracksuits and it was still raining as we chatted in the middle of the pitch. The lads were wondering whether Doolo will leave at the end of season; the opinion seems to be mixed.

'His head must be wrecked from the whole thing,' said Nults.

Later, the Gaffer asked me privately how I felt.

'A little sore from the Rovers game,' I said, 'but I'll be fine after the warm-up.'

'OK Neilly,' he said. Then he named the team and I was in the starting line-up.

He gave a speech about how he's been finding the whole experience stressful.

'It's not easy being down here without my family and with all this going on at the club, but finishing third would be fantastic...'

We played poorly in the first half and came in with our heads down. The boys all seemed fairly low. Muzza was trying to get people up, but the Gaffer was being negative.

We were better in the second half. I was better too, but the game trickled out – not before Muz got sent off for the first time in his life for two yellow cards, which brought five minutes of panic at the end.

After the final whistle the crowd sang a song about me that they sometimes do (singing my name over and over – *Neal Horgan, Horgan, Neal Horgan!* – to some biblical tune or other), acknowledging that it was one of my last games – which was a nice touch.

League of Ireland Premier Division
Turner's Cross, Cork
Cork City 0–0 Drogheda United

The Gaffer, predictably, was unhappy afterwards. He accused some people of pulling out of challenges as they're looking after themselves for another club next year.

Faz reacted to this, giving out to Tommy: 'He can't be saying that. He means me – I know he does.'

Tommy replied, 'Tell him yourself, Faz,' but Doolo had moved off by then.

Then the Gaffer came back and spoke about focusing on qualifying for Europe.

Saturday 24th October

This morning we all headed to the local pool for our recovery session. While we gathered at the entrance, Greg and Lordy heard someone ask over a walkie-talkie, 'Have they paid?'

It was embarrassing.

Dan Connor told us about his meeting with Liam Meaney yesterday (Dan hadn't been paid his full instalment last week either): 'I rang Liam the day before and he said the money would be in, then at the match yesterday he said the same to me but it's still not come in.'

Dan was majorly pissed off with this and continued, '…it'd be different if he said, "Look, it's not there," or whatever.'

Soon after this we were brought into a room where we had a meeting about the match last night which turned into World War Three.

Faz and Doolo had it out one-to-one in front of everyone, with Faz responding to Doolo's comment yesterday about tackling.

'That was aimed at me, wasn't it Gaffer?'

The Gaffer confirmed that he thinks Faz doesn't tackle enough.

'I don't know what it is with you, Faz,' said Doolo. 'Last Tuesday in the second half you got into it; maybe sometimes you need someone to get onto you before you start playing.'

Faz wasn't happy with that and was in the middle of responding when winger Davin O'Neill, in a misguided effort to quell the dispute, interjected: 'I don't know Gaffer – some players are good at tackling. That's their game. Maybe Faz is more of a creative type player and that's where his strengths lay. Look at me: I'm similar, I can't tackle.'

'Wha?' Doolo turned to face Davin with an expression of pure disgust.

Davin tried to dig himself out: 'I'm just saying that I'm the type of player where tackling isn't my strong point, whereas going past a player or…'

The Gaffer, interrupting, turned to Tommy in disbelief and said, 'Tommy, did you hear what Davin just said?'

'Ah, I'm just saying!' Davin protested.

'No, hold on a bleedin' second here. Did you just say that *you can't tackle*? Am I hearing you right?'

The Gaffer then launched into a tirade about a manager only being able to do so much.

The meeting petered out shortly afterwards and we headed to the pool, where Muz thanked Davin for taking the spotlight. 'He didn't even mention my sending off! Thanks Dav!'

'No problem Muz', said Davin, laughing.

For the rest of the pool session the discussion revolved around the possibility of some of the lads moving clubs after the season ends.

Apparently, later in the evening, the Gaffer rang Muzza to ask, 'Did Davin really say he can't tackle?'

Tuesday 27th October

I was able to make it into training this morning in-between lectures. As I walked in the door I noticed that the place was very dark. *I forgot: no electricity.*

It was total darkness in the corridor except for a distant light moving towards me. I couldn't tell who it was until it came closer, then a familiar head showed itself. It was Jerry Harris.

'I brought a torch,' he said, laughing. 'It's very handy.'

The dressing rooms were only a little brighter.

The boys were chatting about Davin killing himself in the meeting with the Gaffer.

'Ah he was f**ked – there was no way out for him after that,' said Muz, who was the only person clearly recognizable to me as he sat near the caged-up window.

Minutes later Davin walked in and announced, 'Well, I'm gonna two-foot everyone in training today!'

We all cheered.

Then No-Show Joe walked in.

'Wa-hey! Haven't seen you in a while,' I said. 'How did the [knee] operation go?'

'Ya, it went well,' answered Joe. 'There was a bone the size of my fist wedged to my knee; they took it out though.'

Minutes later Joey was fuming as he learned that our new physio, Patrick, wasn't in. 'What happens if someone gets injured?' he asked disdainfully.

Then Tommy came in to take numbers for training and spotted me behind the door.

'Ah Hog, you're joining us today. Fair play to ya.'

'Ya Tom,' I said. 'I'm making a guest appearance but I have to leave at 11.25am.'

When we came out into the light of day to train, the Gaffer was out on the pitch with Tommy and there were loads of cones set out around them. The Gaffer called us in.

'Just so yee know, there's obviously no electricity but apparently youse can use Leisureworld for showers or yee can go home for a shower, I don't mind. But I'll say this… I don't expect it to come back on before the end of the season. OK, let's get warmed up.'

The grass was being cut as he spoke, which was at least something. We did a warm-up, passing drills, then crossing and shooting.

At 11.25 Tommy let me know that I needed to go, so I ran off, and on my way in I told the Gaffer that I can't go in tomorrow but I'll be there Thursday.

'See ya Thursday so,' said Doolo without really looking at me.

Thursday 29ᵗʰ October

When I passed the open door of the meeting/lunch room this morning I spotted the Gaffer and Jerry going through our playing kit for tomorrow. Jerry was holding a jersey up to the light of his torch to see what number it was.

I walked into the dressing room, where Muz was still the only one I could really make out. It turned out Stevie was lying on the bench in the middle of the room; I couldn't see him but the lads were giving him abuse for not washing his kit.

We discovered that since the electricity has stopped, the laundry of our training kit has stopped also.

'F**k that,' said Stevie with contempt, 'no point washing it now, there's only two games left anyway.'

Then, out of the blue, Faz turned to me and asked, 'Are you writing a book, Hogs?'

'What?' I answered, taken aback.

'Are you writing a book?'

'No, but I maybe *should* write one with all the stuff that's been going on here recently.'

No-Show agreed: 'It would be some book, Hog.'

Muz added, 'Hogs, if Donal Óg can write one so can you.'

The conversation moved on but I was unnerved. *How the hell did Faz find out? It doesn't matter. There's only one week left anyway.*

I decided to head for the gym but found it locked with a chain. Jerry arrived with his torch shortly afterwards to open it for me. As we walked into the gym he said, 'It's bad, isn't it?' He was kind of laughing as he said it.

'It's bad alright,' I said.

'And I don't think they're gonna bother getting the electricity back for the rest of the season,' he added.

'Why do you say that, Jer?'

'Well, they're saying that they've found that someone's cutting in on the electricity current and they want to find out who it is before they put it back on.'

'You have to hand it to them Jerry – they're world class at making up excuses.'

'Anyway, there's only one week left, thank God for that,' he said before wandering down the corridor with his torch lighting the way.

Thankfully the gym was half-lit as there are a number of windows facing in on it so I was able to do some strength work before returning to the dressing room.

'How long until we're out?' asked Stevie.

Faz answered, 'It's 10.19.' (We had to go out at 10.25.)

'Thank f**k – another five minutes,' said Nults.

The boys started doing impressions of the Gaffer. They've figured out that when he doesn't want to talk to a player (when passing him in the corridor, or in a meeting room, or anywhere really) he'll start singing 'Scooby Scooby Doo' and will pretend he's kinda humming the song as he walks by.

'He's been Scooby-Dooing me a lot lately,' said Stevie.

All too soon, 10.25 arrived and we headed out wearily. We warmed up, did some sharp feet work, passing across the pitch, crossing and finishing without running for crossers, team shape, then set pieces and in.

The Gaffer talked, again, about how this whole season has been mentally draining but third place would be great.

Friday 30th October

In the dressing room at Turner's Cross before the Dundalk match, the boys were saying a good few of the payment cheques to the staff – including Jerry Harris – have bounced.

Jerry confirmed this.

It had been raining heavily all day and the Gaffer told us the pitch was particularly bad up in the corner. We went out to see and it was like a marsh in the corner where I would be playing.

'Best of luck with that, Hogs,' jibed Nults.

We wondered whether the ref would call it off.

Stevie wanted it off as usual: 'It has to be off – look at that!' he said as he took big clumps of soil up with his foot quite easily.

Myself and Nults didn't want it off though. We were happy for the match to go ahead, to have recovery tomorrow and then Sunday off. If the game was off, we knew it would be rescheduled for Monday, meaning we'd have training Saturday and Sunday. On top of that it was my last league game at the Cross and I was excited. I really wanted to put in a good performance to end things – especially at home.

'F**k off Stevie, stop doing that,' we told him. 'It'll go ahead.'

Back in the dressing room the Gaffer checked everyone was in and said, 'OK, so let's not throw away all our good work. Myself and Tommy were just talking and we agreed how youse have been really great to keep getting the results with everything that's been going on. Really great, fellas. But we need everyone tonight.'

He finished by naming the team – I was in at right-back – and then he left us to get changed.

We began the game well, but then they scored an outrageous goal against the run of play. After that, Danny Murphy and one of their players got into argument and the ref harshly sent the two of them off.

So we went in one down at half-time, but fair play to the Gaffer: he was really positive.

'Youse are actually playing great; keep it up and yee'll get yeer rewards.'

He was even soft on Murph: 'It wasn't a sending off fella, to be fair.'

There was no Dan Murray as he was suspended, and things were quieter without him, but the lads were still up for it.

In the second half we dominated and scored two: one a great header from Longy (who, we found out later, was being watched by a Burnley scout), and Faz converted a penalty to take the lead.

Near the end I had a shouting match with the Gaffer near the sideline in regard to my positioning, but I backed down and apologised to him before getting on with the game.

They got another man sent off and we hung on for what was an important win.

League of Ireland Premier Division
Turner's Cross, Cork
Cork City 2–1 Dundalk

On the way into the dressing room I did a few interviews with reporters who asked me whether my last league game at the Cross had been emotional. I answered that there were two games left – our final league game in Galway and a Setanta Cup fixture against Sligo, '…so not really.'

I'm not sure how the final game will feel.

It was great to win tonight – especially as Derry also won to keep up the pressure. We just need a win next Friday against Galway and we're in Europe.

Muzza came into the dressing room afterwards, delighted. 'Well done lads!' he shouted, 'Great f**king result!'

A few minutes later the Gaffer called me over to explain his reasoning in regard to our disagreement. I appreciated the chat, fair play to him.

In the showers the boys discussed how Coughlan had been seen jumping up and down and encouraging us, and singing with the crowd. This despite the fact that the crowd have been singing that they want him out.

'He's some character,' I said, 'I'll give him that.'

'Ya, but did ya see what he wrote in the programme?' asked Stevie, sounding slightly bewildered. 'He said we've got the best training ground in the country!'

Chapter 13

1st to 10th November 2009

Wednesday 4th November

It was very cold this morning, but at least it was bright so we could see our way around the dressing room a little better.

Tommy came in trying to count numbers. 'Joe here yet?' he asked.

But there was no sign of No-Show.

'He comes in when he likes these days,' said Muz.

Timmy was in though, after a few days' absence.

'So you've gotten over the swine flu, Tim. Fair play,' said Tommy, laughing. And then he spotted me: 'And another guest appearance from Hog!'

'Yeah Tom,' I answered, 'but I have to leave at around 11.50 to make a lecture.'

'OK Hog, no bother.'

Bosnian Faz seemed to have taken me up wrong: 'Do you have to give a lecture?'

'No, I just need to *get to* a lecture Faz, but funnily enough I do have to give a speech tomorrow. Everyone does.'

'I wouldn't fancy that,' said Nults. 'What's your speech on?'

'Well we were allowed to choose any topic so mine's on "Whether a professional football league is desirable in Ireland today".'

'Well, is it? Which angle will you take?' asked Nults, shivering in the dark.

'Ya, I'm saying it is.'

'Fair play to ya Hogs,' Nults gave a big smile.

Tommy came back in and told us we had to go out earlier than usual. 'Youse have to get out now, as Hogs has to go early.'

Nults was disgusted: 'For f**k's sake Hogs,' he said, the smile wiped from his face.

As we were tying up our boots someone asked Dan Connor whether he'd been paid.

'Ya, it finally went into my account alright, thank f**k.'

Then the Gaffer came in, walked over to Kevin Long and shook his hand. 'Fair play to ya Longy son,' he said, and turning to the lads he announced, 'Longy's been called into the full Irish under-21 side now.'

We all clapped and Doolo explained that Longy had been selected for the games against Armenia and another team. 'Tom Coughlan will probably be around with a couple of bottles of champagne today,' he said.

'Better tell your old fella to lock up,' said Tommy.

We were all laughing at this as we made our way onto the pitch.

I noticed that my knee was still bloated even though I haven't run on it since the game last Friday. It's a relief to know there's not much left in the season; I really don't think the knee can put up with too much more at this stage.

During training the boys all took good touches and the Gaffer and Tommy were very pleased with us. During our crossing and finishing drill, which was particularly good today, Greg scored an absolute rocket. From the edge of the penalty box he caught a ball from a cross and hit a volley across the goal, the ball powering against the post and stanchion and then back across the goal to the other post before ending in the net. The boys all roared. Nice feeling, that.

Not long afterwards, Dan Connor got injured and had to be carried in, having hurt his knee making a save.

The Gaffer called us for a meeting at the end of training.

'I'm not gonna do too much as the pitch is getting heavy,' he said.

He talked about how Galway have had a good season with mostly young players and how they'll come at us on Friday. 'So youse'll need to be at it, but once youse do your own jobs we'll be fine.'

As we walked into the dressing room I could hear groaning. Dan Connor was lying up on the masseur bench and our physio Pa was treating him. He looked in serious pain.

Thursday 5th November

It was a very cold and windy morning as usual, but I didn't mind. This was my last training session out in Bishopstown... ever. Maybe in other circumstances I would've been sad, but after the way this year had gone I just can't wait for things to end.

Jerry came into the dressing room with a printed page for Danny Murphy – a fax about his suspension for getting sent off against Dundalk last week.

'Do you want to represent him?' Jerry asked me, half-laughing, on which Stevie shouted, 'It must be the first time a mascot has got suspended!' which started all the lads giggling.

Then Stevie, more serious now, said, 'Did you hear about Derry's trouble with the contracts? That might mean we have Europe no matter what...'

'That'd be brilliant,' said Murph, who then turned to young Longy and said, 'Longy son, will you just sign for Burnley on Monday and we'll all get paid? €150,000, they're saying, if you sign before your contract's up. That'll sort the rest of us out and we'll be happy days and playing in Europe next season! F**k's sake son, get it sorted!'

Longy smiled but said nothing.

'What time is it now?' asked Nults, shivering again.

'21 minutes past,' I told him.

The boys were getting ready around us, putting their boots on.

'For f**k's sake, lads!' Nults pleaded, 'We have another five minutes!'

At this point No-Show Joe (who was in fact present) noticed that Nults was wearing his (Joe's) training rain-jacket.

'Nults – that's my f**king rain-top!' he said.

'Ah Joey, I took it home, washed it and dried it and everything,' pleaded Nults.

Gamble, immediately and without sympathy, plucked the top from Nults, who ran off down the darkened hall to search for a replacement in the kit room. But young Craig Duggan, who'd just arrived back from the kit room, told us he'd taken the last one.

Seconds later Nults arrived back empty-handed and all the boys cheered.

'And we're going out now too, for f**k's sake,' he said.

As we emerged onto the pitch it definitely felt like the coldest day of the year so far, and Nults was really shivering as he ran around to warm up. Gamble came out a few minutes later minus the rain-jacket, just to annoy Nults, who ran at him.

Gamble shouted, 'OK, OK – I'm only messing, Nults! I'm using it alright,' and ran back in to put it on.

Then the Gaffer held a meeting.

'Well I've said enough over last few days, so not much to say to youse today,' he said… and proceeded to talk for another 10 minutes in the freezing cold as it began to rain. Needless to say, Nults was not impressed.

At one point the Gaffer started talking about how we should keep ourselves right in the future and not come back the way we did this year. 'I know youse had no manager and all, and youse probably didn't know which way the club was going, but still – youse need to keep yourselves right during the off-season.'

Someone on my right – possibly Nults – whispered, 'That means he's gone.'

Doolo continued, '…youse've all improved and got better and fitter as the year's gone on. We've become a better team too; not so individually oriented I feel. Let's just make sure it wasn't all for nothing and get a result up there tomorrow.'

My knee didn't feel great as we started into the warm-up.

'Last training session Hogs – any tears, mate?' asked Muzza.

'No Muz,' I answered squarely as I limped about, trying to get the juices flowing.

Inside, after training, I wandered down the dark hallway to see our masseur, Keith, and along the way spotted some of the boys in the kit room checking if there was any spare kit they could siphon. Every year's the same.

I came across Dan Connor standing in the dark on his crutches talking to Nults. He was saying his cheque had bounced, and that he'd already spent the money on overdue bills. He'd received a phone call from his bank informing him that his account was overdrawn by a couple of grand, '...and I've rang Liam and left a message on his phone but had no response yet.'

I wandered past and got a rub from Keith. Lordy appeared after a while.

'Did you hear about Dan Connor's cheque?' I asked him.

'Yeah,' answered Lordy, 'I heard. They're after f**king about with my money too. On my payslip it says I've been paid back tax when I haven't been paid it at all. You'd want to get your payslip too, Hog.'

'It's a shambles,' said Keith as he rubbed my legs.

Friday 6th November

I had lectures most of this morning and was supposed to have some this afternoon too, but I was allowed to leave early in order to get the bus at 12.15. As I was getting my stuff ready the guys in my class whispered, 'Best of luck tonight Neal,' which was nice of them.

A result tonight and we'd finish third and be in Europe next year. It had been on my mind all week; I knew it wasn't going to be easy. We were playing away against Galway, and while they had nothing to play for, equally they had nothing to lose by coming out and trying to win the game – whereas we had everything to lose.

A draw would see us stay a point ahead of Derry, who we all expected to win tonight against Dundalk (who hadn't seemed too bothered when they'd played us, sitting comfortably in mid-table). But if we lost and Derry won, we'd finish fourth and wouldn't qualify for Europe.

I was nearly late for the bus. When I arrived, the lads ripped into my college clothes. 'Were you out in that clobber? Thursday night student night, was it Neilly?' joked Doolo.

I made my way down to my seat at the back of the bus, where I found Davin sitting between mine and Greg's places, as he'd started doing lately.

'Last trip, Hogs,' said Muz as I passed him.

'Thank f**k,' I replied.

As the bus pulled off, the boys were reading the stories about Derry in the tabloids. The papers are saying they're at risk of getting demoted for having double player contracts – apparently each player received a copy of what they thought was their contract from the club but then a different contract, with different terms, was given to the FAI. The Derry players didn't seem to know about the double contracts though. In any event, some of our lads have heard that their whole club is f**ked.

'Poor Kearns,' Muz and myself concurred.

There was also an article about how Cork City apparently spent €2.3 million last season. It said Drogheda spent just €100,000 less at €2.2 million, which might shut Doolo up about our money thing for a while. Still seems like a lot, though.

Since then, of course, Arkaga pulled out, leaving the club with the debt.

Muzza muttered, to nobody in particular, 'Just get a result tonight boys, for f**k's sake.'

We arrived at Galway and had our pre-match food. While we were sitting around, Greg told some Denis-themed stories and we talked about past times at the club. New boys like Stevie wanted to know about previous players such as John Caulfield, Pat Morley and – somewhat surprisingly – Lawrie Dudfield.

Then we were called to a meeting.

The Gaffer was sitting at a table at the top of the meeting room and we sat in two rows, all looking up at him. It was an unusual set-up for one of his meetings; he normally chooses to stand. Maybe it was just me, but today I thought he looked like a judge presiding over us all.

He talked about some of the 'absolutely horrendous things that have occurred off the pitch,' and about how we deserve to finish in third for all the playing staff, 'and every one of you.' Then he said, 'I know you must have heard rumours…'

I thought at this point he was referring to his own position, but he continued, '…however, it may not be true, and Derry could be OK after all. Wouldn't it be terrible if they won – which they will do – and all this was cleared up and we lost out on Europe because we didn't get a result tonight?'

Then he named our team: 'Nults, Hoggie [he's been calling me Hoggie rather than Oggie lately, after all this time], Longy, Dan, Mul…'

We got back on the bus and arrived at the ground good and early – around 6.20pm, with kick-off at 7.45pm. In the dressing room, Greg was singing 'Scooby-doo, oh oh,' just out of Doolo's range, which entertained myself and Guntars for a while. Then Faz put on his customised CD and introduced each new track to the lads. The boys enjoyed it and must've been laughing a bit too much: I could tell the Gaffer was getting agitated but he was trying not to show it.

Eventually the Gaffer walked to the stereo, turned it down and said, 'I don't mind yee having a laugh and a joke, but youse need to concentrate now.'

We all know that he *does* mind us having laugh and a joke – at least before a match. He prefers cold, concentrated preparation. I can see where he's coming from, but I like a lighter mood at this stage of the day and a more intense build-up closer to kick-off. However, he's the boss.

I've been impressed with the Gaffer lately. He's bonded with the players to a certain degree, which has helped. We all know it's his drive (as well as Tommy's) that's put us in the position we're in. I still don't like it when he gives out to us about previous years, but I have to admit he's remained very professional. He's probably the one person we needed this year to keep the players disciplined. Alan Mathews did a great job during examinership, but this year has been different again. Any normal person would've thrown the towel in by now, but Doolo's a very determined individual. We all think he'll do well in the future – just maybe not in Cork.

During the warm-up Tommy said some nice things about us: 'Youse have been marvellous professionals, the way you've carried yourselves.'

Tommy's normally good cop, but never to this extent. Perhaps as a result, we had one of our better possession games during the warm-up; the ball was whizzing about with real quality and I felt we'd be OK in the match.

Back in the dressing room, the Gaffer had a board up to show who everyone was marking. He also set out our routines and set plays, which he proceeded to call out. I was on the back post for defensive corners while staying back for attacking corners.

Staying back for attacking corners brings responsibility. I tend to play as the last man back except for the goalkeeper; this means I need to organise our defensive players before the corner's taken, in order to prevent a counter-attack. If the ball ends up in our net from a counter-attack, I'll be held primarily responsible. Thankfully this hasn't happened in a while.

Staying back for corners obviously also limits your chances of scoring goals in your career – just one of many repressive sides of a full-back's playing life. Who really wants to stay back for corners? Nobody. Unfortunately, much of a full-back's role is made up of such tedious responsibilities. In fact, during a game, a full-back's job is often 75% patient reading of the play and 25% actual involvement. The key to dealing with this – from a psychological point of view – is to appreciate the beauty in reading and anticipating the other team, or your direct opponent. A really good full-back will anticipate the game better than anyone else on the pitch and not expect the plaudits for doing so.

Attacking players are often lauded for being able to predict a phase of play four or five passes in advance. However, any top defender will also need to read the game five, or even six passes ahead. In addition, a good full-back – even more so than a central defender – will need to predict turnovers of possession before they happen, as a full-back is more likely to be caught in an advanced position on such a turnover. So it can become a mental game of 'cat and mouse', and as every defender knows, the attacker only needs to get it right once – whereas the defender needs to be correct on every occasion.

That's the dice every defender is thrown, but it's how you deal with such a weighted dice that counts. If you think about it too much, like I would have done on many occasions in my early years, you can be become overly conservative and stifled – afraid to act – and you almost learn to hate the game. Over the last few decades the removal of the tackle from behind and the arrival of the back-pass rule, together with changes to the offside rule, have weighted the dice all the more in a forward's favour.

But the experienced or top defender accepts the weighted dice, sees it as the huge challenge that it often is, and yet cherishes the game even more as a result. He loves the slanted odds. In response, he (or she) realises that he must act proactively, both defensively and offensively. He must not merely stop the danger; he must prevent it from arising in the first place.

Thus the ability to anticipate – to predict a player's bad touch or risky pass, to know in a millisecond what your opponent wants to do once he gets the ball – is the most prized skill for a full-back to attain. This skill comes from instinct or experience, and sometimes, in the modern game, from the lessons learned through video analysis of the other team or your direct opponent.

In any event, once a full-back anticipates the danger, if he can, he should inform the players around him, so as to prevent the opportunity before it arises. If, despite these preventive actions, the threat becomes more serious, then it may be time to raise the alarm to get your players around you into shape – to grab a hold of your opposing player, to sneakily take them out if necessary, using your body in whatever way you can to stop the opponent.

At this stage, whether you're attempting to defend a cross that's created a goal-scoring chance in the box, or you're in a one-on-one and you're the last man, or you're performing a last-second tackle on a player about to shoot, the instinctive and physical attributes come to the fore. However, the top full-back will always attempt to win the mind game first, a few steps before any of these situations arise.

On the other hand a full-back also needs to be on his toes again should his own team win possession, to gather pace and move up the pitch without flinching, to receive the ball, retain it and allow your team to amass forward. And on top of all this, the very best full-backs have the finishing touches: a great cross or an ability to run past the other full-back, to shoot or score. I would not easily fall into the category of a finishing full-back; my game (particularly in the last few years) has been more limited to defending, supporting my winger and providing good, weighted passes for those around me, including my winger, my striker and my central midfielders – and trusting them to produce the finishing touches. That delegation of task would then allow me to re-focus on getting back into position and defending, which I would see as my primary role, before we've even finished attacking.

The modern full-back, free to roam forward on wild runs, is a different creature. Which is more effective – the old-school/conservative style that I probably represent, or the modern type? Who knows. Sometimes a modern full-back suits a team, while a conservative full-back will be more effective for another team. Nevertheless, the one distinguishing feature of any real full-back is that he must prize a clean sheet over and above his attacking attributes. If a player loses sight of this and starts to see himself primarily as an attacker, in my mind, he is no longer a full-back.

The attacking runs, the dangerous crosses, the dead-ball skills: these are all additional attributes. Without the defensive preventive mind, the full-back – no matter how good he or she is at breaking forward with the ball – is not a proper full-back.

So quite often the full-back position isn't total football. It doesn't involve a huge amount of Cruyff turns, double stepovers or over-head kicks. It can be a very limited form of existence on many teams – and particularly in the League of Ireland. But on a ball-playing side, like ours when we're good, it can be truly rewarding.

In the first half tonight that was exactly what we were: a ball-playing side knocking it about, spreading it to our full-backs. So I got a lot of ball to my feet. Tonight I'd say that 80–90% of my passes in the first half were good ones, though I gave two balls away – one of them just before half-time in a dangerous position.

We were 2–1 up going in at half-time, and the Gaffer warned me about that dangerous pass as I went in.

'Neilly, there's nothing wrong with putting the ball in the corner; if someone tells you otherwise, tell them to talk to me.'

I told him I'd just put every ball in the corner in the second half if I was in any doubt. He seemed happy with that.

At the start of the second half I totally scuffed the first ball I got, trying to play it first time and long. Ten minutes later I gave away a silly free kick near our end line, which almost resulted in a penalty. Doolo went mad, shouting at me from a hundred yards away. I put my hand up: 'Alright, alright!'

Muz shouted, 'Come on Hogs!' and circled his right arm in a gesture encouraging me to raise my game. Following this, myself and Stevie (who was in particularly cranky form) had a few arguments with each other. Stevie was in the mood to get on the ball tonight and play from the back; he thought we were sh*tting ourselves in the second half as we weren't playing much ball, and that as a full-back I wasn't showing for possession like I had in the first half. He had a point, but I knew what Doolo wanted of me, and with Europe on the table tonight I thought to myself, *Stevie can go to hell*.

Galway scored to make it 2–2. We were under pressure.

A few minutes later Stevie dropped deep to get the ball from Nults, still trying to play from the back. I showed for him initially but Galway's winger Derek O'Brien was running at me already, having anticipated the pass from Stevie. He was approaching too quickly for comfortable possession, so I moved again to show Stevie that I wasn't available for the pass.

Stevie hesitated but decided to play the ball anyway, and it ended up behind me and out for a throw to Galway deep in our half. Stevie and I had a brief heated argument as to who was to blame. But then we moved on, as the Galway crowd around us were sniffing blood and roaring them on.

They had absolutely no formation; they were just throwing players forward recklessly for the final 20 minutes. Meanwhile we stuck doggedly with a 4-4-2 and I didn't move from my position. Lordy was doing spades of work on my side as usual, but I couldn't help him much – I needed to stay back. They could send balls in behind us and into my space if I moved forward, as they had most of the possession. We just needed to see it out.

Nults made a good save near the end, then there were two minutes of added time. But we hung on.

Relief. Nothing else.

Derry, it turned out, won 2–1, so we finished third by a point.

We're in Europe.

League of Ireland Premier Division
Terryland Park, Galway
Galway United 2–2 Cork City FC

Afterwards I was one of the first on the bus. The Gaffer was sitting at the front on his own; I took the opportunity to thank him for a great season, all things considered. 'I think yourself and Tommy deserve great credit for holding out like yee did,' I told him.

He said, 'Well I tell ya Neilly, it's been very hard from start to finish, and I don't know how it's gonna go after Monday.'

As I sat down at the back of the bus I realised how glad I am to be getting out of this crazy show. I feel sorry for the others though – including Doolo.

The overall feeling on the bus, however, was one of joy, mixed with a sense of pride that was most tangible among those of us that've been with the club during its successful times over the last few years – the likes of Muz, Murph, myself, Greg, Lordy, Nults (No-Show wasn't there) and Jerry Harris. We're proud that we haven't let the club down in its hour of need.

League of Ireland Premier Division – final standings
(November 2009)

Pos	Team	Pl	W	D	L	GF	GA	GD	Pts	Qual or releg
1	Bohs (C)	36	24	5	7	62	21	+41	77	Champ. League
2	Sham. Rovers	36	21	10	5	51	27	+24	73	Europa League
3	**Cork City**	**36**	**17**	**9**	**10**	**42**	**28**	**+14**	**60**	**Europa League***
4	Derry City	36	18	5	13	49	31	+18	59	**
5	Dundalk	36	12	8	16	46	51	-5	44	
6	Sligo Rovers	36	11	10	15	41	51	-10	43	
7	St Pat's	36	13	4	19	29	46	-17	43	
8	Galway Utd	36	12	6	18	36	57	-21	42	
9	Drog. Utd	36	7	11	18	32	50	-18	32	Releg play-off
10	Bray Wand.	36	6	10	20	30	56	-26	28	Releg ***

*	Cork City subsequently demoted and dissolved
**	Derry City subsequently demoted and dissolved
***	Due to the absence of Cork City and Derry City for the 2010 season, Bray Wanderers were not relegated.

Monday 9th November

Tonight's game was called off very late in the day due to a waterlogged pitch. Stevie was delighted.

After it was called off Liam came in. He thanked us for our efforts over the year and said the club would be in touch with everyone in the next few days. We asked him whether the club was going back part-time and he said no, it's staying full-time.

Tuesday 10th November

We had a few drinks tonight to mark the end of the season, which was great crack. Tommy and Doolo came too. Greg sang a few songs and we had a bit of fun with Guntars about his AIB account, and Stevie apologised to everyone for being so cranky on Friday.

Muz announced that I'd be missed, and the boys (at Stevie's behest) very generously sang '*One more year, one more year…*' while pointing in my direction.

'No f**king chance,' I told them. The time's right for me to get out.

Then the boys gave out about the no-show by – guess who – No-Show Joe.

Chapter 14

10th November 2009 to 22nd February 2010

Not long after Liam told us we'd be continuing as a full-time club, Tom Coughlan was quoted in the *Evening Echo* as saying the following:

'We are looking at all aspects of how we run the club. Wages is a big part of this and they need to be brought in line with what we can afford. That may mean part-time football for some, it may mean new contracts for others and some players may just leave as a result...

Paul will be made aware of our plans. There will be changes to the way we operate.

We cannot afford another season like this one. I have a few months now to get this right and I plan to start by sitting down with the manager and informing him of our plans, that will ensure we have a sustainable and viable club going forward.'

(Evening Echo, 10th November 2009)

Reading this, I suspect Doolo will be relieved of his duties as manager of Cork City FC. The way he's being treated has reminded some of the lads of the way Alan Mathews was treated at the meeting in Kenmare last year. For example, Liam had said that 'the club', rather than Doolo, would be in contact with players who are out of contract. Doolo was sitting just to his right as he'd said this, yet there hadn't been so much as a glance in his direction.

Now this article today says that 'Paul will be made aware of our plans', rather than saying they'll sit down with him and work things out together. The article also confirms that some players, at least, will be put on part-time training contracts, which doesn't bode well for full-time footballers.

Liam texted me to say that my P45 is available to collect and I should ring him to find out where. I've called him three times and left a message, without reply.

I just want to leave now.

Wednesday 11ᵗʰ November
Today Liam texted me to say he was in Rushbrook and that I could come and collect my P45 there. When I arrived I discovered that lads had been calling in throughout the day to collect their bank drafts/wages – those who don't have AIB accounts at least.

Liam, who was talking to No-Show, went to get my P45 and I chatted to Joey. He's started a college course on physical development; it's a good thing for No-Show.

As he was leaving he asked me, 'So are you definitely finished?'

'Yeah,' I answered, 'definitely.'

Liam returned with my P45 and a letter about retirement tax also, and said he'd be in contact about the final payslip with the late payment soon. I thanked him and wished No-Show good luck.

Driving home, I felt a weight had been lifted.

Later I spoke with Darragh Ryan, who was relieved that Pats had stayed up. He told me Kearney was down in the dumps up in Derry. Apparently there was a risk at one stage that the Derry players would be liable for having two contracts at the one time, but today it looks like the FAI have accepted that the players didn't know about the second contracts. While the Derry board have resigned, Darragh and I agreed that it'd be great if they stayed in the league, as they're one of the better teams. We also agreed that Alan Mathews has done a great job keeping Drogheda up after winning out in the relegation/promotion play-off.

Monday 30ᵗʰ November

I tuned into TV3 tonight as Trevor Welch announced that Paul Doolin had resigned as manager of Cork City after a meeting with Tom Coughlan. However, RTÉ.ie had a slightly different angle:

Cork City confirm Doolin's exit (www.rte.ie, 30ᵗʰ November 2009)

Cork City have confirmed that they are on the lookout for a new manager after revealing that Paul Doolin will be leaving his position as manager of the club.

Doolin dismissed reports that he was leaving the club when contacted by RTÉ Sport earlier today, but the club released a statement at 8.34pm to confirm the Dubliner's tenure at the club had come to a premature end.

The statement read: 'Following discussions between Paul Doolin and club management, it has been agreed that Mr Doolin will be leaving his position as manager of the first team.'

[...]

The statement concluded: 'The club has begun the search for a new manager and an announcement will follow in due course.'

City finished third in this year's League of Ireland Premier Division despite having to sell a number of their best players because of the club's on-going financial problems.

Under the chairmanship of Tom Coughlan, the club has been beset by a series of financial setbacks since emerging from examinership last year.

Tuesday 1ˢᵗ December

My phone rang while I was in the computer lab at college this morning. It was a private number. I answered and was greeted by a familiar low voice: 'Ah, Hoggie – Noel here.'

It was my old buddy Spillachi.

'How are you, Noel?' I asked.

'Good,' he said, 'but have you heard what's been happening?'

He told me that Doolin hadn't been able to take it anymore and had apparently walked away from his contract.

'Well if that's true, then I can totally understand it Noel, and I'm not really surprised to be honest.'

We agreed that Doolin had done a great job getting us to Europe despite everything.

'Anyway,' Noel said, 'I need you to clear up a few things that I'm hearing.'

'I'm sort of away from it now Noel, so I really don't know what's going on.'

'No, but it's you I want to talk about. I spoke to Tom Coughlan and he said that yourself and Gareth Farrelly are good buddies and are contenders for the job.'

'What?' I couldn't believe what I was hearing. 'Jesus!'

I took the phone out of the computer lab to get some privacy.

'That's the first I've heard of it, Noel,' I said.

'But yee are buddies, are yee?'

'I'm friends with Gareth, but if you're asking about the job I'm saying not in a million years.'

Spillachi laughed at that, and then concluded: 'So you're dismissing that you're in line for it, yeah?'

'Yes Noel, and you can quote me on this: it's the first I've heard of it and there's no way I'm interested as I'm too busy with college.'

I could hear him typing away.

'OK Hog, thanks for that.'

'No – thank you for the update Noel.'

'No problem. It'll be interesting to see who gets it.'

~~~~

Over the next couple of months I focused on my law course whilst watching, from a safe distance, various dramas unfolding at the club. Every other week in the news there seemed to be a new twist to the story.

Roddy in the frame at City (www.breakingnews.ie, 11th December 2009)

Former Bohemians double-winning boss Roddy Collins has entered the race to be next Cork City manager.

The current team manager of Maltese side Floriana was spotted in Cork yesterday and is due to meet club chairman Tom Coughlan on Monday. Collins' family did not settle in the Maltese capital Valletta and moved back to Dublin.

The 48-year-old outspoken Dubliner has a mixed recent track record. Since winning the league and Cup double with the Bohs in 2001 he struggled with Carlisle, Dublin City and Shamrock Rovers.

Stephen Henderson remains the front runner for the City job...

(Article courtesy of The Evening Echo newspaper.)

Cork chairman Coughlan banned by FAI (*Irish Times*, 17th December 2009)

Cork City chairman Tom Coughlan was asked to consider his position today after the FAI issued a €5,000 fine and a ban from "football-related activity for bringing the game into disrepute".

Coughlan was due before the FAI disciplinary committee in Abbotstown today but according to his solicitors the three-man committee failed to turn up in time and later held the meeting in Coughlan's absence. Aside from the €5,000 fine, Coughlan has also been excluded from FAI Council membership, banned from representing the League of Ireland club and excluded from nomination to any FAI committee.

The FAI ban takes "immediate effect and is for a period of 12 months".

Coughlan, who is still free to run the Turner's Cross outfit as it's an independent company, said he will appeal the decision.

"Mr Coughlan is now questioning this decision and has serious reservations about the FAI's attitude to him, based not alone on today's events, but also recent comments made in the national media by Fran Gavin FAI league director and FAI chief executive John Delaney," read Coughlan's statement, issued through his solicitors.

"Mr Coughlan is extremely disappointed that he did not get his personal hearing, despite the fact that he was present at the correct time for the hearing."

Fran Gavin, the FAI's League of Ireland director responded to today's decision by saying: "The majority of League of Ireland clubs operate as independent companies and their directors are responsible for ensuring that they are run in accordance with Irish company law.

[...]

"The FAI cannot dictate who owns clubs as this would conflict with company law and is purely a matter for the club or limited company. When Mr Coughlan was selected last year by the examiner to bring Cork City FC out of examinership, the move was welcomed.

"While we acknowledge that Mr Coughlan invested money in Cork City FC at that difficult time, his subsequent actions have damaged the credibility of both the club and the League.

"Although Mr Coughlan is presently owner and Director of Cork City FC, we now call on him to consider his position in the interests of the fans and the players, as well as the long term future of the club."

The FAI's decision comes in the wake of Cork City's link with Roddy Collins to become their new manager. Collins is currently manager of Maltese side Floriana, who issued a statement saying they had not given Cork permission to speak with their manager.

It is understood Coughlan is prepared to walk away from Cork City if the right price is met by new investors.

Floriana threaten Collins with court (by Daniel McDonnell, *Irish Independent*, 8th January 2010)

MALTESE club Floriana have given Roddy Collins and Cork City a deadline of tonight to apologise and offer compensation with respect to events surrounding the Dubliner's controversial move to Leeside – or else they will pursue legal action for defamation and bring the case to FIFA.

[...]

Cork City said that Collins was a 'free agent' when they appointed him manager on December 23, but Floriana say that is not the case. After trying to secure a release over the phone, the former Bohs, Carlisle, Dublin City and Shamrock Rovers boss officially emailed the Maltese club citing personal reasons for his departure; they rejected that on the basis of his ongoing dalliance with Cork.

[...]

Floriana want Cork City or Collins to buy out the remainder of his contract – a sum valued at €28,000 – or else they will pursue further avenues of compensation and will bring FIFA into the process. Acting Floriana President, Joe Cauchi, will attempt to speak with Cork owner, Tom Coughlan today to see if there is any kind of offer forthcoming from the League of Ireland club.

Collins argues that the terms of his initial deal changed when he held discussions with officials at Floriana in late October/early November about his working arrangements. His family struggled to settle in Malta, which then led to a revision of his circumstances.

The Irish Independent contacted Collins last night, but he said that he didn't want to comment on the argument being pursued by Floriana, stating that the affair is in the hands of his legal people. However, he said that he was unaware of any deadline set for today.

[...]

Another dispute is the last thing Cork City need as they seek to cope with a variety of outstanding problems in the month where their Premier Division fate will be decided upon by the FAI's Licensing Committee.

Earlier this week, Alan Mathews withdrew his legal proceedings against the club, a development which means that his case comes back under the remit of licensing. Mathews is listed as an employment creditor dating back to 2008, thus adding to the bill that the Leesiders need to settle if they are to have any chance of remaining in the top flight.

Worst case I've ever seen, insists players' solicitor (by John Riordan, *Irish Examiner*, 30th January 2010)

The solicitor acting on behalf of Cork City players and staff yesterday described the standoff which has enveloped the League of Ireland club as the worst he has seen during his career in employment law.

Having endured 10 weeks without pay (money received on Christmas Eve had been due since October), the club's employees contacted John Boylan for advice.

And yesterday, at a specially [convened] press conference, Boylan outlined the grievances of staff and players in a carefully constructed two-page statement.

"It's the worst I've ever seen," said Boylan. "If it was an ordinary work job – if it was my office and my secretaries weren't paid for two and a half months and they went through Christmas without being paid I just actually can't imagine that they would keep coming in.

"The idea of people loving football so much that they would take their eye off the ball and put up with not being paid – I just find it extraordinary. I've never actually come across it previously in any walk of life and I'm an employment lawyer for more than 20 years.

"I've actually never come across that. They love football so much and they are all decent, down-to-earth guys, they don't make trouble and yet they manage to put up with two and a half months of not being paid. I find that extraordinary."

Boylan did however rule out any court action.

"I told them that it was a waste of time going into the legal arena because I have acted for previous employees of Cork City Football Club and we have got judgements from the same consortium and they still haven't been paid.

"There was a very long-standing employee Noelle Feeney, who is one of the heartbeats of the club. She was an employee – a registered employee – and she was fired on the spot. We went to the labour court and we won completely. And they have never paid her a penny.

"I will be keeping a close eye on things but having looked at the finances there is absolutely, in my opinion, no chance.

"Alan Mathews has got a judgement, Gareth Farrelly has got a judgement and neither of them have been paid. Noelle Feeney got a judgement nearly nine months ago. To be frank about it I haven't seen any judgement paid except for the Revenue – and the Revenue are the only people who have a real hold over him."

Murray: this is the lowest I've ever felt (by John Riordan, Irish Examiner, 30th January 2010)

DAN MURRAY yesterday claimed he is going through the lowest period of his life as wages owed to him, his fellow players and staff remain unpaid.

The Cork City captain doesn't hold out any hope of ever being paid what he was owed – but claims he would rather be paid nothing under different ownership.

Murray was speaking after yesterday's show of force by employees of the League of Ireland club at a specially convened press conference in the Maryborough House Hotel.

Telling reporters that he had just endured a very harsh Christmas, Murray reiterated calls for Tom Coughlan to strike a deal with a local consortium involving Jim McCarthy of the Quintas Group and Michael O'Connell.

He also admitted that it was hard to predict his future under Coughlan's recent managerial appointment Roddy Collins – a notable absentee yesterday.

"Something is going to happen, I'd say," responded Murray when asked whether or not a backlash was in the offing.

"I'm probably the first to get it anyway. He's not paying me anyway so he can't stop paying me! He can stop me playing but I've still got a contract. There's nothing to gain from them doing anything to me. They are better off trying to work with me. I'm happy to work with Roddy for as long as he wants me.

"The way we see it, we're not going to get paid at the minute. We're probably not going to get paid even with new owners, we may have to come to an arrangement. But as players we would be happier to come to an arrangement with different people and not Tom Coughlan. Every time we've had an agreement with him, he's not done what he said he would do.

"We've heard so many [lies] and I've had it to my face. I just can't handle that. That has probably ****ed me off more than anything else.

"The options for myself to leave are probably running out as you've kept people hanging on for so long. They've gone for other options. It's more important to make sure the club is there – and at the moment I can't see that with Tom in charge.

I can't see us getting a second chance with the Revenue on Monday, for example."

Murray also outlined what had been a less than festive period.

"You can't buy presents or travel home to England to see the family because you haven't any money," he said. "You can't put petrol in the car, can't buy your family presents, borrowing money off people just to pay the bills and put food on the table. I wouldn't wish it upon your worst enemy. It was the worst Christmas I've ever experienced. It's hard to accept what was going on.

"We just want to look after ourselves. We're not on massive money like English Premier League players, where you can afford not to be paid for a few weeks and it won't affect you. We get enough money to pay the mortgage and the bills and if you're lucky, there is a bit more to pay for a few luxuries like dinner out or a night out. Over the last two months we haven't been able to do any of that. I've probably turned into a bit of a hermit sitting at home watching Celebrity Big Brother."

Murray agreed that it was probably the lowest period of his life.

"Yeah, I think it is. I have been lucky enough that I've had a good life and enjoyed most of it. I have good family support and friends but this is totally different. You go to bed every single night wondering what bill is going to come through the door the next morning, wondering where can I get the money. It puts stress on you, and it's the most stressful I've ever been in football.

"Hopefully he [Coughlan] can see sense and get out while he still has something. I don't know what he can gain by doing what he is doing now. If someone can just have a good talk to him and say – right Tom, this is a good time to go, for the good of yourself and Cork City Football Club just leave and give someone else a go.

"At the start I think he had the best interests in trying to do it properly but then as it went on he just dug a bigger and bigger hole and he just wants to fight to get out of it instead of just putting his hands up. I don't know what he's trying to get out of doing what he's doing. Surely he knows now that he is not the best man to run the football club."

Cork City takeover almost complete (by Alan Smith, www.extratime.ie, 12th February 2010)

Cork City's current owner Tom Coughlan is willing to 'step aside from all club affairs with immediate effect' according to General Manager Liam Meaney after a consortium headed up by Jim McCarthy lodged an official bid to take over the club.

It appears that it is now just a case of dotting the i's and crossing the t's as both parties appear to be working rapidly so the club can secure its place in the Premier Division, which kicks-off in the first week of March. The takeover is not likely to see Coughlan walk away with any money, but it will clear all of the club's outstanding debts, which is estimated to be in the region of 500,000 euro.

At a fiery press conference on Friday [February 12], in which Roddy Collins also blasted former players Dan Murray and Dan Connor, Meaney said: "I'd like to announce that Tom Coughlan has received a bid for the entire shareholding of the club from the Quintas group led by Jim McCarthy.

"This offer is being assessed by Tom Coughlan and his advisors. Having regards to the importance and immediacy to this matter, Tom Coughlan has offered to step aside from all club affairs with immediate effect.

"He has offered the interim Chairmanship of the club to Jim McCarthy, and a place on the board to Peter Gray. Jim McCarthy is currently consulting with the FAI in an attempt to allow him accept the Chairmanship so matters can move forward."

If the club are to survive in its current guise, a deal will need to be completed before the end of the weekend, with both the Licensing Committee's decision and the Revenue's winding-up order to be heard on Monday.

""With the licensing deadline looming large on Monday next, I would certainly hope matters will be resolved in the next 24 to 48 hours," Meaney added.

"We've had to fulfil the outstanding criteria that is in place for the Licensing Committee, however, with the new bid in place, they're [Quintas & Peter Gray] undertaking that. I would be quite confident of this bid succeeding."

The FAI could look favourably upon the club's future if the takeover is completed in enough time before Monday's announcement, and it would see them take their place in the Premier Division as well as the UEFA Europa League.

Collins slams players' lack of loyalty (by Alan Smith, www.extratime.ie, 13th February 2010)

Roddy Collins launched a stinging attack at former players, particularly ex-captain Dan Murray, by questioning his loyalty after the defender walked away from the club with three months' wages still owed.

Murray left for Tallaght earlier this month, citing his need for some sort of income as his girlfriend is due to give birth in April. However, Collins couldn't justify his departure and had some harsh words to say about the defender.

"Nobody is irreplaceable. The only disappointment was Danny Murphy leaving the club. In my opinion he's the best left back in the country. The other players can be replaced. Whoever wants to leave can leave if that's their prerogative.

"I knew from day one that Dan Murray was going to leave. Dan Connor? He showed no interest," said a furious Collins after being asked if he will miss 'the 3 Dans'. "You have to show loyalty and respect to the people involved with Cork City Football Club. If you're half a man you accept that there is a

financial disaster going on all over the world and it's not just in your little house in Cork."

Collins also criticised the "abuse that has been going on at this club." He continued: "I can't believe the players ripping the club off and managers ripping the club off. You can quote me on that because it's the truth.

"You don't take blood out of a stone. To hand out the salaries that were handed out at this club was an absolute disgrace. It was a massive abuse of finances and the players are laughing their way to the bank. Loyalty is paramount to any success, whether it's a marriage, a family or a football club."

On his future, Collins remains positive that there is a place for him at the club when the takeover is completed. Also insisting he is not at the club just for a short-term.

"There's no doubt where I want to be. Hopefully whoever takes over the club will know that I'm still available and that they will consider me because it's a great setup. I was away for seven months and didn't know too much but I'm just concentrating on the playing side of things."

If given the chance, Collins believes he can build a young and competitive team for the future. It'll prove difficult for the Leesiders to make any big signings though, with the club putting a €750 wage cap in place.

"I will deliver a competitive team," he added. "Results I can't legislate for but we will have competitive players. We'll see the young players being developed and players who have an ambition to come in and play for the club."

City to be wound up tomorrow (www.rte.ie, 22nd February 2010)

Cork City is to be wound up after the deal to buy the club by the Quintas Group fell through following the Independent Club Licensing Committee's decision to deny the club a Premier Division licence.

The decision of the licencing committee means that the deal to buy Cork City FC from Tom Coughlan will now not go ahead and the club will be wound up by the High Court on Tuesday at 2pm.

Peter Gray, Michael O'Connell and FORAS, the Cork City Supporters Trust, made up the Quintas Group.

A spokesperson for the group said: "With the decision of the Licencing Committee not to grant a Premier League licence, we're unable to proceed with our bid."

Cork denied licence, FORAS get green light (by Alan Smith, www.extratime.ie, 22nd February 2010)

CCIFL Ltd, the holding company of Cork City FC, have been refused a Premier Division licence for the upcoming League of Ireland season. However, it still seems likely that Leeside will be represented by a football club in the LoI for 2010 after FORAS were granted a licence to compete in the First Division.

[...]

The Independent Club Licensing Committee have taken a firm stance on the matter by denying Cork a chance to remain in the top flight, which also means that they will lose their Europa League spot too.

A statement released by the Licensing Committee read: "The Independent Club Licensing Committee met this evening [...] and unanimously decided to refuse the Premier Division Licence application of Cork City Investment FC Ltd."

[...]

Cork can appeal the decision but it now looks likely that FORAS will start from scratch in the First Division after they were granted a licence to compete in the second tier.

[...]

"This is a sad day for us, the FAI and Cork City, as we are now left without top-flight soccer in the country's second city."

~~~~

In all honesty, as well as sadness I felt a sense of relief. On reflection the last few years had felt a lot like watching a person fall ill, and then seemingly recover, before deteriorating further than ever before. As things became progressively worse it was increasingly painful for everyone involved. So on the day the club folded there was a sense that it had been put out of its misery.

Fortunately, fans group FORAS had been preparing for this in the background, and were ready to bravely step forward. They created a new entity – Cork City FORAS Co-op – that would preserve the identity and life of the club. Soon they changed their name to Cork City FC and successfully made their way back to the Premier Division, challenging for the league title and playing in cup finals as well as in Europe. Today things seem to have reverted back to the good old days; so much so that a casual observer might be forgiven for thinking that our troubles in 2008 and 2009 never happened at all.

Chapter 15

Interview with Joe Gamble ('No-Show Joe') – 15th March 2016

Some six years later I heard that No-Show had finally returned to Cork. He'd left the club a few months after me in early 2010, travelling back to the UK to play for Hartlepool first, then had a short spell with Limerick back in the League of Ireland before seeing out his final two years as a professional footballer with DPMM FC of Brunei in the Singapore League. In Brunei he'd played alongside another one of our league winners from 2005, Roy O'Donovan.

I managed to get hold of No-Show's new Irish number from a common friend and he agreed to meet up with me in the Clarion Hotel in Cork for lunch. On arrival it was clear that, although recently retired, he was still in great shape and still acting and talking like a professional. (He ordered a tuna wrap and water, which pressurised me into doing the same.)

He was happy to tell me all about his experiences in Brunei, but before that he was kind enough to look back to the end of 2009 and what had happened to him after the club folded.

~~~~

Neal Horgan: So Joe, do you remember how your time with Cork City FC ended?

Joe Gamble: Yeah, I left at the start of 2010 at some stage between Roddy coming in, the club going under and the fans taking over. It was forced on me really; I didn't really want to leave. But I could tell that I just couldn't sustain myself as a professional footballer in that environment, on that budget, so I left. It wasn't the club's fault or anything. If they'd been able to offer me a full-time wage then I would've stayed.

NH: And so was this your second time leaving Cork City FC in order to play professional football?

JG: Well in a way yes, but in another way no. When I first left back in 2000 the circumstances were quite different. At that time I left the Cork City youth team to go to England and to Reading who were a full-time professional club. Cork City were part-time back then – Dave Barry had been in charge. They had a good side; they'd finished second behind Brian Kerr's St Pats for two years in a row, in 98 and 99. I think Dave had decided to step down, and then Colin Murphy had come in. I played a few games in pre-season that year [2000] for the seniors before leaving for Reading. Actually a few of us had come through at the same time from the youth team and some did very well afterwards...

NH: Yes, I remember that youth side being particularly good. You won the national cup in 2000 under Stuart Ashton and Paul Bowdren – with future full internationals such as Damien Delaney, Alan Bennett...

JG: Yeah, we had a strong side...

NH: Actually I remember feeling annoyed as I was a few years older than you guys – maybe two years out of youths – and then you and Damien Delaney bypassed the reserve team, where I was playing at that time, to go straight into City's first team. To be fair you were both at a different level to most guys in the reserve team. It was clear to anyone who was around at the time that both you and Delaney were very determined to become full-time players in England. I remember playing the Super Cup game in 2000 with you and Delaney against Bohs when you scored – and not long after that you were gone. How old were you then?

JG: I was 18.

NH: So why didn't you go to England earlier? Most of the other best players would've been gone at 16...

JG: I didn't have much opportunity to be honest: I had trials with Ipswich under-16s – I was there for six weeks but I wasn't offered a pro-contract – but then I got into the Irish under-17 team and won Player of the Tournament in a competition involving Portugal, Norway and the US, and after that all the clubs were really onto me. In the space of two months, Crewe, Aston Villa, Bolton, Tranmere and a few other clubs were at my door – especially as I was the only home-based player in the squad.

NH: So eventually, a few years later, you went to Reading. You went on a free [contract] didn't you?

JG: Yes, that's a major problem with Irish football – I went on a free from Cork City when I probably should've been tied down on a contract for two or three years with a buy-out clause, and then the club would've gotten a fee, and my schoolboy club Everton would've gotten a fee too for all their hard work. But for whatever reason I was just able to leave on a free.

NH: Especially as you'd won the national cup with the Cork City under-18s. And you were one of the better players on the team, if not the best…

JG: Yeah, that part of the game here needs to change – and quickly. Do you see clubs anywhere else in Europe letting their young players walk into another professional football club for free – or for a small fee, which I would say is really only a token gesture? I doubt it. In fact it simply never happens. It never happens in Scandinavian countries, or in the countries that were once part of Yugoslavia. They get real fees for their players. Why would they accept less; what benefit is it to the club? Clubs from the smaller countries of Europe with players of a similar standard as here in the League of Ireland can sell players for between 500K and a million or more fairly easily, while we seem to sell or leave Irish players go to England for buttons. I can't get my head around that. It's a business, but we don't seem to have the bargaining powers of the other countries of our size.

NH: You're right: we sell our players for far too little. As you'll be aware, this changed somewhat when we became more professional; the transfer fees that our clubs could leverage started to increase. But now it seems to be back to square one as the league is part-time again. At any rate, you left back in 2000 on a free contract to try your hand in Reading, where things went well for a while?

JG: Yeah, I got in at Reading and did OK, but then I got injured – dislocated my knee. I found it hard to get back in after that, but I went to Barnet on loan and got back playing. Reading were in a good place with really good players; they went on to climb all the way from the First Division to the Championship and then finally to the Premiership – so it was a club that knew what it was doing. I learnt so much from the set-up and the players, and just from the whole process. My four seasons there gave me the platform to carry on playing for the next 12 seasons – but I was gone by the time they'd reached the Premier League. After my injury I struggled to get back in the team and so I came back to Cork City.

NH: ...in 2004 under Pat Dolan. And if memory serves it was against NEC Nijmegen in the Netherlands that was your debut?

JG: Yeah, you're right – the day Billy Woods hit the crossbar twice, which he never shuts up about. And we drew out there in Nijmegen I think, but went through in the return leg at home. Over the years we had some great nights in Europe to be fair.

NH: And we were full-time at that stage under Dolan, weren't we?

JG: Yes, the club was full-time, but I'd have to say that I'd spent four years at Reading who were doing things right, and at Cork we never really managed to become a proper full-time club. We might've been full-time on paper, but that was all really. Any player that plied their trade in England would've been able to explain the differences. And that's no slighting or bashing anyone at Cork City – far from it; they were doing their best to improve things – it's just a simple fact.

NH: What do you mean?

JG: Well, for one, we definitely didn't have the structure that's needed, including a proper backroom staff that a professional club needs. Say, for example, a full-time strength and conditioning [S&C] coach plus a younger apprentice. It's impossible for one S&C coach alone to monitor 20 professional players, their training loads, rehab, prehab, individual programmes, extra physical sessions and so on... We just had the apprentice – a good one at that – on a cheap salary, with little experience and little equipment. Cathal O'Shea was the guy at the time; Rico had brought him in between 2005 and maybe 2008. He couldn't be expected to do everything, especially as he was inexperienced with full-time footballers. In England you'd have guys who were at the top of their game in charge of the S&C for the players – not someone who was just starting out. That's no slight on Cathal – he was a great lad, really he was: he did better than anyone could've done in the same position – but he was only just starting out on his career then.

The same with the physios: they were all very good and experienced in terms of, say, private practice, but in relation to managing and maintaining full-time players... none of the people we had on board had any of that kind of experience.

These are such important roles at a full-time club. Look, if I was a manager and I had a budget for say 20 full-time players but I wasn't given a budget for an experienced, full-time S&C coach and physio, I'd say to the chairman, 'Look, I'll take 18 players and an experienced S&C coach and physio to maintain them.' This would bullet-proof the players – because that's what you're doing, you're trying to bullet-proof them for a tough season ahead. OK, you're going to get injuries – that's the nature of the sport – but you're looking to avoid the stupid injuries from overloads in training, hamstring injuries, in areas where certain individuals have weakness etc. It's so important – as you know yourself – to be at your best every week. If you have an injury and it's not properly managed, then you're goosed. The club would be saying, 'Sorry Joe, you're not playing as you've missed too many games through injury. Your performance isn't where we feel it should be and so we'll not be renewing your contract.' That's the reality.

NH: One of the things I noticed when we came down from full-time weight training in 2009 – when our fitness coach Mark McManus left us as he wasn't getting paid – was that a good few of us started having knee problems. I think it might've been down to the fact that Doolin's training was very grinding on our bodies and we no longer had Mark around to do the group strengthening sessions to keep our muscles maintained and to protect the bones...

JG: Yeah, I was actually involved in bringing Mark into Cork City. I'd worked with him previously; he had experience from the UK with elite athletes – which was great – and I knew he was excellent. But in regard to the injuries after he left, it could've been two things really: it could've been that the muscles were no longer being maintained, like you say, but it could also have been down to the rapid increase in training that we weren't used to from the moment Doolin arrived. While we'd been full-time before that, we probably weren't properly full-time from a physical point of view – so we weren't able to deal with the increase or overload.

Overall there were many other areas where you'd have to say the club fell down in comparison to a proper professional club. Our use of video analysis at the time would also have been poor. In my opinion video analysis is of paramount importance in relation to improving the match-day performance; it gives the players visual feedback so that they can see for themselves what needs to be done. And there's no hiding place. It's black and white, so to speak, and if used correctly it can be very helpful. In fairness I think most clubs in the LOI would have video analysis now though. Again, I'm not bashing or trying to criticise anyone, but my opinion is that we, at Cork City FC, could have pushed the standard every year. Those 1% margins are crucial if you want the edge over your rivals.

NH: But we were successful…

JG: Yes, we won the League in 2005, the FAI Cup in 2007 and the Setanta Cup in 2008 – and we were punching above our weight in Europe too. The standard was definitely improving. We were becoming more and more professional, and it was great while it lasted…

NH: …but then we ran into problems. We were both there during examinership in 2008, and in 2009 when we seemed to be in the High Court every few weeks. It was a very frustrating time as you'll remember. I'd started planning an exit strategy at the end of 2008; were you thinking the same?

JG: Well, I'd signed a contract in 2008 for another two seasons. I remember when I signed it – we'd just played FC Haka at home, drew 2–2. You scored, didn't you?

NH: No – I hit the crossbar and then the post in last 10 minutes.

JG: Are you sure? I thought you scored?

NH: Let's pretend I did, but anyway…

JG: So I was 26 and I figured it was likely to be the most lucrative contract of my life. We'd won the league, the FAI Cup, done well in Europe, and I'd spent my entire life working hard to be a professional footballer…

NH: …and so you felt you deserved to be rewarded for our success?

JG: Yeah, that's true; I felt that while we'd all done well, I'd become one of our more important players. I wanted that reality reflected in my contract – like anyone would.

NH: So you were delighted…

JG: I was, but in the end it wasn't worth the paper it was written on. Do you know when I actually found out that this was the case?

NH: Go on…

JG: A month after signing the contract my daughter Madison was born, and on that very same day – I swear to God, on the day she was born I got the call (I think Maddie might have even been in my arms when the phone rang) – and was told that the club had gone into examinership. To be honest I didn't really take it in at the time; I was so overwhelmed with Maddie that I kind of decided to think about it later. I'd just signed a great contract and I was happy – delighted – to be staying at Cork. But that was the start of it.

Those wages weren't sustainable in Ireland. No way. But I wasn't going to turn them down – who would? I had other clubs in for me at the time: Bohs and Pats. Not many people would know this but I'd actually agreed a pre-contract with Pats which would've started at the end of 2008, but I didn't really want to go – especially when we were expecting our first child. We wanted to stay in Cork amongst our families, and so when Cork matched Pats' offer I was absolutely delighted. My first child and a three-and-a-half-year contract with Cork. *Brilliant*, I thought.

NH: But in the end…

JG: In the end I got one month's pay on the new contract and that was it. Examinership broke and the lads were telling me I might as well rip the contract up. I felt very hurt – especially as I was in the prime of my career and the club owners [Arkaga] must've known when signing me that there was no way they could keep to the agreement. You often hear supporters and club officials talk about loyalty, and it makes me laugh to be honest. The truth is that there's no loyalty in professional sport. As a player, the day you can't perform, for whatever reason – be it injury, age etc – your contract will not be renewed. It won't matter if you've been a one-club man for 10 or 15 years; you'll still just get a handshake and then the club will move on to thinking about your replacement. To be honest, what happened in relation to my contract back in 2008 had a big effect on me. It meant that I became even more ruthless in my approach to football. And it lingers to this day. I still have an underlying feeling that I can't trust anyone in football.

NH: That must've been very tough for you to take. And it was in the papers so it was public knowledge, which wouldn't have helped. Come to think of it, while I do feel we were all let down by what happened, funnily enough, you always seemed to me, during that period, to almost symbolise full-time professionalism in Ireland. And I say that despite your frequent tardiness...

JG: [Laughing] That's harsh – I'm always on time! OK, sometimes I might not turn up to certain club functions... if I could get away with it then I would, and that's where the name came from!

NH: Seriously though, you were always the player that was most annoyed or disappointed when we weren't acting professionally as a club. Remember 'Busgate', for example?

JG: Oh yeah, that was embarrassing. The bus driver wouldn't leave as we hadn't paid him... who were we playing?

NH: St Pats

JG: Yes, Pats. I was going mad. Travel to the game should be a basic enough thing. I remember thinking to myself, *Is this what it's come to? Asking supporters to give the lads a few bob?*

NH: I remember – and have documented in this book – that you stayed on the bus while everyone else got off, apart from the driver.

JG: Really? What was I doing?

NH: You were just sitting there with your head in your hands...

JG: Probably thinking to myself, *Someone tell me this is a f**king wind up!*

NH: So anyway, that was an example of the bad times. But overall, even during the good times when we'd made progress, we never actually became a proper professional club.

JG: No, we never did. Look, we were trying hard to get there – everyone was: Lennox first, Dolan and then Rico – and then Arkaga came in and it all went belly-up. But in truth we were full-time on paper only. We needed more time; the club itself needed more time to develop a full-time culture including backroom staff, players and administrative staff. But as we all know, time ran out – and more importantly, so did the money. You need to have big pockets and people willing to commit to putting their hands in their pockets and not to expect a profit in return. There probably aren't too many such people out there.

NH: You've just come home in the last few weeks from Brunei, where you played with DPMM FC in the Singapore League. Were they full-time?

JG: Yes, we were full-time. There was no expense spared in anything they did, but funnily enough they were a bit raw when I first arrived. It was the opposite of Cork City in the sense that they had the necessary financial backing and a good administrative structure, but on the pitch they lacked a lot of knowledge in most, if not all, departments. They lacked knowledge of basic tactics, how to play against different opponents, of playing systems, warm-ups, game management – literally everything. Steve Kean, whom I'd worked with at Reading, had taken over as manager and brought me in, and we were both amazed that they hadn't had a team gym session for five years. I couldn't get over that. But Steve knew I had a degree in that area, and so in the end it worked out well for me as I took over that aspect for the club while playing for them, which was a great experience. We won the league cup in 2014, and last year, for the first time in the club's history, we won the Singapore League – so we must've been doing something right.

The club had the finances to do it, to change everything they wanted. They were able to bring in an ex-Premiership manager to make wholesale changes, and that's what it comes down to really – having the resources to do that. Full-time football costs a lot of money, so you need investors with big pockets, and a vision for long-term success with structures in places from the bottom up. I always remember a saying that Pat Sullivan [the Limerick FC chairman] used to use: when referring to a table he would say, 'You need to build the legs first'. And I agree with that. We never really had a solid base for full-time football in the League of Ireland, for whatever reason. We never built the legs or the base for full-time football here. When you look at it, there was no plan in place really.

NH: One thing Joe, which I've emphasised in a few articles I've done for the *Irish Examiner*, is that apart from a solid base and financial backing – both of which you obviously do need – if you're going to go professional as a club then the number one thing you need is the support of your association behind you.

JG: Definitely. You can't be pulling in opposite directions.

NH: It did feel like that though, didn't it?

JG: Yes it did. If you look at the FAI it seems one of the biggest problems is financial resources. I just don't think they have the resources to pay for all the things that go with running a football association – all the various under-age and senior teams – as well as running a full-time league. They have so much going on that the League of Ireland isn't getting, I feel, the importance or the priority that it should get. For me this is a mistake. Developing players in this country is crucial. Maybe it's the politics within Irish football, but I wouldn't know much about that. I'm certainly not trying to say that I know more than the FAI about how to fix or improve Irish football, but I do feel that if the FAI were to give even more support and guidance – both financially and morally – to League of Ireland clubs to bring them to a higher standard, then I can only see it as a win-win situation for football in this country. If that needs people to think outside the box, then we need to do that. Something has to change.

Back in Asia, for example, they're more open to change. They're creating an ASEAN super league which will include clubs from countries like Thailand, Vietnam, Malaysia, the Philippines, Singapore and Australia. Those countries aren't, in general, that far away from each other – two or three hours on a plane, which would be nothing to them. So in creating this new league they're trying to increase the revenue – the sponsorship possibilities, the stature of the clubs – and to create a bigger attraction for everybody.

NH: With bigger clubs…

JG: Yes, with bigger clubs, bigger attendances… bigger everything really.

NH: So is the crux of the matter in Ireland that the clubs are too small currently?

JG: Yes, most of the clubs are too small. I always refer to the rugby – that's why they decided to go professional using the bigger provinces of Munster, Leinster, Connaught and Ulster rather than the clubs. I wouldn't support getting rid of any club here, and I don't think the Munster/Leinster thing would work in soccer. But you can see why they did it in rugby: the Dolphin, Cork Con or the other rugby clubs at the time would never have been big enough to support professional players, and it's the same with soccer in Ireland – the clubs are too small at the moment. Having said that, Hartlepool, where I played in 2010, is a small place – way smaller than Cork – and yet it was proper full-time with great structures in place. A training ground situated in Durham University. That's definitely an area clubs in the LOI should look to explore further – associating with universities. I know it's happening a little; there's recently been a link-up between Cork City FC and UCC [University College Cork], but more could be done. Also, Hartlepool had six corporate boxes at the ground. Simple structures – nothing massively fancy. There's not one club in this country that has any sort of corporate box or dinner function on match days, which is another area of possible revenue that isn't looked at – not to my knowledge, anyway.

NH: So do you think if the surrounding circumstances were in place, including a plan towards full-time football with the required financial backing and the support of the FAI, in say five or ten years' time, could Cork City, for example, become a proper full-time club?

JG: Definitely. While we have other sports to compete with in Cork, that doesn't mean we can't have a full-time club in our city. And by full time I mean having a youth structure from U-15 to U-19 with full-time coaches, an environment where players can excel and develop. It could easily happen if the surrounding circumstances were right.

NH: How about the league itself, and the other clubs?

JG: Yeah, the structures of the league need to change I think. You could see that a club like Cork City or Shamrock Rovers might do very well, but other clubs might struggle...

NH: I agree. It seems to me that it suits some of the less supported teams to be part-time or amateur – but the likes of Cork City and the bigger clubs need better opposition if they and the league are going to improve. While Cork City have done brilliantly the last two seasons under John Caulfield, it still looks to me like the league has deteriorated since 2009. The UEFA coefficient for the league would tell the same story.

JG: Well obviously you can't close the door on any club, but you have to say that some clubs never really had much support. You need bigger clubs for the game to go professional – you need proper financial backing and a large fan base, or at least the potential for a large fan base. Cork City, Shamrock Rovers, Bohs, Derry... the support and potential is definitely there for those clubs to become bigger.

NH: Yeah and I agree that the Munster/Leinster thing wouldn't work in soccer, and I wouldn't want it, but I do think that an All-Ireland league could work.

JG: Definitely.

NH: That said, we did play in the Setanta Cup, which was an All-Ireland competition [involving clubs from Northern Ireland and the Republic of Ireland]. That was good: some nice prize money involved for the clubs at one point, and some good TV coverage – including in particular, after our game against Linfield in Belfast, one memorable interview... [laughing]

JG: [Laughing] Ha, yeah, what happened there? Some fella lost his rag, nearly killed the reporter…

NH: Ha, yeah. But seriously, people have said to me in arguing against an All-Ireland league that the Setanta Cup didn't really catch on – but they fail to see that it was really only a 'league-cup' type thing. It wasn't the main competition. If the All-Ireland league was your main competition then it would be different.

JG: Yeah, the Setanta Cup was more of an invitation thing. You didn't take it too seriously; it was good if you won it – and the prize money was decent – but you weren't really judged by it.

NH: So if, on the other hand, an All-Ireland league was the main competition, I think it could be much better than the Setanta Cup.

JG: Definitely.

NH: And you know that's why Arkaga came in back in 2007 – they were backing the All-Ireland league. Fintan Drury and Platinum One were behind it but it didn't proceed. I think one of the reasons it didn't go ahead was because they were proposing a merger of the associations, the FAI and the IFA. I don't ever see that happening, do you?

JG: No.

NH: But you could have a league that doesn't involve the merging of the associations or national teams… like the one you've talking about – the ASEAN super league. They're not talking about merging the associations, are they?

JG: No, just creating a new league – a new entity.

NH: Right, so the national teams stay separated, and perhaps both associations could retain all their club European spots – the four Republic ones and the four Northern Ireland ones. I've looked into this previously and written about it. There was recently a combined women's league called the BeNE League where this happened. It only lasted three years, but it combined the top women's clubs of the Netherlands and Belgium. Whichever Belgian team finished highest took its

Champions League spot, regardless of whether there were four Dutch teams ahead of it. That concept, if approved by UEFA, could really work for a combined All-Ireland league.

JG: Of course it could. I know a lot of people would pull against it, but as a fan now, I want to see full stadiums, better competitive games and a real vibrant league. For the past ten years or so there's been a lot of 'the FAI should do this,' and 'the FAI shouldn't do that,' etc., etc., but I think people need to understand that while they should and could do more, they can't do everything. Anyone who supports football in this country I'm sure would love to see a real buzz in the league, and if that means combining two leagues to make a strong single professional league, then let's give it serious thought sooner rather than later. And it could be done by a neutral party so that the FAI and IFA could be stakeholders in it rather than the main drivers of the competition. That would allow bigger clubs to progress without overstretching the FAI, and it would attract more television, sponsorship…

NH: You would also be moving from a general background population of roughly 4 million to 6.5 million. Every country in Europe with a population of 6.5 million or greater has a full-time league. It just seems to make sense: a bigger audience and bigger clubs would improve the standards of clubs from both domestic leagues.

JG: Yeah, you could definitely see the likes of Linfield, Glentoran and Cliftonville progressing. They're big clubs in their own right.

NH: And you'd be connecting the two biggest cities on the island – Belfast and Dublin – albeit only in a footballing sense, and only for the sake of a combined league. A joint committee or an independent body could run the league on behalf of both associations; nobody loses seats on committees, or any of their current roles. I see it as a win-win. There would of course be security issues, but I'd imagine those could be overcome.

JG: Yeah, well from our point of view anyway, something needs to happen. We can't go on just hoping to be lucky. That said, the under-17 and under-19 leagues here have made great progress and we really have to commend the FAI for this...

NH: You're right, we do.

JG: That's definitely progress, but in terms of our own league, we need to be feeding players into a pro-league here before they progress overseas – like most other small European countries do. We need to develop our own players, otherwise we'll be left behind. The gap between us and other countries is getting bigger all the time. You see it now in England, the money that's being spent on player development. They've a mission statement in England now that they'll win the World Cup in 2026; of course we can't match that, but we need to adopt a strategy that's Irish. We don't need to be copying the bigger countries. We need to establish a real identity in football, and for me that involves creating a pro-league here. If we don't – if we don't change our mindset and structure towards producing professional footballers – then we'll be overtaken by the so-called minnows countries.

You see the technical ability of the likes of Spain now versus their national team 20 years ago: they've improved enormously. I'm not saying we'll ever be like Spain... we won't. But the problem is that everyone else is pushing on, and if we don't, well who knows where Irish football will be. Look at the Cypriot league, the Swedish league – they've had clubs playing in the Champions league recently. We were beating their top clubs ten years ago. They've moved forward, whereas we've moved backwards.

NH: And our league should be capable of being transformed or merged without too much difficulty – unlike if you tried to make dramatic changes to nearly any other European league.

JG: Yes, there'd be too much resistance there; but here, if you think about it, we're ripe for change.

NH: UEFA of course would need to approve an All-Ireland league, but if it's for the benefit of cross-border trade and relations – which it would be – then I really think they'd support it.

JG: As I mentioned earlier, create structures in the clubs, and do it properly, and you create better players for the national team moving forward. A long-term plan for developing players will not happen by simply wishing it to happen – you need to have clear pathways. These are key. So we need to have a pro-league in place with U-19, U-17 and U-15 teams lined up and feeding into the first teams like a pyramid. A further step would be to fund academies at an even younger age – in a similar way to how the FAI/FAS scheme is funded – and linked with the pro-league clubs. Then you'd really be talking. This would create a football industry of full-time coaches and players, with youths coming up who'd be able to maintain their educational commitments while playing in an academy, like in other countries in the UK and Europe.

But you really do need the existence of full-time clubs at the top of the game for the game to change in Ireland – and if you did have this, together with the academies and underage, I think it would 100% increase our chances of creating top players for the future, and ultimately for the international stage.

NH: This already happened to some extent in our time: how many players for the national team were produced from our full-time experiment? If you look at the squad now – Doyler, Longy, Coleman, Hoolahan, Meyler, Ward, McClean, Forde, Daryl Murphy – more than ever before – and this can be sourced back to our full-time period. The league, since its return to part-time, hasn't produced a player for the Republic's national team.

JG: The divide is bigger now for the likes of Forrester, Lenihan and Towell, to name just a few, as the league is more part-time again. And that's not the fault of those players; if they'd come through a full-time club at home first, the jump to full-time football in England or wherever – and to the national team – wouldn't be so big. Although there were many Irish players that would have made the transition to England seem easy in the past, things are more difficult in England now for any Irish player.

~~~~

Joe and I spoke for another few minutes before heading back to our daily lives. As we left I asked what his long-term plans were. He said that while he and his wife Sylvia had always wanted to come home, he knew when he was returning that he probably wouldn't be able to work in soccer in Ireland – the work's just not there.

So he was looking at other options whilst doing his S&C coaching – and quite controversially for a St Finbarr's man (like myself), he was working with our local rivals Blackrock's intermediate hurling team.

We wished each other good luck and I walked back to my office, wondering about what could have been and what might be in the future for the league, and how much Irish football needs the likes of No-Show involved in our game.

(I forgot to mention that he was late to meet me, of course, but at least he turned up…)

Afterword – The Need for Change

The foregoing pages document in painful detail the almost daily need of the players at Cork City FC for reassurance regarding their wages. The relative instability of our employment, combined, of course, with the irregularity of our payments from the club during this period, helps explain this insecurity. However, I'd like to make it clear that most of the players at the full-time clubs around the country during this period weren't just playing to pick up a wage. Like players at every other club in the world, they were looking to do as well as they could on the pitch so as to improve their individual reputations and prospects. Many would have carried ambitions of moving overseas. But most of us were also keenly interested in improving standards within Ireland and in breaking down the barriers (both real and imagined) that seem to hinder professional football in this country. Like any League of Ireland player over the past 60 or 70 years, we also wanted to do well in Europe and bring a greater respectability to our league. And when full-time football was going well for the clubs during this full-time period, we did just that. In fact we brought the league's co-efficient ranking (which rates the top league in Europe on the basis of their clubs' performances over a five-year period) from 39th in 2003 to an all-time high of 29th in 2010. The return to part-time football in the league since 2010 has seen our ranking drop back to 43rd in 2015.

However, the European displays of Cork City and Dundalk in this current season (2016) have brought fresh hope. Of the 2009 Cork City squad, only Ballincollig men Mark McNulty and Colin Healy (who returned to the club in 2011 after his time at Ipswich and a loan spell at Falkirk) remain, and Jerry Harris is still walking the corridors out in Bishopstown – albeit without the need for a torch. That the lights are well and truly back on at Bishopstown and Turner's Cross was perhaps best celebrated with Colin Healy's incredible overhead kick winner against St Pats on 8th August 2014.

There can be no dispute, though, that it has been Stephen Kenny's Dundalk side that have been the leading light back towards higher standards in the league. Their captain Stephen O'Donnell has shown maturity in playing the captain's role both on and off the pitch. His consistent bravery and composure on the ball against any and all opposition is what has allowed Dundalk to play out from the back, in a style that is, perhaps, the most attractive and effective of any Irish side (including the national team) for some time. And 'Stevie', as I remember him from less mature, ass-revealing Cork City days, has recently confirmed, following a magical and remarkable period for the club, that League of Ireland players are not just interested in improving their own prospects but the reputation of our league as well.

Dundalk's Part-Timers Ready to Make Champions League History (by Alan Smith, *The Guardian*, 13th August 2016)

Four years ago Dundalk's very existence was in jeopardy. The team were treading water, while attendances at the Irish club's unsightly Oriel Park ground hit a baseline of 260. Wages were unpaid and a genuine belief festered that the end was nigh. They were spared relegation only because Monaghan United ran into financial difficulties and withdrew from competition, allowing the Lilywhites a two-legged play-off to stay up.

[...]

In three and a half seasons they have brought them to a stage no other Irish club has reached before: a two-legged tie against Legia Warsaw from reaching the Champions League group stage.

Stephen O'Donnell, the captain, has been in a similar position, scoring an extra-time penalty to send Shamrock Rovers into the group stages of the Europa League, an Irish first in 2011. Defeat against Legia would send Dundalk there, too, but already talk has shifted to them being the best Irish side of all time.

For O'Donnell the most pleasing aspect was how they reached this point, defeating Bate Borisov 3-0 in the second leg to overturn a one-goal deficit with a display of clinical, attacking football having already beaten the Icelandic champions, FH. There was no sign of the direct, physical play Irish teams have so often been criticised for. "Usually there's relief after winning but this was pure ecstasy," O'Donnell says. "The way we played was the stuff of dreams."

Even if Legia advance, it will have been some feat for a team that trains in the evening because several members of the squad have day jobs to supplement their income. They are professional in everything but financial reward.

Dane Massey, the left-back, is an electrician, Andy Boyle sells meat and his centre-half partner, Brian Gartland, has been working as a basketball coach. The leading star of their European run has been David McMillan, architect by day, goalscorer by night.

Off the field the club relies on volunteers to keep going because there are only two full-time employees. The general manager, Martin Connolly, is the brother of the co-owner but has previously worked as goalkeeping coach and turns his hands to whatever odd jobs need doing. Darren Crawley, the press officer, works 40 hours a week and has been struggling to find time to deal with the increased attention over the past week. "No one ever thought we would be in this position so quickly from the despair of 2012," Crawley says. Even Kenny's assistant manager, Vinny Perth, is part-time.

There are other challenges, too. Dundalk are fighting to win a third league title in a row but have lost both games since defeating Bate Borisov, their first consecutive defeats since 2013. Europe is a distraction and, as O'Donnell points out, "we don't have the biggest squad".

Retaining their best players has been an issue in the past. Richie Towell, their star in 2015, received an offer he could not refuse to join Brighton in January, but he has found playing time under Chris Hughton a precious commodity.

[...]

The biggest challenge, though, may be keeping hold of Kenny. O'Donnell has worked under Michael O'Neill, the Northern Ireland manager, but believes his current boss is incomparable. "Stephen is definitely the best man-manager I've worked under. He gets the best out of his players, believing in them and making them feel 10-foot tall. To do what he has done, from a blank canvas in four years, is amazing."

O'Donnell is also dedicating their run to the league, which has been maltreated by those in control for far too long, not least the Football Association of Ireland (FAI) chief executive, John Delaney, who currently earns more than three times the prize money for winning the league title and describes the league as "a difficult child".

Dundalk's European foray has run parallel to the FAI making a song and dance about offering each club a desultory €5,000 for strategic planning. Insulted, Derry and St Patrick's Athletic have turned it down and a grim back and forth has taken place between the latter and the association. For context, Delaney earns €360,000 per annum having taken a substantial pay cut in recent years, while the association earned more than €11m in prize money alone from Euro 2016.

There is no shortage of well wishers, including the FAI, whose jumping on the bandwagon has not been met kindly by supporters. One other Premier Division club, Wexford Youths, are providing free buses for their fans to bolster the crowd at the Aviva in Dublin on Wednesday night.

That will be their third home ground of the campaign because the decrepit Oriel was not up to scratch for the Bate game and Tallaght Stadium is not of a sufficient standard for the play-offs.

"The only way to make people not usually interested in the league sit up and take notice is to do well in Europe," O'Donnell says. *"We've made people do that. We want the league to be respected and there are a lot of very good players – this is for them. When people say the league is rubbish, it grates on you."*

Unfortunately, Dundalk, just like Shelbourne back in 2004, fell at the last hurdle before the lucrative Champions League group stages, going down to Legia Warsaw (3–1 on aggregate). Even so, Steven O'Donnell's comments reflected exactly how I felt back in our successful period from 2003–2007; that we were representing Irish football in Europe, fighting for respect and for a better reputation for our league. As such, there were times when it felt like we were guinea pigs in an unauthorised experiment; there was excitement in the sense that we were up against the establishment in Ireland as well as our opponents on the pitch, but in reality we were too weak to swim against the tide. We couldn't do it on our own, divided as we were between clubs that were fighting amongst themselves for players and for results. We needed a plan for all of us, from above.

In retrospect it's clear that we needed 'the Association' to buy into the idea of really progressing the league and its clubs. We needed those seated around the tables up in the FAI to recognise that what we were trying to do was worthy of praise and support. We wanted them to see, for example, that Dan Murray, Joe Gamble and even 'Ding Dong' Denis Behan were doing our city and the whole game in Ireland a service by improving standards here and by helping the club to beat teams in Europe.

We wanted the FAI to herald our great victories against the likes of Malmo, NEC Nijmegen, Djurgardens and Apollon Limassol, as well as the victories in Europe for the other full-time clubs during this period – the likes of Shels, Bohs, Derry, Pats and Drogheda – as signs of real hope and development for football in this country. We wanted them to acknowledge the possibility that with more support, development and sponsorship of our league, it could progress even further. In essence, we needed the FAI to further organise and plan for the continued progress of the professional game in Ireland.

For whatever reason, none of this really happened. They never came on board and there was no plan put in place for the continuation of professional football in Ireland. This is crucial, as in my opinion the lack of an over-arching plan for full-time football in Ireland was at least as significant a factor as the oft-mentioned issues of 'excessive player wages' or 'mismanagement by club owners' in the failure of full-time football in this country between 2003 and 2010, as well as in the death of my football club, Cork City FC, at the start of 2010.

In my opinion the FAI needed to be leading the charge – not individual clubs or individual chairmen. The frustrating thing is that if the FAI really decided to make professional football in Ireland a priority, it could be the most exciting journey that Irish football has ever taken; a journey towards sustainable full-time football clubs, regular meaningful European fixtures around the country, and a better pathway for our best and brightest before they move to other more developed leagues. It could be the maturing of our league, as well as 'the Association', that is long overdue. For this to happen we need the FAI to see the real potential of our clubs and of our people. In short, we need the FAI to believe in us.

Without the support, planning, leadership and clout of the FAI, ambition will continue to be a dangerous thing in the League of Ireland, and survival rather than progress will, unfortunately, remain the priority.

The experience of clubs such as Cork City FC during this period needs be analysed so that we can learn and progress. Worryingly, there is no evidence that this type of analysis has taken place along the corridors of the FAI. In fact, on reading the Conroy Report one could be excused for thinking these events never happened at all – and so I recently decided to write about it.

Questions to Answer if our League Really is to Progress (by Neal Horgan, *The Irish Examiner*, Friday, April 15th, 2016)

When the FAI announced they were commissioning a report into the League of Ireland in 2015, I was hardly alone in warmly welcoming the news. And by the time Declan Conroy published his findings last September, I really hoped that I was about to read a serious and progressive plan for reform of the Irish game.

First impressions were of a substantial undertaking, many of whose recommendations have indeed been well received – such as an increase in prize money, the re-introduction of marketing personnel specific to our league, and the introduction of club ambassadors and a league 'champion' to promote the senior game in this country.

More controversially, there was also a recommendation in respect of changing the format of the two divisions, but, as Conroy's stated purpose was to start a conversation about the league, you could argue that he succeeded in that respect too.

However, all that said, it's my opinion that his report failed to address some of the biggest challenges facing the League of Ireland. And, whatever does eventually emerge from ongoing discussions on the document between the FAI and the clubs, I believe that the most fundamental questions about the future of the domestic game have still to be tackled.

Why in a league of its own?
Those of us who have a serious ambition for football in Ireland have long pined for the progress and status enjoyed by leagues of other countries with a comparable population and size to our own.

The fact that, in the Conroy Report, no comparison was made with any other country's league seemed to me, at first, to be a blatant oversight but, when asked about this omission shortly after publication, Conroy explained that it was not part of his remit. The question then should be, why not? The 'Genesis II' report, 10 years earlier, carried out a comparison with other leagues, including those of Austria and Norway. So why not an updated version? Does our league compare so badly to other countries that a comparison would not be helpful?

Despite the lack of comparative analysis, the Conroy Report still insists on setting out what it calls the "unique" environment in which our league finds itself, at one point stating: "The Irish sporting landscape is uniquely different from most of its European equivalents." It is difficult to understand how it can be proposed that we are unique in any way in a report which does not offer a comparison with even one other country. And I am not being pedantic here. I feel this is an important issue as there's a danger that if we accept we are "unique", then we might be more inclined to accept that we should be judged only by our own standards.

The full-time question
There is another important omission in the report – the subject of full-time football in Ireland.

Nowhere is there any mention that full-time football between 2004 and 2009 brought better results in Europe, improved crowd attendances, attracted bigger transfer fees for our players, and increased the production of more players for the Irish national team than ever before from the League of Ireland.

Nor, on the downside, is there any analysis of the considerable problems that full-time football (in its ad hoc and uncentrally planned format) posed for a number of clubs.

The current predicament of some of our top players, who are effectively full-time from March until November before becoming unemployed from December to February, is something that needs to be considered as a matter of priority.

It seems to me that there are two possible ways forward: Either the league reverts to a purely part-time game, with afternoon training allowing these players to hold down full-time jobs or, challenging though it may be, we seek a transition to a full-time game.

The blame game

There were other troubling aspects to the Conroy Report. For example, in the event of a club experiencing financial difficulty, it seemed to preclude the idea of any responsibility whatsoever falling on the heads of the FAI.

In Chapter 4.2, page 10, under the heading 'Roles and Responsibilities', it states: "While not a universal view, it has become, for some, a conveniently held position... that issues affecting a club's operation or viability are the responsibility of the FAI."

But surely at least some of the issues which affect the operation or viability of a club operating under the authority of the FAI are, by definition, the responsibility of the FAI? And responsibility is the crux of the matter. The health of our national league clubs should be one of the FAI's most important responsibilities, given the crucial position of the League of Ireland at the top of the pyramid above intermediate, junior, and schoolboy clubs.

Beyond reruns of the old blame game when things go wrong, we need an association that understands it plays a crucial role in deciding how clubs are run and how the league should position itself going forward. In short, an FAI that is really part of the league.

A way forward

I think the SSE Airtricity League, in a strategically reformed or (ideally) merged state, has the potential to become a fully professional and well-respected league as appropriate for our *population, environment, and resources. The reasons why this is currently not the case are due, principally, to our poor performances in European competitions, the league's low co-efficient, a lack of stadiums of quality, and an inability to offer full-time football.*

In my opinion, we need the FAI to make the attainment of professional football in this country a priority. I would prefer if there was a concerted effort by all of those involved in the game to plan for this, rather than a concerted effort to try to stay positive about the league as it is – with all its defects. I'm sorry if that's deemed to be negative but that's how I feel – and I hope nobody needs to be convinced that I write as someone who loves the League of Ireland.

I had hoped that this general and relatively brief critique of the Conroy Report might form part of a healthy discussion on the Report's overall merit. However, since then we seem to have accepted its findings and recommendations *carte blanche*, and without question or debate. But the recommendations that the Conroy Report provide are problematic for a number of reasons. Firstly, the mandate of the Conroy Report was stated as follows:

1. *Seek views as to how the Clubs and the League currently operate.*
2. *Hear views on how best the Clubs and the League can move forward*

So the mandate was to seek and hear views, yet there is no mention of recommendations. Perhaps this can be forgiven, as recommendations based on the findings are surely to be welcomed. Unfortunately, the findings as published are not readily identifiable in the recommendations.

For example, one of the questions asked by the Conroy report as part of a survey of fans was as follows: *'Please*

*outline ONE development you would like to see implemented
by your Club or the FAI in the SSE Airtricity League in the
next 5 years?'* The number one answer, according to the
report, was *'All-Ireland League. Four Regional Leagues. One
division with better spread of clubs.'* (SSE Airtricity fans'
survey question 21, page 71, Conroy Report.)

This would be consistent with the Genesis Report's main
structural recommendation, which involved a gradual move
towards an All-Ireland League. This would, it argued, given
the greater market involved, offer a more sustainable model for
professional football in Ireland on both sides of the border.
Declan Conroy is one of the people who is specifically
mentioned in the Genesis Report as having being consulted by
Genesis; it is somewhat surprising, then, that there is no
mention in the Conroy Report of an All-Ireland League as a
possible structural model for Irish football – particularly
surprising given the above number-one answer and because Mr
Conroy must have been very aware of the Genesis Report (the
existence of which is not referred to in the Conroy Report
either).

Furthermore, at page 42 under the subheading
'Managers/coaches,' regarding consultations made by Conroy
Consulting with various League of Ireland managers, the
'prospect of a full-time league' is the first item listed as being
'among the main issues raised.' Despite this, the *'prospect of
a full-time league'* forms no part and earns no mention
amongst the numerous recommendations of the Conroy
Report.

However, we need to be careful if we are critiquing, as the
Conroy Report itself seems to include a deterrence for anyone
who wishes to question or criticize.

At page 50, under the heading *'The Brand, Marketing and
Promotions'* and the subheading *'Negativity'*, is stated the
following:

Yet the League suffers from a certain negativity that dominates. While some of this is undoubtedly cultural, a concerted effort by all parties within the game must be made to engage more positively around the brand. As a start, the game needs everyone from within to avoid being negative in public.

This is one of the more alarming comments in the report. On top of this and more recently still, the former St. Pat's, Ireland and Faroe Islands manager Brian Kerr stated that the FAI uses the participation agreement (agreed between the clubs and the FAI back in 2007) 'as a muzzle on the clubs,' adding that the 'clubs are afraid to challenge the FAI' (*Soccer Republic*, RTE, 9th August 2016).

Given our history of poor performances in European competitions, the league's low co-efficient, our lack of quality stadiums, our dismally low attendances around the country and our inability to offer full-time football in Ireland, we shouldn't be pretending that everything is fine. We need to talk about the League of Ireland and its problems. It's time to remove the muzzle.

The approach of the Conroy Report and the FAI reminds me, in some ways, of my father and grandfathers, when I was a young child, only wishing to discuss the glory days of the League and Cork clubs, rather than the death of Cork football clubs in the 50s, 70s and 80s. But the Irish soccer community is not a young child; we need and deserve a critical analysis of why full-time football didn't work in the 2000s, so that we can decide for ourselves whether it could be viable at some stage in the future in a better organised (and possibly more centrally planned) way.

However, despite what seem – to me at least – to be important and clear limitations of the Conroy Report, it appears that 'the Association' are pleased with it. FAI chief executive John Delaney released a statement on 25th September 2015 welcoming the report's findings and labelling it the 'the most comprehensive and thorough review of senior domestic football in Ireland' (www.the42.ie, 25th September 2015).

While as a player who played through this period it's frustrating that our experiences have not been acknowledged in the Conroy Report, much more significant, in the absence of FAI support for full-time football, is the ongoing danger that a club or two will strive towards professionalism without the backing that the FAI could and should provide. In such a scenario I would not be surprised if the chaos that engulfed Cork City in 2008 and 2009 repeats itself at some club in the near future.

As such, when I ask readers in the introduction of this book to 'abandon all hope', the 'hope' I mean is the hope, still held by many in this country, that everything will work out OK if we continue to trudge along the way we have for the last 60 years – without any transformative changes or any ambitious and integrated design for professional football in Ireland.

Thankfully, and despite ongoing concerns about our senior League of Ireland clubs, there have recently been some positive moves by the FAI. The introduction of under-19 and under-17 national leagues represents the first steps towards the creation of a viable domestic player pathway for our best and brightest towards the professional game. The proposed under-15 and under-13 national leagues will only further encourage our top young players to find a route to the professional game through the League of Ireland, rather than the traditional risky emigration at 16 years of age to professional clubs in the UK. However, the level of professionalism of our top league – the League of Ireland – will continue to be the determining factor in whether we can keep our top players here, until they are more mature. Sending our kids to England or elsewhere as legal minors, away from their friends and family at such a young age, should be the exception rather than the rule. At the moment that risky emigration remains standard practice for our best players – but the new under-age national leagues offer hope of change.

It should again be highlighted, on the topic of player pathways, that the full-time era between 2003 and 2010, for all its flaws, produced more players for our national team than ever before. In contrast, the reversion to part-time for the league since 2011 (or whatever strange mix of full-/part-time currently exists at our top clubs today) has meant that the League of Ireland has not produced a single player for the national team over the past five years.

So we need professional football for the individual player, for the national team, and for the health of Irish football overall. We need the FAI to lead and plan the route to professional football in Ireland – by way of a 10- or 20-year plan if necessary. The League of Ireland should not just be an after-thought. For too long now it has remained in the shadows, and we in Ireland have remained 'off-the-radar' in terms of the professional game that is enjoyed in most other countries in Europe.

So when somebody today says, '*Sure haven't we seen how it [full-time football] is unsustainable, when all those clubs went belly-up back in the 2000s,*' in response one could perhaps refer to this book as evidence of the uncoordinated and often chaotic manner in which it was attempted. To dismiss the idea of full-time football in Ireland forever on the basis of what happened between 2003 and 2010 does not stand up to critical analysis.

But how to dismantle the other commonly held responses that seem to confirm why we shouldn't or can't have a professional soccer league in Ireland?

Let's deal with the size issue first. '*We're just not up to it; we're too small.*' But we know from talking to Robert Mežeckis in Chapter 7 that Latvia, with a population of about 2 million people, has 8 full-time clubs. OK, so this might lead to another question... '*Latvia doesn't have the GAA. They don't have a national game that dominates over and above football in their country.*' Well, that might be true, but Finland, for example, have a full-time league even though ice hockey is their national sport. So the existence of a national or dominant team sport other than soccer (assuming that is the case in Ireland), though important, isn't an absolute barrier to professional soccer in a county either.

(I would also argue that the existence of the GAA in Ireland isn't only an impediment to soccer here, and that the situation is more complex. Soccer receives benefits from the GAA's existence which, probably due to historical or political reasons, remain under-acknowledged. For example, the physical and psychological benefits of playing GAA for a soccer player have recently been declared by players such as Seamus Coleman, Kevin Doyle, Shane Long and Damien Delaney.)

'*But the population of Finland [5.4 million] is greater than ours,*' might be the response at this stage – and this, of course, is true. However, Irish rugby has managed to go professional in Ireland despite the existence of the GAA and despite our low relatively low population. This, in turn, may be followed by another statement: '*But rugby is different to soccer. They've always been wealthier and had more access to funds, and it is a less played sport in Europe and thus easier for, say, Munster to win the European Cup than for something similar ever to happen to an Irish football club.*'

Of course rugby is different. Of course they had the advantage of a viable Celtic league to help grow the game. And, of course, Irish club rugby had a greater ability to actually win trophies in Europe than Irish soccer clubs will ever have. As to a greater access to money, I'm not so sure. Soccer has a much richer potential market in Europe and the rest of the world than rugby. Dundalk's recent windfall in the Champions League shows the type of funds that are available for progress through even the early rounds of soccer's European competitions these days.

One crucial thing that Irish rugby did was to plan for the professional game from above. This, in my opinion, was the most important factor in its success. It was the IRFU leading the charge, not individual clubs. Central planning was crucial for the professional game here. Another difference was that the IRFU was willing to do something that the FAI seemingly does not do: that is, to pass on a portion of the gate receipts or earnings from the national team's matches or events to the domestic clubs. The FAI, as far as I am aware, do no such thing. Icelandic soccer, on the other hand…

Here's how Iceland chose to spend some of their Euro 2016 money (by Paul Fennessy, *The 42*, 22nd August 2016)

Thanks to Iceland's Euro 2016 heroics, the country's players earned their Football Association a fee of €14 million for reaching the quarter-finals at Euro 2016.

With smaller football associations such as Iceland's often having to make do with very limited resources, the Uefa prize money will likely serve as a huge boost to football on the island, which has a population of just over 330,000 people. Interestingly, from the money earned, the Nordic country chose to distribute €3,409,670 (453 million króna – roughly 25% of the total fee) to its football clubs, according to the Football Association of Iceland's official website.

Some teams received more than others based on their league performances in recent seasons, though each club were given roughly €19,000 at the very minimum, while of the 47 recipients, 13 received six-figure sums (in terms of euros).

The figures make for interesting reading from an Irish perspective, particularly in light of the recent controversy surrounding the FAI's distribution of €5,000 for each of the 20 SSE Airtricity League clubs to assist in the completion of five-year strategic plans, with St Pat's and Derry City subsequently saying they would reject the offer, amid widespread suggestions that the funds being made available were derisory.

So in a similar vein to the IRFU in Ireland, the Icelandic FA appear to be supporting their football clubs by way of their national team's exploits. Perhaps this is something that could be done in Irish football too?

Another common response when discussing the prospect of a professional league in Ireland might be: *'But they don't have the English Premiership at their doorstep.'* However, most Scandinavian countries are as intertwined and saturated with English football as we are – and they still have full-time clubs. See also Latvia, Lithuania and Slovenia, which operate full-time professionalism in the shadows of the relatively nearby Bundesliga.

So overall we can point to examples, mainly around Europe but also within Ireland, which address many of the concerns of those who think we cannot have a professional soccer league here. This is why a comparison with other countries (which formed part of Genesis's report but did not form part of the Conroy Report) is so important.

Obviously it is impossible to find an identical country to compare ourselves with – a country that could address all of the issues raised form an Irish point of view at the same time. However, after we've addressed each of the objective criteria underlying the apparent barriers to professional football in this country – such as population size issues, issues in relation to the strength of other domestic sports, issues in relation to funding and the proximity of a strong neighbour – we're left with the subjective criteria.

This, I feel, is the crux of the matter and why we don't have a professional league in Ireland. Some people in Irish football seem to want it; others don't seem too interested, or have other commitments. In truth, on this issue we have always seemed very divided amongst ourselves and lacking real leadership and vision.

Recent troubles involving the FAI and League of Ireland clubs St. Patrick's Athletic and Derry City confirm the divisions within Irish football today. The issue being disputed involves the announcement by the FAI of a payment of €5,000, by the FAI, to each of the 20 League of Ireland clubs, for 'Strategic Planning.' The FAI have stated that they are doing this in order to follow on from one of the recommendations from the Conroy Report. But Derry City and St. Pats refused to accept the payment and a war or words ensued. St. Pat's eventually published a statement on their website (www.stpatsfc.com/news) that included the following:

[...]
Our game is in crisis. That is why the clubs established the PCA (Premier Clubs' Alliance), so that the Premier League clubs would consider their responsibilities and attempt to engage with the governing body with a view to effecting change. Ten months since we brought these issues forward, nothing material has happened. We have made the Association aware of the seriousness of the challenge facing the senior clubs – and the domestic game at all levels – but there has been no serious engagement. To demonstrate its commitment the PCA appointed Senior Counsel, Michael Cush, to lead its engagement with the FAI but, to date, his efforts have been largely rebuffed. It may appear strange in a week when two of our clubs brought such distinction to our domestic game to talk of the League being in crisis, but that is by no means an exaggeration.

It is not the FAI's role alone to address the crisis. The responsibility for this lies with various stakeholders, including the clubs. The board of St Patrick's Athletic is perfectly prepared to accept its part in this, however all the senior clubs are beholden to the Association, which has utterly failed to create a suitable environment in which a sustainable, commercially sound League which would nurture young talent and generate public support. It is ten years since the Association took control of the League of Ireland. In that time it has displayed nothing approaching leadership.

Derry's response took a similar tone:

Derry City to snub 'disgraceful and disrespectful' €5K FAI grant (*The Irish Independent*, 4ᵗʰ August 2016)

Derry City have decided to reject the €5,000 grant recently announced to be coming from the FAI to SSE Airtricity League clubs, calling it 'disrespectful and disgraceful.'

Last week, the FAI confirmed that they, along with the Premier Clubs Association, would be allocating a €100,000 grant to be shared equally among the 20 SSE Airtricity League clubs.

However, speaking recently to the Derry News, the Derry City Chairman, Sean Barrett, was adamant that the club would not be availing of the money in question.

"I think it's absolutely disgraceful the way they have treated the clubs." Barrett said.

"The FAI received €11 million and to throw something like that at us is disgraceful when we as a club on its own have had at least six players coming through Derry City Football Club to go on and play international football.

"For us to be treated like that is not only disgraceful, it's disrespectful and we will be not be accepting that figure. We will be telling them to keep the money. We won't accept it."

Indeed, Mr Barrett claimed that the sum in question would mitigate little of the costs incurred when running a club and, in fact, claimed it to be disrespectful.

"Affiliation fees alone are €15,000. There's the affiliation fees and then there are things like fines; for example we were fined €750 for one flare incident.

"To ask anyone to do a five-year plan and then to give them to what equates to £4000 is disgraceful. It doesn't scratch the surface. We're not even prepared to accept it.

He concluded; "It shows the lack of respect for the league. We have had six players play for the national team but they don't seem to care about the league. It's absolutely disgraceful," he said.

So here we all are. Fighting amongst ourselves, divided, with everybody seemingly blaming everybody else for the problems. Overall there does appear to be a tangible lack of real leadership with regard to the future of the League of Ireland. But we are not the first country that has faced these types of problems. Back in 2002/03, Australian soccer was facing turmoil similar to what's happening here in Ireland. Their domestic league, the National Soccer League (NSL), was in particular trouble.

From www.austadiums.com/news, Wednesday 23rd October, 2002:

NSL crowds plummet
The troubled National Soccer League is suffering by the game's lack of exposure on TV with crowds at their lowest level for seven years.

With TV rights holder Channel Seven refusing to air any NSL action this season, thousands of disgruntled fans and sponsors are being left out in the cold.

After five rounds, the average attendance is 4,381 – down 15 per cent on last season's figures. This equates to 66,651 less fans walking through the turnstiles, costing clubs valuable income.

Even the league's marquee club, Perth Glory, has seen its crowd numbers drop while last season's second most supported side Newcastle United has lost up to 20 per cent of its crowd.

Glory chairman Nick Tana was quoted by AAP as saying: "We can't identify the specific reason for the drop in crowds".

"Whether or not it's the lack of visibility of the league and the lack of free-to-air television I don't know.

"But if you look at the rest of the league, theirs (attendances) have dropped off as well. If the league is not visible in the marketplace as a marketable product, there'll be a detrimental effect."

Despite their problems, Perth and Newcastle are still the best supported clubs in the NSL, while the champion Olympic Sharks and South Melbourne continue to lose fans at a worrying rate.

In response to growing concerns, the Australian government commissioned a report entitled 'Report of the Independent Soccer Review Committee into the Structure, Governance and Management of Soccer in Australia' (April 2003). Chaired by David Crawford, it was thus coined 'the Crawford Report.' Unlike the Conroy Report, the Crawford Report published direct comments from many of those interviewed under the heading *'Stakeholder Comments'*. A total of 92 named stakeholders make comments that are published from page 47 to page 66 of the document. Many of these comments highlighted the fractious and dysfunctional state of Australian soccer and their domestic league, the National Soccer League (NSC) at the time. They were also surprisingly similar to the comments made by St. Patrick's Athletic and Derry City recently in respect of football here in Ireland. Here are a few examples:

Richard Bennett: 'I feel that the problems start and end with the administration of the game at the highest levels and filter down to a disgruntled general football [soccer] community that is fast becoming apathetic. In other words how do you grow the game if the followers are jaded and frustrated with a catalogue of embarrassing mismanagement and in-fighting? Certainly the general sporting public sees the game as endemically mismanaged at all levels and the media only reports and reinforces these negative aspects. I would like to comment that time is of the essence, and that commodity is fast running out. If the game is not prepared to be shaken out of its slumber then I can only see stagnation and more of the same tokenism and more wasting of resources leading to a football wasteland in this country.'

Ken Kendrick: 'I find it very hard to believe that with hundreds of thousands of Aussie kids playing the game every weekend, and over 150 Aussies playing on the world stage, that the NSL [National Soccer League] (with all its mismanagement, infighting, petty squabbles and self seeking agendas) has managed to turn the world game into such an abysmal failure in Australia.'

Murray Jesson: 'In my 23 years here [in Australia] I have watched with sadness and dismay how state and national administrators have shot themselves and the game in the foot to advance their egotistical ambitions.'

Chris King: 'It has been the same issues that have not been addressed. These issues have always had a great impact on the sport at all levels from the juniors right through to the top level. The ongoing division within the game is the killer of it … because of power and the belief of those with it that they are doing the best for the game. People at all levels of the game find ways not to work together for their own self interests rather than go out of their way to find a means of working together for the betterment of the game.'

Dimitrios Mavratzas: 'The state of the game of soccer in this country is at an all time low ebb. Soccer Australia is in public disarray; the national team with its full complement of players has not been seen in action for nearly a year [when written in November 2002]; the NSL stumbles along to ever decreasing crowds without a formatted sense of direction … the financial affairs of Soccer Australia have been headlines in all sections of the media, further ridiculing the game of soccer here in Australia.'

Colin Pope: 'The NSL seems discarded with no promotion or marketing and limited media exposure. Futsal is a forgotten part of the sport. Juniors are catered for, but only because of the mums and dads who put the time and effort in for the children and not for themselves. Clearly the structure is not working. A board that is there for the game and not themselves is needed. The fans and players are not truly represented. The state federations appear to have some similar problems as Soccer Australia, only not as big. The decisions are made along lines other than the best long and short-term interest of the game as a whole. There is little planning currently evident to anyone outside Soccer Australia.'

So the Crawford Report clearly wasn't interested in avoiding negativity. It was also different from the Conroy Report as it had a mandate that included, amongst other things, the provision of recommendations:

The Committee's terms of reference require it to prepare a report that includes:
1. *a critical assessment of the existing governance, management and structure of soccer in Australia*
2. *solution-based recommendations to deliver a comprehensive governance framework and management structure for the sport that addresses the needs of affiliated organisations and stakeholders. These recommendations may include adjustments to*

existing governance systems and/or integration of activities and operations

3. *identification of potential impediments to reform and strategies to overcome those impediments*
4. *a plan to implement the recommendations.*

(Page 1, The Crawford Report)

Also unlike the Conroy Report, this report was to review the entirety of the game, including the performance of 'Soccer Australia' – the existing governing authority in Australian soccer. It was also to be carried out by a committee of independent experts as follows:

- *Mr David Crawford (chair) – retired National Chairman of KPMG and current director of several major companies including BHP Billiton, Foster's Group, Lend Lease, National Foods and Westpac Banking Corporation.*
- *Mr Johnny Warren – former captain of the Socceroos and highly regarded football analyst and commentator.*
- *Mr Bruce Corlett – Chairman of Adsteam Marine Limited and Servcorp Limited, current non-executive director of several companies including Trust Company of Australia Limited and Stockland Trust Group, and past chairman of Australian Maritime Safety Authority.*
- *Ms Kate Costello – lawyer and former academic, chairman of Bassett Consulting Engineers, chairman of SAAB ITS and director of SAAB Systems, member of the Australian Institute of Company Directors' Education Committee and management consultant specialising in corporate governance.*
- *Mr Mark Peters – Chief Executive Officer, Australian Sports Commission and experienced national and international sports administrator. He has considerable experience in reviewing the structures and management of sports and national leagues.*

(Page 39, The Crawford Report)

As such, this committee, commissioned by the government, enjoyed the benefits of being able to rely upon expertise from top businessmen, academics, lawyers and sporting individuals. (It is uncertain whether the Conroy Report had such an array of expertise to leverage.)

The following extract, published two years after the Crawford Report, shows that the report's recommendations didn't go down so well with the existing governing body:

The Fathers of Australian soccer's success *(Theage.com.au, November 19th, 2005)*

FAILURE is an orphan and success, so the saying goes, has a thousand fathers.

Australian soccer, for so long the problem child of Australian sport, is poised to become the glamour star of the sporting landscape, thanks to the Socceroos' stunning success over Uruguay in dramatic circumstances last Wednesday night.

There are many with justifiable claims to a key role in the triumph. The coach, Guus Hiddink, his assistant Graham Arnold, Hiddink's predecessor, Frank Farina, and the players themselves, of course, who did all the work in Montevideo and Sydney to finally end the 32-year World Cup drought and win a place in Germany next year.

But from an overall perspective, the real architects of this triumph — and the men who can claim to be the fathers of success — are Football Federation Australia chairman Frank Lowy and his chief executive, John O'Neill, the man Lowy expensively (and controversially) recruited from rugby union only 20 months ago.

They have wrought a revolution on the game, both domestically and internationally, and, with the public glowing over the Australian success, it is easy to forget how far the game has come in such a short time, and how it all nearly did not happen in the first place.

Following the debacle in Montevideo four years ago, when Uruguay defeated the Socceroos 3-0 and progressed to the World Cup in South Korea and Japan, there was near universal agreement that there was an inescapable need for massive change in the Australian game. Prime Minister John Howard even entered the debate when FIFA boss Sepp Blatter came to Sydney, joining state premiers Steve Bracks and Bob Carr to support the idea that Australia should bid to host the World Cup.

But the politicians made their pledges of support with one key proviso — that the people in charge of the sport embraced the need for wholesale reform and huge structural change before the state and federal coffers would be opened and any public largesse put their way.

For the (largely) ethnic powerbrokers who had controlled the sport for so long, this challenge posed grave difficulties.

Yes, they wanted the game to move on, to take the central position in Australian sporting life and culture that they and all its fans believed it should.

But, for the main, they were very reluctant to surrender the positions of power and influence they had amassed in control of state federations, clubs and on the board of Soccer Australia, despite all the evidence suggesting they were incapable of running the game efficiently or broadening its supporter base.

THE Federal Government's route to revolutionising the game was through the Australian Sports Commission headed by Mark Peters, a man who was committed to pursuing a reform agenda for the game.

The ASC, with the backing of federal Sports Minister Rod Kemp, commissioned the Crawford report, a long investigation into the governance, organisation and structure of soccer conducted by insolvency expert and leading financial adviser David Crawford.

Crawford's findings were manna from heaven for those who wanted a revolution in the sport, but bad news for the entrenched old guard who wanted to retain their fiefdoms. He advocated wholesale change, a new league and a raft of revisions, which were resisted by many.

Lowy, the Westfield property and shopping developer whom BRW's latest rich list last year valued at $4.8 billion, was the man both Howard and the ASC wanted to take charge of the moribund, debt-ridden Soccer Australia and turn the hulking ship around.

Lowy, a soccer-loving Czech-born migrant who encapsulated the emigrant dream of success, was an inspirational choice, even if he initially needed convincing to take on the burden. The now-septuagenarian businessman had bitter memories of his time in the sport in the late 1970s and early 1980s when the club he controlled, Sydney City, was a dominant force in the newly established National Soccer League. Lowy, weighed down even then by the internal politicking, wrangling and self-interest, walked away from the game he loved, and it was touch and go whether he could be persuaded to return.

But a request from the prime minister is powerful motivation, and Lowy said he was ready to take on the new challenge and become chairman of Soccer Australia. He brought with him a high-profile slate of candidates for election to the board, including Melbourne events supremo Ron Walker and advertising guru John Singleton, all with enormous pull in business, commercial and media circles.

It looked like a no-brainer, but it was not that simple.

While some state federations recognised the inevitable and accepted the need for change, others, including Victoria, took their time to get behind the new high-profile candidates.

The so-called "rump board" of Soccer Australia (those who had not resigned or left following the Crawford findings) held firm and forced elections. To the horror of all those desperate for change, it became clear there was no certainty that Lowy and his colleagues were going to win the day.

Meetings were held in private rooms, deals were done in the corridors and cafes of hotels near Sydney airport as the horse trading intensified while the election dates loomed.

Eventually, common sense prevailed, the old guard stood down and Lowy and his group assumed control.

Within months, the old debt-laden Soccer Australia had been killed off and wound up, with a new body, the Australian Soccer Association (which later morphed into Football Federation Australia), being formed.

[...]

But in the administrative area the winds of change blew fiercely. Lowy, whose presence guaranteed that the top end of town finally would take approaches from soccer seriously, was determined to find the best administrator he could to drive the cultural revolution the game needed. He settled on O'Neill, the former merchant banker and rugby union supremo who had just masterminded the most successful rugby World Cup in history.

O'Neill, by his own admission, was an unlikely figure to spearhead the revamp. He openly made it clear that he did not know soccer and that his children were keener on rugby.

But, from his days running the Australian Rugby Union, he was acutely aware of the potential the game offered. He voiced publicly what all executives of other sporting codes would acknowledge only privately, that when he was in charge of rugby, he could not believe his luck that the then-soccer administration was so bad.

With Lowy's backing, O'Neill ignored the post-Crawford recommendations of an NSL taskforce calling for the establishment of a new league with 10 teams and announced the creation of an eight-team competition, with only one club from each major city in Australia and New Zealand.

There were to be minimum capital requirements of $5 million a club — much greater than required for the old NSL teams — and a raft of other conditions that consortiums bidding for the teams had to satisfy. Crucially, the clubs chosen were to be "broad-based" and capable of attracting the support of the whole community rather than narrow sectarian groups.

The successful ones were to be given a five-year guarantee of exclusivity in their region — a guarantee O'Neill argued was necessary for the new clubs to establish themselves and build supporter loyalty in their market places.

The howls of protests from the traditionalists were as loud as they were inevitable, with people querying his knowledge, commitment, understanding and empathy for a sport he knew nothing about.

But Lowy knew that O'Neill's proven track record of success would open doors through the commercial sector, and his appointment would make it clear to the media and corporate Australia that this time the soccer revolution was serious.

This, after all, was a man who had been one of the architects of the move to professionalise rugby union through the creation of the Super 12 competition, the most significant turning point in the 100-plus year history of that sport.

The duo drew up three key objectives.

The first was to successfully establish the new domestic competition, to be known as the A-League. The second was to end Australia's international isolationism in world governing body FIFA's tiny Oceania Confederation and move to the burgeoning soccer region of Asia. And the third was to qualify for the World Cup.

All three have now been achieved.

Further on in the article, the Rugby Union expert John O'Neill explains:

"Frank and I have taken quite a few risks in the past 18 months, and they have been calculated to achieve the trifecta this year — to qualify for the World Cup, to launch the A-League successfully, and the most important strategic move in the history of this game, our integration with Asia, next year.

"Those three achievements will secure the long-term future and viability of this game in Australia. I think 2005 will go down as a year to remember (but) we have got to keep our feet on the ground.

"We have got a participation level that is the envy of many other sports. We have got an A-League that looks the goods, and we have got a national team that is performing at the very highest level. We are a very serious player now in mainstream sport and I really think our positioning vis-a-vis the other football codes has been substantially enhanced.

"I am not saying we are going to be the No. 1 football code in Australia within X number of years, but certainly our chances of achieving that have dramatically improved."

Obviously Australia is a far bigger country than Ireland, with many key differences, including the existence of greater resources, a much greater population and the ability to run a franchise league (without the relegation/promotion required by UEFA). However, the similarities between the state of their domestic league (the NSC) in 2003 with the League of Ireland today are too numerous and obvious to ignore.

In 2003, the NSC was in terminal decline, with decreasing attendances, a disinterested general public, and constant in-fighting between the stakeholders. They also faced considerable competition from other established and better-organised field sports.

But, unlike the Conroy Report, and in the face of these very real challenges, the need for *'wholesale reform and huge structural change'* was seen as crucial both by the findings of the Crawford Report and by the likes of Lowy and O'Neill, whose jobs it became to implement the transformative changes.

The result of all this? Despite some initial growing problems over the first few years, some 12 or 13 years later the ambitious idea of the A-League appears to have been turned into a resounding success.

Growth in soccer numbers across nation due to success of Socceroos and Matildas, growth of A-League (Andrew Carswell, *The Daily Telegraph*, June 26th, 2015)

WHEN it comes to soccer, success trumps scandal any day of the week.

While the sport's governing body FIFA is imploding in a maelstrom of bribery allegations, the "beautiful game" is booming in Australia where it counts most — at the grassroots level.

Thanks to the Socceroos' success in winning the Asian Cup, and making the finals of the past two World Cups, the sport has recorded a 7 per cent increase in participants at a club level in NSW during the past year.

This weekend in the Socceroo breeding ground of Manly Warringah, clubs fielded under-18 teams down to five grades, thanks to a staggering 37 per cent growth in the number of players in one season in the age group.

Connor McColl, a goalkeeper with the U15 Doonside Hawks, is sticking to the roundball code rather than switching to rugby league.

In the booming under-9s age group, a record 138 teams hit the grass, an increase of 13 per cent, while the under-10s recorded 18 per cent growth.

Football NSW chief executive Eddie Moore attributes the rapid growth to the success of the Socceroos and Matildas, as well as the growth of the A-League.

"At the top end of the game there are some really good stories and lots of excitement around the sport," Moore said.

Chris and Karin Parker and their two kids Chloe (8) and Cameron (5) love the original football code.

"The colour at that level of the game is very positive and people get it. They want more."

Already, a total of 225,832 players are registered to play club soccer this year, plus an additional 28,700 players in school competitions across the state.

In Sydney's west, where the rise of the Western Sydney Wanderers has spawned a new generation of soccer fans, registration numbers across the region have increased 9.7 per cent since 2014.

"If we were to include school, indoor (Futsal), church, ethnic, community and corporate competitions in Western Sydney, football (soccer) in the west would easily have more than 150,000 participants," Football Federation Australia spokesman Kyle Patterson said.

The Australian example came to my attention thanks to former Cork City player Roy O'Donovan, who currently plays with Central Coast Mariners in the Hyundai A-League, where he was the club's top scorer in the 2015/16 season. I met Roy on his off-season back in Cork this year (2016).

I know Roy quite well as he had played in front of me on the right wing when we won the League of Ireland title with Cork City back in 2005. A gifted winger or striker, he was a proud northsider who brought an element of steel and pace to our Cork side – qualities that had been somewhat missing until his arrival. Years later, after spells with Sunderland, Blackpool and Coventry, amongst others, he had ended up playing again with Joe Gamble in Singapore before a move to the A-League transpired.

Roy mentioned to me that the A-League was a huge success, that the average attendances across the league (though stable over the last few years) had grown from an average of 4 to 5 thousand in the old NSC in 2003 to nearer the 12 to 13 thousand mark in the Hyundai A-League in 2015. He also explained that the professionalism of the clubs had much improved, so much so that the clubs were getting further in the Asian version of the Champions League and were attracting bigger and better sponsors. He told me that their footballing association, the Football Federation Australia, were succeeding in bringing football into parts of Australia where it hadn't been successful before, and how an over-arching plan – complete with a centrally controlled league, fully integrated with underage football – was having huge benefits on the game there.

As an example of what he meant, he explained how the pre-season that he was heading back to in a few weeks' time would involve a mini-tournament amongst four A-League teams in an area that is underdeveloped from a footballing point of view, but with big potential – think for example in Ireland of a Kerry, a Tipperary or a Mayo. Three of the clubs would be from any part of the country and the other would be the nearest A-League team to that area. These clubs and players would be going to schools, businesses and underage clubs to foster goodwill for the A-League in the area in the hope that it would help draw players, sponsors and media to the relevant team that were the closest A-league representative. And that same process was taking place with the other teams in different parts of Australia at the same time.

I was struck by how much of a 'well thought-out' idea this was and how it involved a lovely co-operation between the clubs, but also that it presupposed the existence of a central authority that was really committed to the league. It seemed that the previous authority, Soccer Australia, hadn't been able to bring this type of growth or leadership to the domestic game and so it was, eventually, disbanded.

In Ireland it does not have to go this way. We have very good people involved with the FAI but it's time for them to show real ambition and leadership, in the face of the considerable challenges that we face; the type of ambition and leadership that was shown by the likes of Frank Lowy and John O'Neill in Australia. The Australians have shown in their country, despite the existence of other dominant field sports as well as an apparent disinterest from the general public, that strategic and ambitious planning can bring real success to the domestic game and can add huge benefits to the overall game in the country.

If the FAI were ambitious for our league and gave the attainment of domestic professional football the priority it deserves, then we could still see real progress for our domestic leagues and for soccer in this country over the next 10 to 15 years. But this type of progress firstly needs a realisation that major transformative changes are needed, which implies an understanding that all is not OK with the League of Ireland today. Unfortunately, instead of a plan for the major structural changes that are required, we seem only to have a plan to keep negativity away from the media and away from the League, and to reduce the number of teams from 12 to 10.

If we continue going down the road we are on, fighting amongst ourselves, then there is a danger that we may at some stage need the government to step in and sort out the growing mess. I'm hoping this never happens, but only time will tell.

Finally, at this point I must admit to a clear limitation of this book. As my stated intention was to present the view of the 2009 season though the players' eyes, this book therefore lacks the valuable perspective that a financial expert or accountant might offer to a period that was defined by financial insecurity. It must, however, be clear to anyone looking back on the period – from the safe distance of 6 or 7 years – that the prevailing economic climate was also a major contributing factor in how matters played out. And the experts seemed to agree...

Examinership Law in Ireland A Rescue Remedy or a Temporary Safe Haven for Insolvent Companies? (Article by Sharon Sheehan, Examiner in Professional 1 Corporate Law, Published by the CPA (Certified Public Accountants) Ireland, March 2010)

[The] sharp increase [in examinerships in the Republic of Ireland] between 2006 and 2007 can undoubtedly be attributed to the burst of the Celtic Tiger bubble and the resulting recession. What is more significant perhaps is the impact these increased applications have had on the success rate of examinership. Between 2002 and 2006, approximately 95 per cent of companies entering into examinership survived as viable entities. However, success rates have declined significantly ...

It is worthy of note that of the companies that had examiners appointed to them since 2007 to June 2009, only 30% successfully came out of examinership and continue to trade...

This deterioration in the success of examinership can be largely attributed to the credit crunch and the resulting difficulties in attracting new finance to companies to ensure their survival during the examinership process.

These findings can only serve to mitigate whatever blame was placed, justly or otherwise, at the feet of Tom Coughlan, our white knight, for the death of our football club. At one point as matters were getting hairy, Coughlan admitted that he had made 'a balls of it' and I agree with this. But at least he was able to admit it. And in the end, despite everything that unfolds within these books, I would have to agree with Coughlan, who on finally resigning his position in January 2010 declared that 'the structures of the league are the problem, not just Tom Coughlan' (*Irish Examiner*, 29th January 2010).

As the old adage goes: the first step in fixing any problem is acknowledging that there is one. I, for one, hope that the FAI, following on from some of their recent positive steps with the new underage structures, finally acknowledge and embrace the need for more transformative changes to the League of Ireland. And I hope that, in the near future, they will lead the way with the ambitious but achievable plan for professional football in Ireland that is long overdue.

But I have my doubts too.

Acknowledgements

Thanks to Robert Mežeckis and Joe Gamble. Thanks to the *Irish Examiner*, the *Irish Independent*, the *Irish Times*, the *Guardian*, RTE, the *Evening Echo*, the *Herald*, *The Daily Mirror*, Extratime.ie, the 42.ie. Breakingnews.ie, Touchlineviews.com, St. Patrick's Athletic, *The Age*, *The Daily Telegraph*, austadiums.com, Sharon Sheehan and the Institute of Certified Public Accountants in Ireland for kindly consenting to the reproduction of your respective articles. A particular thanks to Liam Mackey of the *Irish Examiner*, Daniel McDonnell of the *Irish Independent*, Emmet Malone of the *Irish Times* and Alan Smith of the *Guardian* for (amongst other things) taking the time to read the book and to offer quotes for the cover. Thanks to Kostis Pavlou (www.kostispavlou.com) for the design of the cover.

Thanks again to George Laval of www.lavalediting.co.uk for all your help and guidance. Thanks to my colleagues, solicitors Gearoid McKernan, Dave Cowhey, John Cooke and David McCoy for their constructive advice and support. Thanks to Patrick O'Riordan B.L. and Judge Olann Kelleher for their advices. A big thanks to Gerry Desmond of Cork City FC programme fame for his assistance with the proof. Thanks to Mary, Tara, and Trish Horgan and Caroline Kilty for your continued support and input. Thanks to Eoin Horgan and John Fuller for your kind consideration of matters on my behalf. Thanks to John Breen from Waterstones of Patrick Street, Cork for your kind assistance.

Thanks to Ruth Fuller and Ciara O'Leary Fitzpatrick of Fuller Marketing (www.fullermarketing.com) for your expertise, guidance and enthusiasm in marketing the book. Thanks to Alan Bennett, Mark Herrick, Anthony Buckley, John Dunleavy, Ian Turner, Damien Delaney, Liam Kearney, Roy O'Donovan, Kevin Doyle, Shane Long, David Meyler, Billy Woods, John Cotter, John Caulfield, Colin Healy, Derek Coughlan, Declan Daly, Tony O Donoghue, Colin O'Brien,

Dan Murray, Gerry Harris, Mick Ring and Stephen O'Donnell for helping in various ways.

Thanks to Alan Mehigan for your kind assistance with several matters.

And again thanks to the players, members, staff and fans of Cork City FC and of the League of Ireland.

Who's who: CCFC playing staff, Season 2009

Name	Position	Nickname
Paul Doolin	Team Manager	Gaffer/Doolo
Tommy Dunne	Assistant Manager	Tommy
Dan Murray	Captain/Defender	Muzza/Muz
Dan Connor	Goalkeeper	Dan
Mark McNulty	Goalkeeper	Nults
Roberts Mežeckis	Defender	Robert
Neal Horgan	Defender	Hoggie
Danny Murphy	Defender	Murph
Pat Sullivan	Defender	Sully
Stephen Mulcahy	Defender	Mul
Kevin Long	Defender	Longy
Greg O'Halloran	Defender/Midfielder	Greg
Cillian Lordan	Defender/Midfielder	Lordy
Ian Turner	Defender/Winger	Turner
Stephen O'Donnell	Midfielder	Stevie
Joe Gamble	Midfielder	No-Show (Joe)
Colin Healy	Midfielder	Healers
Shane Duggan	Midfielder	Duggie
Craig Duggan	Midfielder/Forward	Craigy
Alan O'Connor	Midfielder/Forward	Al
Billy Dennehy	Midfielder/Forward	Billy
Fahrudin Kuduzović	Midfielder/Forward	Faz
Davin O'Neill	Midfielder/Forward	Davin
Paul Deasy	Forward	Deas
Denis Behan	Forward	Denny/Beehive
Guntars Silagailis	Forward	Guntars
Tim Kiely	Forward	Timmy
Gareth Cambridge	Forward	Gareth

Jerry Harris	Secretary	Jerry
Jerry Kelly	Groundsman	Jerry K
Caen Harris	Kitman	Caen
Mark McManus	Fitness Coach	Mark
Dr. Gerard Murphy	Club Doctor	The Doc
Alex Mason	Physio No. 1	Alex
Patrick Hanley	Physio No. 2	Pa
Keith Warren	Masseur	Keith
Éanna Buckley	Club Administrator	Éanna

sportsproview

www.sportsproview.com

Printed in Poland
by Amazon Fulfillment
Poland Sp. z o.o., Wrocław

60515411R00183